THE HIDDEN LAMP

The Hidden Lamp

Stories from
Twenty-Five Centuries
of Awakened Women

Compiled and Edited by
Zenshin Florence Caplow
and Reigetsu Susan Moon

Foreword by Zoketsu Norman Fischer

Wisdom Publications
199 Elm Street
Somerville, MA 02144 USA
wisdompubs.org

Library of Congress Cataloging-in-Publication Data
The Hidden Lamp : Stories from Twenty-Five Centuries of Awakened Women / Compiled and Edited by Zenshin Florence Caplow and Reigetsu Susan Moon ; Foreword by Zoketsu Norman Fischer.
    pages cm
Includes bibliographical references and index.
ISBN 0-86171-659-0 (pbk. : alk. paper)
1. Buddhist women. 2. Women in Buddhism. 3. Religious life—Buddhism. I. Caplow, Florence, 1964– editor of compilation, writer of added commentary. II. Moon, Susan, 1942– editor of compilation, writer of added commentary.
BQ4570.W6H53 2013
294.3092'52—dc23
                              2013007111

ISBN 978-0-86171-659-3   eBook ISBN 978-1-61429-133-6

20 19 18
9 8 7 6 5

Cover design by Phil Pascuzzo. Author photo by Victoria Leonard.
Interior design by Gopa&Ted2, Inc. Set in Berling LT Std 10.4/15.4.

Wisdom Publications' books are printed on acid-free paper and meet the guidelines for permanence and durability of the Production Guidelines for Book Longevity of the Council on Library Resources.

♻ This book was produced with environmental mindfulness.
For more information, please visit wisdompubs.org/wisdom-environment.

Printed in the United States of America.

Please visit fscus.org.

Table of Contents

Stories and Reflections

I. CLAPPING HER HANDS AND LAUGHING: STORIES OF SEEKING AND AWAKENING

II. Bring Me a Mustard Seed: Being Human

III. Why Do You Call Yourself a Woman? Words in the Midst of Wordlessness

IV. I Saw You Fall Down So I'm Helping: The Path of Practice

Foreword

IT IS A GREAT RELIEF to finally have access to this rich material. The editors have been kind enough to share the manuscript with me as they proceeded, so I have been using these stories and commentaries for some time, savoring them, sharing them with friends. You, as reader, will also plunge in with your experiences and reflections, because this text comes from the rawness of spiritual life actually lived, as you live.

It's instructive to compare this "hidden" collection of koans and stories to the traditional Zen koan collections on which it is modeled, and for which it's a foil. The three principal Chinese collections (all now in English) are the *Blue Cliff Record* (twelfth century), the *Book of Serenity* (twelfth century), and the *Gateless Barrier* (early thirteenth century). Most well-known Zen stories are from these texts. As the editors note in their introduction, it's hard to miss the fact that these collections come from an almost exclusively male practice milieu, and their style reflects this: terse, uncompromising, powerful, full of slang and humor, sometimes (but not always) useful—and, in general, withholding.

The traditional collections often make reference to two opposing but complementary teaching styles: "the grasping way" and "the granting way." The grasping way, the withholding way, gives you nothing because there is nothing to give. Whatever there is to be gotten must be hard-won through struggle. This is the way of the solitary hero. The granting way is the kindly way of clear and helpful teaching, in which even your confusion and suffering is part of the path. Practice always takes place in the context of others, so awakening is not something you "get" as much as the relief you experience when you recognize that your life is always right (even when it is difficult) and always shared.

It's likely that in actual practice throughout the centuries, Asian monastics experienced both ways, according to temperament and circumstances. But the classical collections seem not to reflect this. At least for the Western reader, lacking cultural and literary context, the granting way seems more or less absent in the style and presentation of these old tales and commentaries. Now that *The Hidden Lamp* has seen the light of day, this absence is filled finally with presence—with bodies, voices, emotions, lives. Included here, that is, are not only the long-missing stories of women, but, along with them, a spirit and attitude of open-handed teaching that the commentaries and the text as a whole reflect.

It's instructive too to compare compositional methodologies. Although both the *Blue Cliff Record* and the *Book of Serenity* were compiled by two authors (the *Gateless Barrier* has a single author), these works are not collaborative: one author simply takes the work of his predecessor and comments on it. *The Hidden Lamp* is, by contrast, a true collaboration, not only between the editors, but also in its inclusion of many commentators. And not only is the temporal scope of stories expanded, as the subtitle mentions, to twenty-five centuries, so is the range of who is included. Many of the commentators are Zen teachers, but many others come from a wide range of Buddhist traditions and lineages and teach in many different ways. This all-around openness and expansiveness offers many stunning moments unimaginable in other more traditional koan collections, like the alternative version of the story of Buddha's home-leaving in which, with great regret for what they both know he must do, he makes love to his wife Yasodhara on the night of his departure, and the resulting pregnancy parallels his spiritual quest. Or the straightforward practicality of Roshi Jiyu-Kennett's words about enlightenment: "But if you don't keep your training up, heaven help you; you'll be worse off than you were before." All this goes to say that the virtue of the important work you now hold in your hands isn't only that it offers for the first time spiritual stories of women, collected and commented on by women, but that it completes something that has been incomplete for some time, and in doing so it offers a style of spiritual teaching particularly necessary for our trying times. This collection by and about women is not just for women. It's for everyone—men as well as women. In bringing forward the voices of women, the balance that Buddhism (and all religion) has always promised but so far not delivered is now possible. This collection is for everyone who is looking to complete the broken circle that exists in all our great religions—and in our hearts and world.

Zoketsu Norman Fischer

Introduction

THIS IS A BOOK of meetings. In these one hundred stories about awakened women, people meet together intimately, without turning away. They bring up the Dharma together, sometimes kindly, sometimes fiercely, sometimes serving each other tea. A hundred contemporary women have joined the conversation, reflecting on the teachings of these old koans and stories.

We too have been meeting for a few years now, as we have worked together on this book. As we write this introduction, we are in a house by the Pacific Ocean, making each other cups of dragon well tea, working across from one another at an old wooden table, with pages and pages of beloved stories piled like leaves between us. Out the window, the tips of the beach grasses are shining in the dunes.

We call the book *The Hidden Lamp* because, while the lamp of Buddhist women's wisdom has been burning through the centuries, its light has been hidden from view. In this time, more than ever, we all need that light to guide our way. Many of the more familiar Buddhist and Zen stories are about monks living in monasteries. Here you will meet all kinds of people on the spiritual path: not just monks and nuns and teachers, but also husbands and wives, teenagers, hermits and cooks, courtesans and uppity grandmothers. Yes, this is a book that features women, but there are men here too, in almost every story; this is a book of human stories, human teachings.

The book addresses an absence for both men and women within Buddhism (and most other religious traditions, for that matter): the invisibility of women ancestors and their wisdom. In every family, we have both grandmothers and grandfathers. If we heard only the wisdom of our grandfathers, something in our own hearts would be incomplete. It's the same in the Dharma. So it's time for these stories of women to become part of a shared vocabulary and heritage for all Buddhists, just as the stories of the Buddha and other great teachers of the past are already known.

Never before in the history of Buddhism have women been so prominent or empowered as Buddhist teachers, nor, until now, have scholars and translators brought to the West so many of the old stories about women. So finally the lamp can be uncovered, for the benefit of everyone.

Stories and Koans

Stories have been part of Buddhism from the start. The Buddha's own teachings were full of parables and stories about Indian life in his time. There are even poems and stories of the first women who practiced with the Buddha, and several of these are included in this book.

A type of story called a *koan* first appeared in ancient Chinese Zen Buddhism. Koans are particularly powerful and succinct stories, most often about encounters between Zen teachers and students. They can be playful and humorous, mysterious, opaque, or even combative. We use "koan" and "story" interchangeably in this book. The very few stories about women in the great Chinese koan collections are here. The book also includes stories and koans about women from ancient India, Japan, Vietnam, Korea, Thailand, India, and the West.

In one way, all of these stories are koans. They are short, powerful narratives about meetings between Dharma practitioners and about experiences on the path. Nonetheless, some readers may feel that only stories from the classical collections are truly "koans." Whatever they are called, they are our and your birthright, whether you are a Vipassana practitioner, a Tibetan Buddhist, a Chan Buddhist, a Rinzai or Soto Zen student or teacher, a Pure Land Buddhist, or a reader exploring what it means to be a human being.

The word *koan* is a Japanese form of the Chinese word *gung an*, which means "public case" or "public announcement," since these encounters often took place in the Dharma hall in front of an assembly of Zen practitioners. Heinrich Dumoulin writes, "A koan, therefore, presents a challenge and an invitation to take seriously what has been announced, to ponder it and respond to it."

D. T. Suzuki, whose writings first popularized Zen for Westerners, described koans as inexplicable paradoxes or riddles, and this somewhat misleading idea about koans has persisted. Ruth Fuller Sasaki, one of the earliest Western Rinzai practitioners, differed in her view of koans. She wrote, "The koan is not a conundrum to be solved by a nimble wit . . . Nor, in my opinion, is it ever a paradoxical statement except to those who view it from outside. When the koan is resolved it is realized to be a simple and clear statement of the consciousness which it has helped to awaken."

It is thought that koans first evolved from teaching dialogues between Chinese Zen masters (*Chan* masters in China) and their students in the Tang dynasty period (618–907 CE). These dialogues were collected as "records" of a particular master's teaching and were also gathered in records of whole lineages of teachers, called "lamp collections." The Chinese koans may or may not reflect actual historic events and encounters, and some koans may have been written hundreds of years after the events they describe took place. But regardless of their historic accuracy, they can be appreciated as powerful expressions of awakened teaching.

Later, starting in twelfth-century Song dynasty China, particular koans were chosen from the earlier records and assembled in what we think of now as the classical koan collections, particularly the *Blue Cliff Record*, the *Gateless Gate*, and the *Book of Serenity*. With these collections, the commentaries and verses on koans developed into high literary and religious forms. But very few stories about women were included in the classical collections.

New koans also evolved over time. For instance, in Japan's Kamakura period, in the thirteenth century, a whole new set of koans arose out of the experience of the samurai class as they encountered Zen practice, and these include a surprising number of koans about women.

As we have shared these stories and koans with our fellow practitioners, we have noticed that some people feel a wave of anxiety at the word "koan." They associate koans with something mystifying and impenetrable, with right or wrong answers, and with grimacing Zen masters holding big sticks. But these stories are intended as mirrors for your own life and practice. Each story is a gift from one woman ancestor to you, whether you are male or female. You can sit quietly with it, find inspiration or encouragement within it, or take it all the way to the heart of your life. Only you can know exactly what the gift may be.

How Are Koans Used in Zen Practice?

No one knows exactly how teachers and students practiced with koans in ancient China, but Dahui Zonggao (1089–1163) is generally credited with being the first teacher to have his students meditate on phrases from the koans as a method of awakening. Over time, as Zen spread throughout China and then to Korea, Vietnam, and Japan, each school and lineage of Zen developed its own way of working with koans.

Asian and Western Zen teachers keep these various traditions alive. Within the Japanese Rinzai lineages, Korean Zen, and some Japanese Soto Zen lineages, practitioners spend years working their way through a koan curriculum, presenting their understanding to a teacher in private meetings. In some lineages, completion of the curriculum, usually involving hundreds of koans, is a requirement for becoming a teacher. This kind of koan practice is a full-bodied and whole-hearted encounter; it is, as John Daido Loori writes, "one's own intimate and direct experience of the universe and its infinite facets." Many of the commentators in this book have trained in this way, and their commentaries give us a glimpse into the feeling and intensity of Rinzai koan practice.

There is also a traditional Soto Zen approach to koans that began with Eihei Dogen, the thirteenth-century Japanese Zen master who founded the Soto school. In this tradition, instead of looking at a single phrase as in Rinzai Zen, one works with koans by unfolding and expanding on their teachings. Dogen models this approach in his many essays in *Shobogenzo*, taking what Steven Heine calls "the scenic, or panoramic route."

Many modern Soto teachers approach koans as "family stories." Classical koans are anecdotes from the lives of the great teachers, including those whose names are chanted every day in Zen monasteries. They express the particular spirit of the teacher, and by engaging with and studying these stories, a student develops a subtle feeling for the spirit of Zen practice. Soto teachers also encourage students to work with "the koan that arises from your own life"—a compelling Dharma question that comes out of personal life circumstances.

Recently, some Western Zen teachers have begun working with koans in another, somewhat radical way: exploring them in open discussion in a group, so that everyone's insight can shine a light on the old story. And in the last decade, some Western Zen practice centers have begun to chant the names of women ancestors, including women from the time of the Buddha and women teachers in China and Japan. Many of the koans in this book bring to life the teachings and spirit of these same women.

Why Do Stories about Women Matter?

Buddhist teachings on nonduality emphasize that there is no "male" or "female" in any absolute sense. So why create a book of women's koans? No matter who we are, or how awakened we are, we practice the Dharma in our complicated, gendered lives—it's the only place we *can* practice. A human birth is supposed to be an advantageous birth because only as a human being in a human body can one awaken. Our gender identities are more plastic, more mind-constructed than we used to think, but still, in our own eyes and the eyes of the world, we are shaped by "male" and "female."

Women have had to struggle mightily in order to practice Buddhism. It was hard for women in Buddha's time and it stayed hard for them for centuries. In ancient China, Japan, and other Asian cultures, women were not allowed to ordain without the permission of male family members. They were kept home to be householders, slaves, laundresses, cooks, wives, rearers of children. Some scarred their faces so they could enter a monastery but not disturb the monks with their beauty.

For much of Buddhist history, it has been a commonly held belief of laypeople, monks, and even nuns that it is not possible to be enlightened in a woman's body. Furthermore, many monastic men believed that women were dangerous obstacles to awakening because of their desirability. It's still hard for women to practice in many places, as either nuns or laywomen. Even now, women in many Buddhist lineages cannot be fully ordained, and in some places in Asia it is considered a sign of a woman's spiritual attainment if she remains silent and doesn't teach. These painful anachronisms are slowly changing, thanks to the efforts of courageous women and their male allies.

Buddhists all over the world practice in traditions where historical women's voices are rare and many of the teachings and practices emanate from a largely male point of view. By bringing forward both historical and contemporary teachings of women, we hope to help address this long-standing imbalance.

Who Are the Women in These Stories?

The women in these stories, and the men who supported them, are our ancestors and our relatives. There really was a woman named Ryonen, for example, who burned her face with a hot iron in order to be admitted to a Zen monastery in seventeenth-century Japan. She later became an abbess and founded her own temple. Then there are the stories—probably a combination of myth and history—of the first Buddhist women: Kisagotami, who came to the Buddha with her dead baby in her arms, or Mahapajapati, the Buddha's aunt and foster mother, who finally won admission for women to the Buddha's sangha. Did they really do what the stories say? We can't know, but it doesn't really matter, does it? Somebody did something like that for us—we wouldn't be here practicing without them. Great Granny Miaoxin, Auntie Kisagotami, Cousin Lingzhao Pang, Great Uncle Zhaozhou— their faces seem to peer out at us from old daguerreotypes.

Many of the Chinese and Japanese Zen koans are about nameless old women, selling tea or rice cakes by the side of the road or working in their fields. These figures lack any worldly power—they are women, they are old, they have no social standing, they are laypeople, they are without men to give them credibility—and yet they are powerful teachers. Their grandmotherly kindness often takes fierce forms. One burns down a misguided monk's hermitage, another roars like a tiger at a famous Zen master, another refuses to serve rice cakes to a sutra scholar who doesn't understand his own precious texts. Zen is full of stories of iconoclastic outsiders, and these old women are the ultimate outsiders. They are just the ones to puncture a foolish monk's pride and inflated sense of purpose.

Another striking aspect of the stories about women is how many explore the body, desire, and sexuality—topics that are generally absent from koans about men. There are koans in which lustful monks approach women, and the women are unafraid and unapologetic about their sexuality in their response. A monk exposes himself to a visiting nun, saying, "My thing is three feet long." The nun responds with, "And my thing is infinitely deep." Another woman tells a monk that her vagina is not for him to enter—it's the place from which he and all the buddhas came into the world.

Many of these stories turn the stereotypes of women upside down. A young woman who sells herself to a brothel is a bodhisattva, supporting her starving family. A helpless old woman isn't really so helpless after all, as she wields her fire poker on foolish monks. And a teenage girl meets the greatest Zen master of her time, Hakuin, and bests him in their Dharma encounter.

There are extraordinary men here too, who supported and respected women as equal practitioners in the Way: Ananda, who persuaded the Buddha to receive Mahapajapati and the other women into the sangha; Zhaozhou, whose encounters with nuns and old women are some of the greatest of Chinese Zen koans; Layman Pang, who practiced in partnership with his wife and daughter; Hakuin, who was so fierce with his monks but so admiring of the enlightened laywomen in his community; and Dogen, who in "Raihai Tokuzui" extolled the spiritual power and virtues of women Zen masters, and remonstrated with monks who denigrated women.

Many of these stories explore the possibilities of practicing in the context of everyday life, in a family, as a householder. Some show us women in traditional secular roles as wife, daughter, servant, slave, grandmother. Others show us women breaking out of these roles and joining the ordained sangha. We see women awaken while cooking dinner and we see them awaken as nuns. Sometimes, when the woman has an enlightenment experience while performing the tasks of a housewife, her reaction is to throw down her pot, hurl the tray of doughnuts to the ground, stop bothering to cook for her children, or leave her husband in order to ordain. Although this is more or less what the Buddha did, the abandonment of family seems more shocking when a woman does it. There are also stories of the women who awaken but remain happily in lay life until the day they die, surrounded by their children and grandchildren.

You will also find stories here from the teachings of eminent modern teachers who have recently passed away. We believe that koans are a living tradition, that teaching encounters are happening all around us, and that modern teachers are fully in Buddha's lineage. Questions that were asked one or two thousand years ago are still being asked today: *What do you do about loneliness? How do you know when you are enlightened? What do you do if you are trembling with fear?* Each generation keeps the Dharma alive.

And of course, in the great tradition of Zen humor, some of these stories use laughter to wake us up. You may find yourself chuckling at the teenager Satsujo comparing her butt to the Lotus Sutra, or at

Shariputra's utter bewilderment after the goddess turns him into a woman, or at Yuanji knocking over her brother's upside-down corpse and telling him he was always a trouble-maker. A good guffaw can be the Dharma too.

How Were the Stories and Koans Chosen for the Book?

We began by searching for koans and stories about women in English translation. We were able to find more than two hundred of them, far more than anyone would have predicted. In many cases there was just one koan about a woman buried in a volume of hundreds of koans. Where there was only one translation or source, we obtained permission to use it; otherwise we consulted a number of translations to develop our own version. In some cases we used only one part of a longer koan or story.

Because we chose to limit the book to one hundred koans and stories, this required a painful paring down of our original collection. The ones we didn't include are not necessarily any less wise or wonderful than the ones we did. We chose the stories that spoke to us and that represented different times, places, teachers, and traditions.

Instead of arranging the stories chronologically or geographically, we have chosen to organize them in an intuitive way, grouping stories together that resonate with each other.

Each story uses the form of spelling and pronunciation that is closest to the original, although diacritical marks are not used. For instance, the female bodhisattva of compassion is referred to as Kuan Yin in the Chinese koans and as Kannon, the Japanese form of her name, in the Japanese koans. For the Chinese koans, the names are generally in the modern Pinyin romanization of the original Chinese. The glossary provides alternative, and in some cases more well known, versions of some names. The great Chinese master Zhaozhou, for example, is sometimes better known in the West as Chao-Chou or Joshu.

Contributors and Reflections

In the classical koan collections, like the *Blue Cliff Record*, each koan
has a commentary written by the compiler. In this book, each story
has a short reflection by a different woman teacher.

Because there are many more than a hundred contemporary women
teachers, we established general criteria to help us choose whom to
invite. Generally, we invited women who have been teaching the
Dharma—or in a few cases writing about the Dharma—for a long
time, though we invited both prominent and less well-known teachers.
Some of the women we invited were unable to contribute, but most
accepted our invitation with generous enthusiasm. Because of the
richness of women's practice at this time, there were many powerful
women teachers whom we were not able to invite or who were not
available. We wish we could have included them all.

Our intention from the beginning has been to bring a diversity of
voices and perspectives to the book. We invited women who teach
in a wide range of Buddhist traditions, including Zen (from Chinese, Japanese, and Vietnamese traditions), Pure Land, Vipassana,
and Vajrayana. We invited women of diverse ethnicities, racial back-
grounds, and sexual preferences. We invited both nuns and laywomen.
We invited women from all over the world.

Due to our own limitations as translators, we were unable to invite
women who don't write in English. This limits the range of the book
to some extent, but ultimately our commentators represent all major
Buddhist traditions and come from thirteen different countries in
Asia, Africa, North America, Central America, Australia / New Zealand, and Europe.

There is one significant way that the reflections in this book differ
from the commentaries in traditional koan collections (besides the
obvious difference of being written by women!). Each contributor
explores the question of how the story speaks to her in her own life
and Dharma practice, and this encourages us, the readers, to do the
same. It is, after all, in our very vulnerability as humans, subject to old

age, sickness, and death, that we find our freedom. And many of the stories affirm this. It's encouraging to know that when we feel lonely or afraid, this doesn't mean we are not strong enough to follow the Dharma path. Our teachers and ancestors have been there before us.

None of the reflections on the stories, no matter how esteemed their authors, are final answers in any sense—this is why they are called "reflections." Each is one woman's perspective, opening the curtains on a view from a particular window into the landscape of the koan.

Each reflection is followed by a series of questions that have arisen for us as we, the compilers of the book, have lived with the story. This echoes the traditional structure of the classical koan collections, where each koan is accompanied by a commentary and a "pointer."

These stories are invitations extended to you across the centuries. An old woman at the side of the road has some tea and rice cakes for you. Asan's rooster crows for you. Ziyong borrows the voice of the mountains to speak to you. Dipa Ma reaches her hand across the aisle to you when the plane encounters turbulence. A Brahman wife tells you that you're not the only one who burned the family's curry dinner and that you too can wake up at the sound of the sizzling.

All these stories are pointing to spectacular, profound, and potentially life-changing teachings. We twenty-first-century Buddhist practitioners can take these stories and koans into our own practice; we can bring them to life in our bodies and hearts; they can put us in touch with our relatives, both known and long-lost, and wake us up to the truth that we are all connected, *all* of us, across time and space. Everyone is invited to the family reunion.

Zenshin Florence Caplow and Reigetsu Susan Moon
Shoalwater House, Tokeland, Washington

Suggestions for How to Practice with *The Hidden Lamp*

First of all, how you read and approach this book is entirely up to you. You may have your own way, formal or informal, of practicing with koans. But if working with koans and teaching stories is new to you, or you'd like more guidance about how you could use this book in your life and practice, here are a few ideas.

- You can engage with these koans and stories, whoever you are. You don't need to be a Zen student, a scholar, or an experienced meditator.

- The introduction may provide a helpful overview of how we approach koans in this book, and the history of stories and koans in Buddhist practice.

- This book can be read from cover to cover, or not. Although there is an internal order to the koans and stories, it is not necessary to read them in order. They are not arranged chronologically.

- Koans, particularly the Tang-dynasty Chinese koans, can initially seem opaque or difficult. We have found it helpful to let go of trying to "understand" these koans in an analytical way. They are more like dreams or poetry than news reports.

- Approach the koans and your responses to them as mirrors for your own life at this moment.

- Reading a koan is different than other kinds of reading, and requires slowing down. Read the koan several times before going on to the reflection. Feel what you feel in your body as you read: excitement, poignancy, confusion? Is there a particular phrase in the koan that intrigues you?

- You can take a phrase from the koan that particularly moves you, write it down, and bring it up during the day in your ordinary activities or meditation practice. This is an ancient way of working with koans.

- If you'd like to know more about the koan or the characters in the koan, there is a glossary in the back of the book and another section with sources of translations for each koan. You can also learn more about each commentator in the contributor biography section.

- Buddhist practice, although deeply personal, is not something most people can sustain entirely on their own. Teachers and Dharma groups are the lifeblood of the Dharma. If you have a teacher, consider exploring a koan or story together. If you are part of a sangha or Dharma study group, it can be fruitful and fun to work with these stories in a small group. Read them together, sit with them together, write poetry in response to them together, dramatize them and act them out, or write your own. Be willing to be surprised at what a group of ordinary people can see and teach each other.

Suzuki Roshi, in a talk about koans, said:

> Koan is not something to explain. We talk about it to give some suggestion, you know. It is suggestion. We don't talk about what koan means directly. We give you just suggestion, and according to the introduction or suggestion, you work on koan. That is how we explain koan and how you listen to koan.

Clapping Her Hands and Laughing

Stories of Seeking and Awakening

1. The Old Woman of Mount Wutai

CHINA, NINTH CENTURY ···

N OLD WOMAN lived on the road to Mount Wutai. A monk on pilgrimage asked her, "Which is the way to Mount Wutai?" The old woman said, "Right straight ahead."

The monk took a few steps, and she said, "He's a good monk, but off he goes, just like the others." Monks came one after another; they'd ask the same question and receive the same answer.

Later, a monk told Master Zhaozhou Congshen what had happened and Zhaozhou said, "I'll go and investigate that old woman myself."

Next day Zhaozhou went to the old woman and asked, "Which is the way to Mount Wutai?"

"Right straight ahead," she replied.

Zhaozhou took a few steps.

The old woman said, "He's a good monk, but off he goes, just like the others."

Zhaozhou returned to the monastery and told the monks, "I have checked out the old woman of Mount Wutai for you."

NANCY BROWN HEDGPETH'S REFLECTION

Years ago, before practicing Zen, I read an article about Dorothy Day, the Christian activist. She had recently died, and the article included one of her favorite poems, written by Rabindranath Tagore:

I slept and dreamt that life was joy.
I awoke and found that life was duty.
I acted, and behold, duty was joy.

I cut those lines out of the magazine, tucked them in my wallet, and carried them around for years. They captured a longing I had for a life that was all of a whole—what I called at the time "being fully human." In this koan about the old woman of Mount Wutai, I recognize my own seeking in that of the pilgrims: looking for some way of living that would seem complete, compassionate, and wise.

When I read this koan, I imagine an old woman who lived most of her life near a crossroads on the way to Mount Wutai. As a younger woman perhaps she raised children, cared for her husband and parents, cleaned, cooked, tended animals, and raised food for her family. Maybe, over her long life, she had witnessed many pilgrims who were seeking the mountain, seeking the Buddha's wisdom, seeking some special experience that might change their lives so they could embody that wisdom themselves. Many had asked her, "Which is the way to Mount Wutai?" (Or: "Please help me; I'm suffering.") How did she answer when she was a younger woman? Perhaps literally: "Go left" or "Go right"; after all, she knew which way led to the mountain. Over the years of her life, a stream of sincere seekers passed by.

We live our daily, ordinary lives right alongside of our seeking: "There must be more to this living; everything I care about changes, dies away; everything I wish were different doesn't change enough or not in the right way." We see—for ourselves—that getting things or money or influence doesn't ease the longing; even being loved doesn't ease the longing. And there is more: "Not only do those I love change and die but so do I." And "What is this 'I'?"

Over time, perhaps the woman who lived on the way to Mount Wutai matured and ripened into the very compassion and wisdom that the pilgrims were seeking. Instead of pointing the exact way she offered an experience that stopped their minds and raised a question: What does she mean by "Right straight ahead," when the way is not straight, and why does she say it to everyone?

One of the attractions of this koan for me is that the language of the old woman is so much that of my late teacher, Zen Master Seung Sahn. The teaching with which he ended every retreat and every letter was, "Only go straight, don't know; try, try, try for ten thousand years nonstop; soon get enlightenment and save all beings from suffering." This has everything we need: question, courage, faith, direction, compassion, and vow. The old woman of Wutai, from her experience, boiled it down to "Right straight ahead."

How do we go "straight ahead, don't know"? This question—any sincere question in the moment of asking it—returns us to a mind that is before thinking. In this moment of asking we and this universe are not split apart. How is it just now? What is the job of this moment? What a simple and portable practice!

I live on a farm, and we plant many vegetable seeds. Those tiny seeds contain an unbelievable force that brings together earth, nutrients, microbes, tilth, water, heat, gases, sunlight. When the seeds germinate, their tender forms move earth and rocks and go in whatever direction is needed to grow. As the plants mature and flower they offer us the oxygen and nourishment we need to live, as well as color, variety, medicine, and many other benefits. Finally, the plants make new seeds before they wither, decompose, and give back to the earth what is left. In fertile ground and with proper conditions their seeds will start the cycle over again.

I imagine this phrase "Right straight ahead" as a wonderful seed that the old woman of Wutai planted in the fertile ground of the pilgrims— the ground of not knowing, of being willing to ask. Her seed is still being planted and cultivated in us as we open to it. What an inspiration! May each of us create fertile soil and plant seeds beneficial to all.

What is the point of spiritual seeking, and what do you hope to find there? Have you ever overlooked the wise person right in front of you, clothed in a seemingly ordinary form?

2. Anoja Seeks the Self

 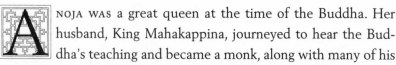

NOJA WAS a great queen at the time of the Buddha. Her husband, King Mahakappina, journeyed to hear the Buddha's teaching and became a monk, along with many of his attendants. He sent a messenger back to his court with the news, and when Anoja asked if the king had sent a message for her, the messenger said, "He gives all his royal power to you; enjoy the glory and pleasure."

But instead Anoja said, "The Buddha could not have arisen only for the benefit of men, but for women as well." So she and her attendants also made the journey to hear the Buddha and to ordain. Mahakappina, now a monk, was present, but the Buddha, using his magic powers, made the king invisible. When the queen and her attendants heard the Buddha speak, they all became "stream enterers," the first of four levels of Buddhist realization. Then the Buddha asked Anoja, "Would you rather seek the king or seek the nature of the self?"

Without hesitation she replied, "The nature of the self."

SANDY BOUCHER'S REFLECTION

Anoja speaks to me as one of those strong, perceptive women who understood the Buddha's message and the opportunity he offered, and saw no reason it should be limited to men. But as I look more closely, her story highlights the choices I myself face in daily life.

As a queen, Anoja was accustomed to ease and luxury, used to having the power to control others; she must have been tempted to stay and do what her husband invited her to do: continue to "enjoy the glory and pleasure" of royal dominance. I certainly would have been tempted to stay if I were her, for in my twenty-first-century life I cling to my creature comforts and resort to my regular escape routes of food and drink, entertainments and relationships, to keep me moving in the same old grooves, filled with the same old discontent. The story doesn't tell us whether Anoja agonized over her decision. Did she hesitate? Did she lie awake wondering what to do? Did she engage in a process of introspection and self-questioning? I know I would have, and I don't know if I would have had the courage to make the choice she made.

Anoja realized—even from afar and never having seen the Buddha before—that he was offering something more precious than all the wealth in her kingdom, more powerful than all the freedoms and powers that she had been taught to cultivate. When I am most clear I also understand that in giving up my attachments I attain true freedom from suffering.

She set off with her attendants to meet the Buddha, and he realized that she was on her way. He was well versed in the magic arts, but also he must have had quite a sense of humor, for he hid the king-now-turned-monk by making him invisible, setting up the conditions for Anoja to be tested a second time.

Queen Anoja and her ladies-in-waiting and other attendants had evidently lived many virtuous past lives and were karmically ripe for enlightenment, because just by hearing the Buddha speak his wisdom that day they entered the great stream of Dharma. When the Buddha saw that Anoja and her attendants were established on the path, he proceeded to question her.

No doubt he was wondering, "Is this woman really serious about this Dharma stuff, or did she come here just hoping to pry away her ex-husband because she misses him so much?" He asked Anoja the crucial question, knowing that Mahakappina was there watching and listening. Did she long for the security and pleasure of a relationship with her (presumably) beloved partner, or did she truly wish to discover what it is to be a human being? Another temptation—this time not material goods and worldly power but the sweet safety of an intimate relationship.

How many of us have faced this choice between a relationship and what we knew to be the path of growth and clarity? In college my brilliant French-major roommate was dating a grad student. When she won a Fulbright grant to study in France for a year, her boyfriend insisted she refuse the opportunity and stay home with him. Thrilled by the romance of it all, I supported her decision when she gave in to him. Not too many years later, involved in my own passionate love affair, I turned down a fellowship in a prestigious graduate writing program for the sake of romance, choosing the familiar path of short-term gratification. It was a move that turned out badly on several fronts.

The Buddha asked Anoja, "Would you rather seek the king or the nature of the self?" and the story indicates that she responded "without hesitation." We can't know her inner process, but I imagine that she perhaps did hesitate as she felt the lure of the known and comfortable, and then the pang of loss as she made her choice to move forward on her path.

Anoja's story brings a truth home to me: often in order to do what is most authentic and appropriate I must step away from the familiar. I have to let go of my belief in the person I was yesterday and venture forward into new, more spacious territory. Anoja's story offers a model for choosing the more life-enhancing path, taking a chance on liberation.

What do you seek, truly? And what are you willing to renounce for it? Is it necessary to leave your home in order to find what is within you?

3. Joko Beck and the Thought of Enlightenment

UNITED STATES, TWENTIETH CENTURY ···

OKO BECK had finished a talk and asked if there were any questions. A young man raised his hand and bluntly asked, "Are you enlightened?"

Her response was immediate. Laughing, she said, "I hope I should never have such a thought!"

PEG SYVERSON'S REFLECTION

I have thought about this exchange many times over the years since I first witnessed it. I had not been studying with Joko very long, and everything she said surprised me. The young man in this encounter is like the professor in the story of Nan-in serving tea. Nan-in, a nineteenth-century Japanese Zen master, was visited by a university professor who came to inquire about Zen. Nan-in politely served his guest, pouring tea into his cup until it was filled to the brim. He continued pouring, overflowing the cup, until the professor finally said, "It is overfull! No more will go in!"

"Like this cup," said Nan-in, "you are full of your own opinions and speculations. How can I show you Zen unless you first empty your cup?"

The young Zen student in this story seemed to be asking Joko a question, but his head was already filled with his own opinions and speculations about "enlightenment." He was no doubt wondering: "Can this teacher really help me? Can I trust her? Does she have any credentials?" So much is bound up in the student's simple question. "Who should I follow? Who can help me get enlightened?"

Of course it is important to have discernment when we work with a teacher. Still, beyond the issue of qualification or capacity is the nature of the relationship itself. Joko's playful, humorous response changed the entire field of her relationship with this student and with everyone who was there. But it opens to a much deeper mystery. As I heard Joko's response I marveled at her words, and I still do. They echo the renegade Zen master Ikkyu: "I don't remember making a mistake called enlightenment."

My own encounters with Joko were just as unexpected and penetrating. Early in our spiritual work together, when I was a single parent juggling three jobs and a full-time graduate program, she asked me what had brought me to Zen practice. I knew that this was not a casual question. For weeks I reflected on it, and finally I came in for *daisan* (private practice interview), met her piercing gaze, and said, truthfully, "I just want to be a better mother for my son." She tartly replied, "Well, that's a story!"

I was startled into wonder and, for just a bit, completely lost my bearings. I barely managed to stand, bow, and leave the little room where she was even then ringing the bell for the next student. I felt as though she had suddenly tossed a pitcher of ice water in my face.

But at some level beyond language, I knew she was right. My "story" was suddenly quite clear: the core belief that I was perpetually failing at some performance of "being a good mother," despite having neither models nor even any idea what such an ideal might be. No, I was always just coming up short, always scrambling to improve, and still failing. In fact, deep in my heart, I held this lacerating belief as a virtue—a sign of both my noble aspiration and the humble recognition of my terrible failings. It was poignant and heartbreaking. Yet this very story was actually coming between my son Ben and me, a filter through which I was always anxiously and apologetically and sadly viewing our marvelous life together. That single retort in Joko's tiny daisan room changed the entire course of my relationship with Ben.

Simply staying present with him without the story was infinitely more challenging, and yet the intimacy it opened was vast and luminous.

We live with a yearning for something always just out of reach. Without it, we would never come to practice Zen in the first place. We have many ideas about our practice, about ourselves, and about the world. Our cup is full. Like every other inexperienced Zen student, I was striving to be awakened. I wanted to be a light in the world, to have the genuine insight, true compassion, and profound wisdom to offer something truly needed—care for others that was *real* care. There is nothing wrong with a heartfelt aspiration for awakening, of course. But "I hope I should never have such a thought"? The ringing clarity of her words illuminates our secret agenda, our constant negotiations, calculations, and manipulations, our efforts to finesse life-as-it-is, and reveals our hidden longing for enlightenment as ultimate comfort, confirmation, achievement, or holiness. The demolition of this self-centered dream is the revelation of the true path.

How do you follow the spiritual path without trying to achieve enlightenment? And is there a problem with a thought about enlightenment?

4. The Old Woman and the Pure Land

N CHINA and Japan many millions of Buddhists have been—and in Japan still are—devotees of the Pure Land doctrine. According to this doctrine a bodhisattva made a great vow, which in time fulfilled itself as the manifestation of the Buddha Amitabha (infinite light), who created a Pure Land paradise in the West for those who would take his name with faith. From this Pure Land it was easy to attain final nirvana.

An old lady of this faith was walking along the road when she met a Zen master, who said to her, "On your way to the Pure Land, eh, Granny?"

She nodded.

"Holy Amitabha's there, waiting for you, I expect."

She shook her head.

"Not there? The Buddha's not in his Pure Land? Where is he then?"

She tapped twice over her heart and went on her way.

The Zen master opened his eyes wide in appreciation and said, "You are a real Pure Lander."

EMILA HELLER'S REFLECTION

Pure Land Buddhists believe that through their faith in Amitabha, the buddha of infinite light, they will be freed from suffering. The Pure Land is a paradise of beauty and liberation and awaits those who truly believe. Are we all not eagerly looking for such a place of liberation? This koan is a simple story pointing to a profound Dharma teaching.

An old lady is walking along the road. She meets a Zen master, who asks her several disparaging questions, but she seems neither disturbed nor impressed by him. She answers his questions with gestures and silence. Wide-eyed, the Zen master sees that she has actualized a true understanding of the Pure Land. She knows it is neither an external place nor something to attain. She just walks along the road, not seeking outside of herself, not seeking an idea of freedom or emptiness or Buddha, not trying to teach or explain. She is alive with her faith and she didn't have to say a word for the Zen master to experience her full presence.

For many years I walked the hills at Green Gulch Farm Zen Center where I live, trying to settle this body and mind. I was haunted by many forms of suffering and ached for release. A koan in the *Book of Serenity* encouraged me:

> The World-Honored One pointed to the ground and said, "This is a good place to build a sanctuary." Indra, Lord of the Gods, stuck a blade of grass in the ground and said, "The sanctuary is built."

It was healing to walk during those years with a mantra crafted from this koan: "Right here is a holy place; right here I'll build a sanctuary." Over and over and over again I recited these words, reminding myself that right in the place where I walked, where I stood or sat or lay down, beyond craving, beyond knowing and not-knowing—this is where an opening could occur.

It was an uphill practice. Having grown up in Manhattan, I felt mostly fear in the wild, although you could hardly call Green Gulch wild. The paths were wide, the view spacious, and yet I feared predators from without and was tormented by negative thoughts within. To meet my demons I expanded my repertoire of mantras to include other phrases that spoke to me. I changed slightly the opening poem of the *Visuddhimagga*: *The Path of Purification*:

> The inner tangle and the outer tangle,
> the whole world's in a tangle.
> Tell me, oh Buddha,
> how to untangle the tangle . . .

I never read beyond this poem in the text. Instead I untangled brambles in the physical world of Green Gulch and patiently and impatiently committed myself to untangling my own tangle, which I hoped would benefit others. Taking refuge in a community of practitioners for so many years gave me the gift of knowing that we are all suffering, and my faith is that there is the possibility of an end to suffering. It takes years to quiet a mind filled with craving. And though I cannot touch my heart and say with full confidence that the Pure Land is right here, nonetheless, slowly, a root has begun to tap into the place and the time where I am, and that is a great relief.

We pilgrims on the path are like the man in the Lotus Sutra who wanders around the world in poverty while all the time a priceless jewel is sewn in his ragged coat. As Yunmen told his assembly: "Within heaven and earth, through space and time, there is a jewel, hidden inside the mountain of form." All of us have the jewel, all of us are the jewel. But even when we believe this, the restless mind keeps asking, "What is Buddha? Where is Buddha?" The wise sages have answered in various ways: "The oak tree in the garden; three pounds of hemp; a flowering hedge. This very body is Buddha along with mountains, rivers, and the great sky." How do we stop traveling the dusty world in search of the answers? How do we find the old lady's confidence that the jewel is within each of us?

The Buddha spoke as a doctor, diagnosing our illness and dispensing medicine to cure us. We are taking the medicine by sitting still, studying the mind and vowing to end the suffering that we experience within and without.

> Walking the hills
> Stumbling and confused

I seek the Way.
When the longing ceases
My heart stills.

How far do you have to travel to find the Buddha?
What do you do when someone says to you,
"There, there, dear, you'll be just fine"?

5. Manseong's No Cultivation

NE DAY a nun asked Manseong Sunim, "How do I cultivate the Way of the Buddha?"

"No cultivation," answered Manseong.

The nun persevered: "How, then, can I obtain release from birth and death?"

"Who chains you to birth and death?" Manseong asked in return.

BARBARA RHODES'S REFLECTION

I picked this koan because to me it strikes right at the heart of what a student and teacher can be for each other. The nun's questions were direct and clear. The teacher's responses were also like that. No hesitations, no filters, just an intimate exchange.

I think it must have taken a lot of devotion and much courage for this nun to get to the point of meeting a great master and asking her these sincere questions. We are born into this life with no idea of who we are or where we came from. It is actually thought to be very rare for a human being to meet a great teacher and even rarer to break through all delusions and attain enlightenment. I've heard it likened to the chance of a sea turtle coming up for air in the Pacific Ocean and putting her head directly into the center of the only floating tire in the whole ocean.

So why did Manseong say that no cultivation is necessary? Perhaps "cultivation" is the wrong word. All the Zen teachings say the Way is right in front of you; it's as easy to see the Way as it is to touch your nose when you're washing your face. Looking for the Way is like a peacock looking for its feathers, a fish looking for water. So there is nothing to cultivate. Nonetheless, we have to do something in order to be able to recognize and digest our various delusions. The magnificent gift that we all have is our doubts and questions; they are the diamond double-edged sword that can cut through our confusion and bring us home.

It's wonderful that the nun had a teacher to ask, but what if she hadn't had a teacher? Then what would she do? What did the Buddha do? He sat down and with complete earnestness asked his questions. As the story goes, he was at the end of his rope, nowhere else to go, nothing else to do. I trust that this nun was also this ripe, had already been questioning and looking into this great question of life and death way before she sought Manseong's wisdom.

When we begin a meditation practice it is often quite shocking to see our very busy mind. I have heard many people say they initially felt worse after beginning to meditate. Previously, they had never slowed down enough to realize what a thought-producing machine their mind was. Some thoughts are easy to drop, but there are others that take a great deal of courage to even face, let alone eventually learn from, appreciate, and then release.

My teacher used the metaphor of a cow chewing on its cud. This very fibrous diet must be swallowed, regurgitated, chewed on some more, swallowed and then passed through four stomachs. It's not easy! So yes, maybe cultivation is not the right word, but for most of us, it takes a huge amount of digesting our karma before we can begin to breathe more easily and perceive the Way.

Earlier I said that it is rare for a person to meet a great teacher, but that doesn't mean that great teachers are rare. Teachers with Manseong's skill are generously provided for us by this compassionate universe. We meet our teacher when we have exhausted all our other options and know there is nothing else to do. I met my teacher when I was twenty-four and all I knew was that I couldn't sustain the sometimes-magnificent states of mind I reached on LSD. I began reading books on Zen, and they made complete sense to me. "Something" appeared to me while I was on LSD and told me to go to the East Coast and find a teacher. I listened to it. Within two months I was living at the Providence Zen Center and studying with Zen Master Seung Sahn. I had great doubts and questions about the meaning of life, but those doubts and questions were my ticket home.

The koan says at one point, "the nun persevered." That is exactly what we need to do. Keep chewing, keep swallowing, and never, ever stop listening. When student and teacher sit down together, the student speaks, the teacher listens; the teacher speaks, the student listens . . . The Way has already appeared.

Who chains you to birth and death? Look in the mirror, then go have a cup of tea. Only you know if it's hot or cold.

Could you say to a person in prison, sentenced to die for a crime she didn't commit, "Who chains you to birth and death?" Is it possible that our desire for spiritual understanding could prevent us from realizing spiritual understanding?

6. Bhadda-Kundalakesa Cannot Answer

B HADDA-KUNDALAKESA was a wandering Jain ascetic famous for her debating skills. Whenever she came to a new place, she set a branch of rose apple in the ground and put out the word that whoever wished to debate her should trample the branch.

When she was seventy years old, she came to Savatti, and Buddha's disciple Shariputra came forward to engage her in a public debate. First she asked a series of philosophical questions of Shariputra, and he was able to answer them all. Then he said, "You have asked many questions. I would like to ask only one."

She said, "Please ask, venerable one."

He asked, "One—what is that?"

She was unable to answer.

He said, "If you don't even know that, how could you know anything else?" and began to teach her the Dharma. She was so moved by the teachings that she fell at his feet and asked to take refuge with him, but instead he told her to come and meet the Buddha.

The Buddha recognized her spiritual maturity and said to her, "One phrase that brings peace is better than a thousand words that have no use."

When she heard these words she was freed and became an arahant. Then the Buddha ordained her, saying simply, "Bhadda. Come."

BETH KANJI GOLDRING'S REFLECTION

One of the great beauties of Bhadda's story is that—like the stories of Angulimala the murderer and of Milarepa, who practiced black magic—it speaks of transformation within this lifetime. Whatever harm we have done, however great, it is possible through sincere effort, sustained by wise teaching, to put it fully behind and to enter into freedom, compassion, and intimacy. Bhadda's story speaks to us not only of realization but of redemption. As one who has done harm in my life, I treasure this possibility.

Bhadda-Kundalakesa's early life illuminates this. Bhadda came from a prosperous middle-class family and was kept secluded because of her willful, passionate nature. One day, from her window, she saw a handsome, high-born thief being led to execution. Bhadda insisted on marrying him. In some versions of the story an innocent person was executed in his place.

Shortly afterward, her husband told Bhadda he wanted to fulfill a promise to a mountain deity. He told her to come with him and wear her most precious jewels; he then led her to the top of a cliff and tried to throw her over. She, having asked to make one last obeisance to him, threw him over instead. Repulsed at where her passion had led her, Bhadda turned away from the world. During her ordination as a Jain ascetic, as a special penance, each hair was pulled out individually by the roots. It grew back curly; hence the name *kundalakesa* (curly-haired).

By the time Bhadda encountered Shariputra and then the Buddha, she had spent many years in determined, impoverished, isolated mendicant practice. Debate, a form of conversation that precludes intimacy, was her primary means of communication. Behind her apparent success, the pain of this isolation must have been unbearable.

What is "the One" that Shariputra asks her about? Perhaps one possibility is that the One is the intimacy that has been Bhadda's deepest longing and birthright, a birthright she first mistook for sexual passion and then turned away from as a consequence of doing harm. Shariputra's question breaks down her walls, showing her the limitations of what she has achieved. This opens a space in her life closed for many years.

The Buddha speaks to her of another One: one word that brings peace, rather than the many words of isolating debate. This opens the possibility of another life, of intimacy with all beings, free of pain, guilt, and isolation. In that moment Bhadda's mind, ripened over many years, finally fully releases. The Buddha then says, simply, "Bhadda. Come." Bhadda enters the order of nuns as a fully enlightened being.

In the Zen tradition there is a saying that "not knowing is the deepest intimacy." When I first encountered this concept in 1979 I found it repellent. I wasn't content with "not knowing" and deeply feared intimacy. It has taken many years for me to find myself at home with the intimacy of not knowing. Perhaps, in addition to the issue of redemption, it is also my long quarrel with both not knowing and intimacy that draws me so strongly to Bhadda's story.

In 2000, I started working with destitute AIDS patients in Cambodia, believing I had finally found work that was morally unambiguous. What I soon learned was that the work brought me up against my resistances to being fully and completely present, completely intimate. I had a supportive supervisor and a compassionate but unsparing Buddhist teacher. These two were vital to my ability to sustain the effort to be present. Seeing my resistances was often the core of my work.

Over time the resistances lessened. I began to feel deep oneness with the patients, a sense of our being held together in boundless compassion. Over more time I began to trust this experience of oneness, to welcome and expect it. I am not alone in this: there are eight Khmer lay chaplains in our organization, and several of them can touch depths of intimacy that humble me.

All of us who do this work know that the intimacy we feel with our patients is utterly sustaining and nourishing for us, that we are truly the beneficiaries of our patients' willingness to allow us to be present.

We are, all of us, far from full realization. But in those moments of boundless intimacy we may well taste what might be possible for one who is fully awakened and intimate and at peace with all beings.

How do you know when to stop talking? How do you give up the "knowledge" that keeps you apart from others? What does "not knowing" have to do with intimacy?

7. Chiyono's No Water, No Moon

CHIYONO WAS a servant in a Zen convent who wanted to practice zazen. One day she approached an elderly nun and asked, "I'm of humble birth. I can't read or write and must work all the time. Is there any possibility that I could attain the way of Buddha even though I have no skills?"

The nun answered her, "This is wonderful, my dear! In Buddhism there are no distinctions between people. There is only this—each person must hold fast to the desire to awaken and cultivate a heart of great compassion. People are complete as they are. If you don't fall into delusive thoughts, there is no Buddha and no sentient being; there is only one complete nature. If you want to know your true nature you need to turn toward the source of your delusive thoughts. This is called zazen."

Chiyono said, with happiness, "With this practice as my companion, I have only to go about my daily life, practicing day and night."

After months of wholehearted practice, she went out on a full moon night to draw some water from the well. The bottom of her old bucket, held together by bamboo strips, suddenly gave way, and the reflection of the moon vanished with the water. When she saw this she attained great realization.

Her enlightenment poem was this:

> With this and that I tried to keep the bucket together,
> and then the bottom fell out.

Where water does not collect,
the moon does not dwell.

MERLE KODO BOYD'S REFLECTION

For several years now, I have kept a picture of Chiyono and her bucket on the bulletin board above my desk. It is a delicate nineteenth-century woodblock print of a young Chiyono standing in pale moonlight, a bottomless bucket at her feet, a puddle of water spreading across her path. The artist is Yoshitoshi.

I was drawn to Chiyono's verse the first time I heard it. I was seized by the words, "With this and that I tried to keep the bucket together . . ." But I did not know that she is also thought to be Mugai Nyodai, whose name we chant in our morning dedication to our women ancestors. She was the first Japanese woman to receive Dharma transmission and founder of the first Zen Buddhist convent in Japan.

When I first heard Chiyono's verse, I had been practicing for ten or twelve years. I was keenly aware of the constant tension of "keeping the bucket together." I understood that the intent of practice was to relax my grip on the old bucket, but conditioning runs deep and the sense of personal identity is strong. Hearing the words "with this and that" I felt the exhaustion of years of vigilance, all aimed at protecting my idea of myself. I felt the exhaustion of being my own obstacle.

Our Zen practice is medicine to this conditioning. All the practices within Zen challenge the illusion of the perfect bucket—zazen, the teacher-student relationship, ritual, sangha relationships. As much as I may wish to appear competent at all times, I cannot immerse myself in Zen practice without a willingness to come apart. Sometimes it's appropriate to stop patching things back together. What, then, allows us to leave the bits and pieces scattered on the ground, like the splinters of the bucket around Chiyono's feet?

We are conditioned to keep the bucket from falling to pieces. Unique personal circumstances can intensify this general conditioning. I was in the first generation of southern black children consciously raised to enter integrated schools. In such circumstances, everything seems to ride on "keeping it together," especially in public, and so we were conscientious and hyper-vigilant in order to prevent disaster.

And yet we Zen students have chosen a path that calls us in the opposite direction. In spite of our conditioning, we are called to awareness rather than vigilance. We are on a path of "no water, no moon." Our conditioning tells us that it is a risky path, and yet we sense its offer of freedom and feel called to take it.

Ironically, it was precisely that conditioning of "keeping it all together" that gave me the courage to walk into a Zen center for the first time. I had been trained to tolerate the circumstance of being "other," to maintain a public identity in places where I was allowed but possibly not welcome. Like the schools and libraries of my childhood, Zen centers offered something that I deeply needed, a place to experience my life in the world more deeply. I hoped I would be welcome at a Zen center, and I also knew that it could be otherwise. To walk into this uncertainty, I relied on being outwardly upright while keenly aware of inner fears.

As Zen students we live between Chiyono's first two lines and her second two lines, between keeping things from falling apart and letting them fall apart. Knowing how to "keep things together" is a valuable skill. It was knowing how to care for things that led Chiyono to continually patch the bucket. When it fell apart, she made excellent use of that circumstance as well. Our liberation deepens with the refinement of our capacity for flexibility and discernment.

The liberation I was raised to seek is one aspect of the liberation we speak of in the Dharma. In the community of my childhood, our efforts were directed primarily toward gaining entrance into schools, access to employment, to housing, to services that made life more comfortable. But awareness of our essential and undeniable freedom comes with awareness that we, and all things, are without self. The one who is liberated must be allowed to disappear like the water and the moon. Moving between patched bucket and bottomless bucket, I can exercise my freedom to keep things together or let things come apart, according to the circumstances. I have come to trust the true freedom of living where the moon does not dwell.

Where does the moon go when its reflection disappears?
Where do we go when we let go completely?

8. Ohashi Awakens in a Brothel

HASHI SOLD HERSELF to a brothel to support her impoverished family after her samurai father lost his position. She served diligently and became a poet and calligrapher, but she was plagued by sadness for her former life. Later she met Hakuin, who advised her that enlightenment was possible in any circumstance. He gave her the koan "Who is it that does this work?"

Ohashi was terrified by lightning. One day, during a violent thunderstorm, she sat zazen on the veranda of the brothel in order to face her fear. A bolt of lightning struck the ground in front of her. She fainted, and when she awoke, she saw the world in an entirely new way. Hakuin later certified her enlightenment.

Ohashi was eventually ransomed from the brothel by one of her patrons, Isso, and they were married. Later, with Isso's permission, she became a nun and was renowned for her wisdom and compassion. After Ohashi's death, instead of making the customary memorial tablet, Isso had a statue of Kannon carved in Ohashi's likeness and donated it to Hakuin's temple.

JUDITH RANDALL'S REFLECTION

Ohashi sold the only thing she had. Strong and courageous, this young woman did what needed to be done. Valuing her family's well-being above her own, she faced her fear and entered into an impossible solution. Her generosity flowed out over her fear. What must it have been like to have the idea come to her? To imagine giving away her body, her very life? To ponder it? To tell her family, and then to leave them and the only life she knew, not knowing if they would ever see one another again? Imagine the dilemma and shame of her samurai father, trained to value honor above life. Imagine the arrangements, the travel, the first customer. Practicing renunciation, giving over, she was already on the bodhisattva path. In her own way, she *was* valuing honor above life.

Ohashi's chances of meeting Hakuin and receiving his teaching were extremely rare. One had to be born into a male body to become enlightened, according to traditional teachings, and prostitution certainly didn't count as "right livelihood." Hakuin told her that *enlightenment is possible in any circumstance*. This bell of Hakuin's teaching rings in our ears even now. This circumstance, right here, right now. My circumstance, not someone else's. He gave her the koan "Who is it who does this work?"

Writing to my Dharma pen pals in prison, who are practicing deeply in an environment that seems anything but conducive to samadhi, these words encourage me and encourage them. Reading news of torture, murder, the hideousness of war, I feel deep despair about the cruelty that human beings are capable of doing to one another. When I remember Hakuin's words, space opens and my heart softens toward torturer and tortured. Hearing the life stories of my Dharma friends, amazed at the terrors they've lived through, I am awed by their resilience. Who is it who sits in the jail cell? Who is it who wields the torture? Who is it who has lived *this* life?

Ohashi intentionally sat zazen in the midst of her terror of lightning. She offered herself to the experience, letting go of control over the outcome. Yielding to the unknown, she gave over, not relying on anything, fiercely determined. The moment the lightning struck—a very loud CRACK of thunder, brilliant light, the rain pounding down—she had no thought, no reaction, no feeling. She fainted, and upon awakening, she "saw the world in an entirely new way." Did she think she had died? In a sense, she had.

Being asked to sit in the Dharma seat and give a talk is quite frightening for me. When the invitation comes, panic and shortness of breath rise up in me. My body contracts. A great *"No! I can't!"* shouts silently inside. Then shame: "All your training and practice comes to *this?*" My mind freezes like jammed radio waves, and I can neither think nor receive any internal guidance.

Yet I yearn deeply to share the power and beauty of this practice. It is this yearning and some kind of fierce determination to meet what arises that helps me move forward. I reach out to trusted Dharma friends and teachers and meet the fear again and again. "Who is it who gives this talk?" I ask, grateful for Hakuin's question.

Ohashi's life says: see the fear, just say yes, and see what happens. When I can do this, another world opens up, a world where ideas begin to gather around a subject, where energy fills the belly and calms the mind. The "I" that thought it was giving this talk and was so anxious steps aside. Something begins to enjoy engaging the process.

Ohashi's life says: Fearlessness is not the absence of fear, but the willingness to walk into it. When I walk into my fear, practice there, sit upright in the middle of it, completely open to the experience, with no expectation of the outcome, anything is possible.

Ohashi's life says: When our circumstances look impossible or terrifying, there is a way. It may look like the way is even more impossible than the circumstances, but if we step into it, with eyes and heart open, take one step off the hundred-foot pole, something will be revealed.

If it is possible to be enlightened in any circumstance, could you be fully present even in work you dislike or consider unwholesome? Can fear itself wake us up? What happens when you face a fear completely?

9. Seven Wise Women in the Charnel Grounds

···

EVEN WISE SISTERS planned a spring journey. One of them said, "Sisters, instead of going to a park to enjoy the spring flowers, let's go together to see the charnel grounds."

The others said, "That place is full of decaying corpses. What is such a place good for?"

The first woman replied, "Let's just go. Very good things are there."

When they arrived, one of them pointed to a corpse and said, "There is a person's body. Where has the person gone?"

"What?!" another said, "What did you say?" And all seven sisters were immediately enlightened.

Indra, Lord of the Gods, was moved by their awakening and showered flowers down onto them. He offered them whatever they needed for the rest of their lives. One of the sisters replied, "We have everything we need. But please give us a tree without roots, some land without light or shade, and a mountain valley where a shout does not echo."

"Ask anything else, holy ladies," replied Indra, "and I will gladly provide it. But I don't have those things to give you."

"If you don't have them," said the woman, "how can you help others liberate themselves?" At this, Indra took the sisters to visit the Buddha.

When the Buddha learned why they had come, he said, "As far as that's concerned, Indra, none of the arahants has the slightest clue either. Only great bodhisattvas understand this matter."

Bonnie Myotai Treace's Reflection

There is much to love and study in this story and many ways to appreciate it. But I don't want to overlook the simple picture: a group of women freely discerning how best to use their time and taking some time to be alone together. So one of the first teachings here is the quiet reminder that women may need some time to walk with one another as these women do, literally, "amid the burning."

It is much harder to maintain the walk of awareness without other women. Receiving the legacy of our grandmothers and mothers helps us. So does knowing that our sisters are beside us and recognizing that we are here to make a better world for our daughters and granddaughters.

But the story of the wise women also reminds us that facing what needs to be faced—walking toward the charnel grounds—can strike us as basically unpleasant. Aren't there always sweeter ways to spend a day, if one has the option, than in the contemplation of death and impermanence?

But the lead woman cuts through: "Sisters, just go. Very good things are there." As we take the step off the edge, here is a reminder to trust the perfect air. Our wise woman gently turns aversion on its head: the place where release from the suffering of decay will be realized might just be exactly where we least expect to find it.

The women make the journey we all make to face mortality. Arriving at the charnel grounds, they awaken. But they look at the sky, and it rains flowers. One of them asks, "Who praises us and showers us with flowers?" Indra, the god of the Earth, answers that it is he who is celebrating the women's awakening, and he asks for the honor of taking care of all their needs for the rest of their lives.

In order to connect with the depth of the story here, and the gorgeous turning that's about to happen, we have to connect with what is realized amid all the decaying corpses. What state of mind requires no support? What empowers the woman to say to this god that she already has everything he has to give her?

We can say that the women in that charnel ground were whole and perfect, but that had been true before they went on their walk. What changed? When they saw the corpses, when their minds settled, they became, in a sense, beings who were no longer turning from pain or mystery. When that occurs, what becomes available? Something invulnerable—and inarguable.

Still we need to be careful. What Indra offered is what many women do without every day. I recently came across the haunting citation that fully seventy-five percent of the world's poor are women. That single, bald percentage shook awake something that's hard to put to rest: the matter of who eats and who goes hungry, of who has a roof and who goes unsheltered, of who is cared for and who is abandoned when ill or aged.

It is likely that the wise woman who talked back to Indra was not poor by worldly standards, but still, it would not be easy to turn down such an offer. Nevertheless, from her awakened state, the wise woman was able to claim with confidence that they had everything they needed. And with that natural confidence, she was able to take the meeting to greater depth. She simply redrew the sky. She is not turning Indra away but standing in utter intimacy. And a subtle point, one that I often find hard in my life, is to realize that a caress of raining flowers—or some such sign—can't be depended upon to affirm our every difficult choice. To the degree I depend upon that, I look outside myself, losing myself and my voice.

To "talk back," in this sense, is to live from the heart of the matter. It is to remember that we are the daughters of ancient springtime, of beginningless time. Finally, an answer to "What do women really want?" The tree without root, the valley without north or south, the shout without echo: each moment so full it has no measure, no boundary, no remainder. Then, as we reach for food, or ordination, or to take the lead when it is called for, we "stand alone between heaven and earth" (as the Buddha proclaimed after his birth)—and walk together.

Where does a person go when the body dies? As long as we're alive,
we need certain impermanent things, like food and shelter,
but do we also need something that is everlasting?

10. Asan's Rooster

ASAN WAS a laywoman who studied Zen with Master Tetsumon and was unremitting in her devotion to practice.

One day during her morning sitting she heard the crow of the rooster and her mind suddenly opened. She spoke a verse in response:

> The fields, the mountains, the flowers, and my body too
> are the voice of the bird—what is left that can be said to
> hear?

Master Tetsumon recognized her enlightenment.

SUSAN MURPHY'S REFLECTION

As one whose morning meditation is blessed by not one but *two* roosters, I can understand Asan losing track of all that she thought she was with the help of a rooster. We did have three, but the exceedingly handsome Jubal Farnsworth was snapped up as an unexpected bonus by a fox, when Jubal rushed to defend two hens deep in meditation upon their eggs. That left the young and beautiful Pericles and his pal, Shadrach, who makes up for stumpy tail plumes with his pompous way of walking.

There's no choice at six in the morning but to enjoy their cries that claim the whole world—repeatedly. The creek music flows right through, and the wind, too, unimpeded. At best there's no irritated person left to hear; at worst, I'm given handy reminders to get out of my own way. To meet Asan where she is we have to discover what "unremitting" and repeated practice might be. And then the chance of no-one-left-to-hear becomes distinctly possible.

Repetition can be useful—the word "practice" already implies something about that. But roosters take it further. They know that there is no harm whatsoever in repeating a good sound. And anyway, no natural sound ever comes again; each appearance in the world is its own freely accepted extinction.

"Repetition never analyzes but merely insists," as acoustician Murray Schafer says (also on behalf of roosters). "Repetition makes the listener participate not by comprehending it but by *knowing* it."

When this whole body becomes an ear, with no impediment of thought, sounds can at last bring the world whole. And it is the *whole* world that finds out and clarifies the true person.

It's not only roosters who can deliver this lucky break but the creak of a floorboard, the clink of china, somebody's sneeze in the early morning meditation hall—any sound that finds little or nothing of you in the way and fills you completely can let you in directly to the shocking open secret: "What is left that can be said to hear?"

For Zen master Ikkyu it was not roosters who awakened him but a crow calling in the early morning, as he lay in a rowboat on Lake Biwa: *KARRRHHHHH!!!* How generously they give themselves away, these wondrous forms of "nothing left to hear." Always at hand to ease us back completely into "the fields, the mountains, the flowers, and my body too." What is that body, at such a moment?

How patiently they wait for us, the cries of the world, always ready to meet us when we suddenly let ourselves back in. Calling out repeatedly, just to let us hear what love sounds like when there is nothing attached to it. Like the girl in the old Chinese folksong, who knew her lover was somewhere out there in the dark, so she called time and again for no good reason to her maid, just so her lover could hear her voice: "Little Jade! Little Jade!"

*AURrroockkkauurrrocckkkarrrrhoooooooo*OOOOOO*!!!*

No-one. No-thing. No-rooster. No-me. Not even fields, mountains, flowers, waves gently slapping the sides of a wooden boat—though they are there, too.

But look, it's not just about lying back and having the whole world advance and confirm your utterly unexpected self as the cry of a bird. It's what you do next. When the mind suddenly opens, the cries of the world grow no less acute. Ask Kuan Yin, goddess of mercy, who hears all the cries of the world with no picking and choosing, no barrier in her heart.

The hen, it is said in Chinese lore, listens with her heart to hatch her eggs: a useful pointer to the ripening of a practice. And listen well, says the hen. We don't know when we will be snatched by one fox or another.

In a life-world on the brink of crumbling in mass extinctions, while human forms of insanity are roundly certified as "business as usual," how will you actualize the cry of the rooster with this whole great body and mind of fields, mountains, and flowers? As Linji said, "When you know who you are then you can be of some help."

You won't be alone. Asan will be there, and one or two roosters; in fact we're *all* in this together. The ongoing cry of the world—how helpful it is, how vast! How important to tune in. And how interesting "*you*" turn out to be!

Is there a single thing in this world that would not be qualified to awaken us? If so, what would disqualify it from such a holy task? Why is it that the most ordinary everyday experience, like washing the dishes, can one day suddenly be extraordinary?

11. The Old Woman's Enlightenment

JAPAN, EIGHTEENTH CENTURY ···

N OLD WOMAN went to hear Master Hakuin give a lecture. He said, "Your mind is the Pure Land, and your body is Amida Buddha. When Amida Buddha appears, mountains, rivers, forests, and fields all radiate a great light. If you want to understand, look into your own heart."

The old woman pondered Hakuin's words day and night, waking and sleeping. One day, as she was washing a pot after breakfast, a great light flashed through her mind. She dropped the pot and ran to tell Hakuin. "Amida Buddha filled my whole body. Mountains, rivers, forests, and fields are all shining with light. How wonderful!" She danced for joy.

"What are you talking about?" Hakuin asked. "Does the light shine up your asshole?"

Small as she was, she gave him a big push, saying, "I can see you're not enlightened yet!" They both burst out laughing.

SHINGE ROKO SHERRY CHAYAT'S REFLECTION

The unnamed old woman is a prototype often cast as someone initially dismissed, but whose cutting wisdom takes male protagonists by surprise—there are many stories from China and Japan in which monks' puffed-up views of their own attainment are skillfully skewered by such a figure.

The old woman in this koan may have been a follower of Pure Land Buddhism, which developed in fifth-century China and took root in

Japan in the twelfth and thirteenth centuries. She would have been taught that by living a meritorious life and by continuously praying to Amida, the Buddha of Infinite Light, she would be reborn in the Pure Land, leaving the suffering of this life behind and entering Amida Buddha's radiant realm in the Western Land.

Hakuin was a ferocious and daunting teacher when dealing with his ordained trainees, but he cared deeply for the peasants who lived in and around Hara, where his temple was located, beneath the looming presence of Mt. Fuji. With compassion and humor, he was able to make Buddhist teachings keenly relevant to these villagers, whose heavily taxed lives were filled with hardship and privation, sickness and early death.

How shocking it must have been to the old woman to hear Hakuin's words, "Your mind is the Pure Land and your body is Amida Buddha." How could it be that her own mind, filled with all its delusory thoughts, was the Pure Land? How could her wrinkled, decaying body be Amida Buddha? Still, Hakuin had said, "Look into your own heart," and with the trusting nature developed by her faith in Amida Buddha, that is what she did.

It's the same for us, after all. No matter how many times we've chanted Hakuin's "Song of Zazen"—which begins "Sentient beings are fundamentally buddhas" and ends "This very place is the Lotus Land of Purity; this very body is the body of the Buddha"—until we awaken to this living truth, we'll "seek it far away." How do we awaken? Only by looking into our own hearts, probing ever more deeply, can we realize what the Buddha taught: "*Attha dipa*: You are the light." Unfortunately, that essential trusting nature is often overridden by our sophisticated and skeptical worldview. And beset by the fracturing, multitasking circumstances of our twenty-first-century lives, how many of us can steep ourselves in our Zen practice, "day and night, waking and sleeping." Yet if we are true students of the Way, this is what we must do—take up the koan, or the current challenge presented by our lives, and bravely plunge into it.

As is frequently the case with a profound breakthrough, it was while the old woman was simply doing her daily tasks that she experienced the actuality of what until then seemed but a promise. We must take note, however: she was just washing a pot, but she was completely absorbed in Hakuin's statement.

Filled with the joy of her enlightenment, feeling the endless dimensions of that light within and without, she ran to Hakuin, who immediately tested her, with words crass enough to shake a realization that wasn't genuine. His question "Does the light shine up your asshole?" was the equivalent of a similarly coarse expression in our time, "Oh yeah? Stick it where the sun don't shine!"—words that would expose any lingering duality of sacred versus profane, Amida Buddha's realm versus this realm.

No longer a timid mouse, the old woman responded like a dragon, with the confidence that comes with genuine insight, challenging Hakuin, revealing the sameness of their awakened mind within the differentiation of male / female, renowned teacher / status-less student. Instantaneously they burst into great laughter, mirroring each other in joyful recognition.

For months on end, I worked on a seemingly impossible koan with my teacher. I knew my responses fell short of the challenge; I sensed that the koan demanded an aggressive physical act. When at last I was able to express my realization with full confidence, great laughter burst forth from both of us. And in seeing into that koan, I also saw how much of my life up to that point had been crimped by trying to be what others thought I should be; my concern for propriety was the very thing that had kept me from the beautiful freedom of direct, spontaneous action.

Is there any place where awakening cannot reach?

12. Qiyuan Gives Birth

 ASTER SHICHE asked his student, the nun Qiyuan Xinggang, "Buddha nature is not illusory. What was it like when you were nourishing the spiritual embryo?"

Qiyuan replied, "It felt congealed, deep, and solitary."

Shiche said, "When you gave birth to the embryo, what was it like?"

Qiyuan replied, "It was like being completely stripped bare."

Shiche said, "When you met with the Buddha, what was it like?"

Qiyuan said, "I took advantage of the opportunity to meet him face-to-face."

Shiche said, "Good! Good! You will be a model for those in the future."

SUNYA KJOLHEDE'S REFLECTION

When I first read this interchange between Shiche and Qiyuan, with that potent phrase, "nourishing the spiritual embryo," some long-ago experiences immediately leapt to mind. In my very first sesshin, when I was nineteen, I suddenly felt as if I were wrapped up in a mysterious birthing process. I had just started working with the koan "Mu" (Case 1 of the *Gateless Gate*), and somehow Mu—the whole universe, in fact—seemed to have all funneled into my own belly and to be swirling around in there. In a very physical way I sensed that something was trying to be born through me. At the time I hadn't a clue as to what was happening. It was an intense and confusing experience, particularly for someone so immature and so devoid of maternal instincts.

Maybe because it all seemed so odd, I never mentioned it to my teacher, Philip Kapleau, in our quick *dokusans* (private Dharma interviews). There was nothing like this in the tantalizing enlightenment stories I had read. Even if I could express what I was feeling, it never occurred to me that any man would relate to it. And yet, looking back, I believe Roshi would have understood. What a perfect metaphor for Zen practice: giving birth to the Unborn, to our own selfless Self!

"Nourishing the spiritual embryo," a phrase adopted from Taoist teachings, has long been used in Zen to refer to deepening and maturing practice. However others may have used it, for many women an image like this can be a lot more accessible than the traditional advice to "bore through Mu like an iron drill," or the purported words of the Buddha, "It's like a strong man pushing down on a weaker one."

I remember the turning point, in another seven-day sesshin, when it hit me that none of these very male images was working for me— when I finally had the confidence to toss it all aside and find my own way. Working with Mu, I realized, was like surrendering to and merging with a lover! Letting Mu walk, letting Mu eat, letting Mu do it all . . . suddenly practice opened up, shifting into something alive and juicy and intensely close.

And then Qiyuan's response to her teacher's question: "It felt congealed, deep, and solitary." Anyone who has, even for a moment, found herself in the dark radiant depths of meditation will recognize at once what this nun is getting at with these few potent words. "Congealed, deep, and solitary" beautifully hints at this state where the mind finds itself pulled in to the very heart of the universe—like some celestial body leaving its familiar orbit and entering the gravitational field of a huge planet. Only the breathing, only Mu. All sense of "myself" and the world "out there" burns up in contact with this powerful force field.

Through sincere practice we become more and more simple, plain, empty. Like a great broom, practice itself sweeps right through our ego-tainted motivations, cleansing our hearts and minds. I went to every sesshin I could get to that first year. Then, early on the last morning of a weeklong sesshin, after working on Mu through the night, I found myself in dokusan, feeling "completely stripped bare." Stunned, I remember asking my teacher, "Can it really be so *plain*?" I meant plain as in "obvious," but even more, I meant it as in "nothing special." Only then did I realize how strongly I had expected and longed for something glorious, something to crow about, a badge of excellence!

That afternoon, at the sound of the last bell signaling the end of the final dokusan of sesshin, Mu broke wide open. Nothing was ever quite the same again. As I experienced later when giving birth to my children, you have to simply get out of the way and let the great mystery roll right through. In a sense we're all pregnant with this wondrous buddha nature. And yet, paradoxically, until we've allowed it to fully come through us, it remains only an embryo, only a potential.

And once we have even just a glimpse of this true one, our whole life becomes an opportunity to "meet him face-to-face." Moving through the checkout line at the co-op, hiking with children in the woods, greeting the rising sun, steaming vegetables, sitting in zazen . . . will we take advantage of these opportunities or not? Everything depends on how we answer this question—not with words and explanations, but with our whole being, moment by moment.

Is our buddha nature, which teachers say is always with us, like a little person inside our bodies? Do we need to take care of it, and does it matter to our buddha nature who we are or what we do?

13. Chen's Mountain Flowers

CHINA, SEVENTH–NINTH CENTURIES ·······························

 HEN WAS a laywoman who traveled far and wide, visiting famous masters. After she realized enlightenment, she composed the following verse:

Up on the high slopes, I see only old woodcutters.
Everyone has the spirit of the knife and the axe.
How can they see the mountain flowers
reflected in the water—glorious, red?

JOANNA MACY'S REFLECTION

Laywoman Chen has seen a lot of the world in her journeys from one spiritual master to another. She has kept her eyes open. She's noticed what's going on. Even up on the high slopes, where the trees grow sparse and vegetation thins out, she sees what people are up to, busily hacking away at anything that can serve as fuel.

The old woodcutters are only doing what's been done for generations, taking from Earth whatever can be used. They've grown so accustomed to sawing and chopping, it's how they define themselves and their purpose for existence. Their tools—knife and axe—shape their perceptions, direct their movements, become, in a sense, who they are.

I love how Chen observes this. I am moved that her quest for enlightenment has not closed her eyes to what is being done in and to the workaday world. It still summons her attention, even after she finally realizes enlightenment.

I appreciate this because my attention, too, is so preoccupied with what we, collectively, are doing to our world. I cannot drive it from my mind. My spiritual practice calls me to come to terms with the destruction we humans are causing. I wouldn't want an "enlightenment" that would keep me from knowing and feeling the ways our actions are unraveling the very web of life. I want to be present to the suffering that comes with "the spirit of the knife and the axe"—the spirit of bulldozer and chainsaw, of deep sea drilling and mountaintop removal, of factory farms and genetically modified seeds.

There are different ways of responding to this hacking away, and my customary response is one of outrage and opposition. I want to make these actions stop. And in order to stop them, I'm ready to harangue those involved, to shame them and show them how wrong they are, and try to take away their tools and their funding. I don't think to aim for anything more. And indeed, outrage and opposition do save some mountain flowers.

How different is Chen's response. Instead of staying riveted on what the woodcutters are doing, her mind turns to what they are missing. The mountain flowers are right there in full view. The blossoms are real and red, glorious to behold. See how the water repeats them in its quivering mirror. Chen returns us to our senses. And that is what she wishes for the woodcutters: to see and feel the life around them. Look! Right here on a branch of this tree you're chopping, see the bright flowers! As she snaps them awake from their habitual behavior, the world comes into focus.

That's the kind of "stopping" she aims for. That's the kind of stopping where one comes back to oneself—and oneself is the place where real change can occur.

Is it possible to enter and witness the wilderness without taking something away from it? Why is it so easy to forget to pay attention to the beauty all around us?

14. Ganji's Family

CHINA, NINTH CENTURY ··

HE WORKMAN GANJI practiced the vow of Samantabhadra. He, his wife, and his daughter all mastered the Way. Once they invited the monk Yantou to pass the summer in their house.

One day as Yantou was mending his robe, Ganji came into the house and stood by him, watching. Yantou picked up the needle and pricked Ganji. Ganji immediately attained enlightenment and went to his room laughing. He put on a robe and bowed to Yantou in thanks.

His daughter asked, "What are you laughing at?"

Ganji said, "Don't ask."

His wife said, "If it's something good, everyone should know."

So Ganji told them what had happened and his wife was instantly enlightened. She said, "After thirty years, every time I drink water it will fill my throat."

Their daughter, hearing all this, was also instantly enlightened.

ANGIE BOISSEVAIN'S REFLECTION

It's rare to meet householders in our Zen teachings, much less a whole family, like the family we meet in this koan. Yet it is largely householders who practice Dharma in the West, not the monks and occasional nuns and old ladies represented in most Zen stories. And in my thirty years or more of Zen sitting practice, I have been deeply embedded in the ordinary and everyday life of my family.

I find this little story encouraging on many levels. I discovered the Dharma by chance while exploring a rough mountain road with my

59

husband many years ago. To our surprise, our road dead-ended at Tassajara Zen monastery, just as they were opening their first summer guest season. Invited in, we learned to sit zazen that day, and after a splendid dinner, were invited to hear the teacher speak. As a child I'd walked through my little town wondering if anyone in one of the houses I was passing knew about the something I had no words for but that I longed for. Sitting in the zendo at Tassajara that night, I was stunned to hear Suzuki Roshi somehow express what I had longed to hear. I had found my bearings at last.

Though I had my hands full in those years, with three little boys, I began to sit early every morning, and our whole family returned each summer to Tassajara for brief weekends. Eventually someone suggested that I might be interested in meeting a Zen master who lived close to my house. Thus I met my teacher, Kobun Chino Oto-kawa Roshi.

For many years, my practice, with Kobun's encouragement, was home-based, with dips into sesshin as often as I could manage. As my boys grew, I was more and more involved with the sangha, especially after Kobun moved to New Mexico and left a few of us who were senior students to develop the small centers, Kannon-do and Jikoji, that he had just begun. Still, whenever he returned he would encourage us to focus on home practice, as well as on our so-called "spiritual" practice. "If you think people at home are not practicing while you are at sesshin, you are making a mistake," he told us. This was a powerful lesson on the nature of Dharma as ubiquitous and seamless.

However, when Kobun referred to me as a "transmitted housewife," during a goodbye ceremony as I was leaving Jikoji after twelve years as its director, I was astounded. And yet, I had to admit that it was true. Through simple ceremonies, he had slowly ordained, empowered, and transmitted me and other householder students, confirming our practice of the Dharma just as we were.

I have always loved the image of Samantabhadra, the bodhisattva who peacefully rides a white elephant through the villages of the world. She/he vows to praise and pay homage to all buddhas, vowing always to protect, teach, and demonstrate Dharma, and to dedicate all personal merit to the benefit of all beings. He/she is a powerful metaphor for us as wives, mothers, grandmothers, and for all who work in the world. Practicing Samantabhadra's vow to aspire to awakening in order to benefit all beings in exactly the place where you find yourself—this was an inspiring model also for the humble workman Ganji and his wife and daughter. Samantabhadra's slow and benevolent movement through our world unites the ordinary and the holy, nirvana and samsara, all expressed as one place in one time, made seamless by simple and powerful compassion.

In the koan, Ganji and his family expressed their generosity by providing hospitality to a visiting monk. The monk, quietly sewing (I imagine him sitting in the sunlight, taking refuge in Buddha with every stitch), woke Ganji with a little prick of his needle. How generous, this prick, and how funny! Ganji's laughter roused his wife and daughter, and—good for them!—the women insisted on being included in the joke. Hearing the story, they felt the prick, and the whole family was enlightened.

A prick like this can travel through many generations, so that wife, daughter, and even you and I are included, right here, right now. Of course, it's annoying that the women in this story are nameless, but look again: it's the nameless wife who caps the meaning with the simple image of drinking plain water. This water . . . so clear, so delicious . . . every single time!

How can you tease a friend into joyfulness?
Can you—or should you—keep your own joy a secret?

15. The Woman Lets It Be

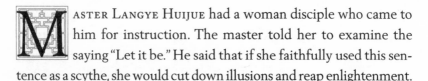

MASTER LANGYE HUIJUE had a woman disciple who came to him for instruction. The master told her to examine the saying "Let it be." He said that if she faithfully used this sentence as a scythe, she would cut down illusions and reap enlightenment.

The woman followed his instructions faithfully. One day her house burned down and she said, "Let it be." Another day her son fell into the water and when a bystander ran to tell her she answered, "Let it be."

One day she started to make fried cakes for dinner as her husband lit the fire. She prepared the batter and heated the oil, then poured a spoonful of batter into the hot oil.

When she heard the sizzling sound, she was immediately enlightened. She threw the pan to the ground and jumped up and down, clapping her hands and laughing.

Her husband shouted at her, "What are you doing? Have you gone mad?" She answered, "Let it be."

Then she went to Huijue and he confirmed that she had indeed harvested the holy fruit.

TAMARA MYOHO GABRYSCH'S REFLECTION

"How long have I been coming to see you?" asks the student.

"A long time," answers the master.

"Yes, but every time I come here, you always say the same thing and I never seem to get it."

"Just keep going—you will see it eventually."

"But it's taking forever! Why does it take so long?"

"Just let it be."

"You keep saying that. I do, but *nothing* is happening."

"My point precisely. So, just let it be. When nothing happens, something will happen. Just keep going."

The student sighs. "Okay, yes. I will."

When we study with a teacher year after year, hearing the same thing over and over, something as simple as "Let it be" can transform into a burning question: "*How* to let it be?" It may wear us down without any signs of success. Continuing to practice wholeheartedly, the question gradually penetrates each molecule of our being. Who knows when the surprisingly mundane sound of a sizzling cake might suddenly crack open our own Dharma eye?

I have worked in the kitchen at Zen River Temple for many years as *tenzo*, or head cook. I'm used to stir-frying copious amounts of carrots, peppers, and zucchini. Unexpected things can happen with the most ordinary of ingredients (like the time I made carrot soup and swore it tasted like dishwater until the moment I added a dash of lemon zest and dill). Paradoxically, letting all the ingredients "just be" always tastes better than interfering too much with them. If I listen to the flavors and ingredients, I know when to stop and just let them be. With practice, there's faith that each meal speaks with its own voice.

Cooking, of course, requires both training and practice, and in the beginning we may need to depend on recipes and cookbooks. In a similar way, if we want to truly "let things be" in our lives, we would do well to follow this woman disciple's example. She used the ingredients and recipes her teacher gave her and practiced cooking with them. In this case, the recipe was "Let it be."

At first glance, this phrase might look like the perfect excuse to do nothing, or a justification for complacency. Don't be misled! Letting things be doesn't mean that we cease functioning, stop thinking, or get rid of the self once and for all (as most of us erroneously seem to hope). In fact it is quite the opposite. It is like waking from a stupor to find everything is very much alive and buzzing.

Let it be, and in that moment our attachment to self can fall away, and appreciation for this life as the life of the Buddha, Dharma, and Sangha—as one mind—can't help but express itself. A simple grain of rice left in the rice cooker is as valuable as a nugget of gold.

Maybe, when her home burned down, this disciple found herself looking forward to a fresh start. Maybe her son was an enthusiastic swimmer who was diving into the water every free moment he had. Maybe seeing her fried batter fly through the air and land on the floor was thrilling. Who knows? When we actively let things be, surprises can happen. A failed sponge cake can perhaps become an excellent trifle.

Life becomes much more interesting when we let things be. In the practice of paying no attention to this illusory self—the cause of all our anxieties—the way is paved for the true, original self to somersault into view. It's always there, it's just that it's been thoroughly ignored—until our own frying pan hits the floor with a crack! This can happen in an instant, and that's when practice really begins. Our true self now simply acts as a conduit for the unborn Buddha mind. From this perspective, we are free to choose how to live this life according to our innate wisdom. We can know what to do and how to do it, without being hampered by the conditioned patterns the dualistic self so much enjoys. In other words, there's no need to buy into our delusions. And not being attached to delusions, this ordinary life can open up like a rainbow in a storm.

Simply practice the recipe of leaving the self be and the light of our original nature can shine. Then peace of mind is ours. And when we are at peace, all sentient beings simultaneously are at peace.

If we ignore the details of daily life, things fall apart. But if we don't ignore them, we may lose ourselves in those very details. Is there a middle way?

16. Awakening While Cooking

A MARRIED BRAHMAN woman went to hear the Buddha teach, and she was so moved by the Dharma that she became a lay disciple. Later she heard the nun Mahapajapati teach, and she wanted to ordain as a nun herself, but her husband would not allow it. She continued to practice as a lay Buddhist as best she could, still carrying out her obligations as a Brahman's wife.

One day, as she was cooking curry in the kitchen, the meal caught fire and, with a great crackling, burst into flames. In that moment, she had a deep insight into the teaching of impermanence, and she attained the third stage of awakening. From then on she gave up wearing jewels or ornaments, as if she were already a nun. When her husband asked about this, she told him she was no longer capable of living a domestic life. So together they went to Mahapajapati and at last the wife ordained, to her great joy. Shortly afterward she became an arahant.

VIVEKA CHEN'S REFLECTION

How can I live out the Dharma wholeheartedly? This is a burning question if, like me, you share this Brahman woman's urgency to bring the Buddha's Dharma to life.

Although my Dharma sister in the story wished to become a nun and devote herself completely to the Dharma, in those days women were not allowed to ordain without the permission of their family. Sadly, her husband was not initially ready to voluntarily part with his wife.

Reading this, I feel fortunate that in 1997 I was able to train for and complete the powerful ritual of Buddhist ordination within the conditions of my socially engaged life. In the Triratna Buddhist Order (formerly Friends of the Western Buddhist Order) we are ordained as *dharmacharinis* (dharmafarers), which is neither a monastic nor householder path. Rather, we commit to wholeheartedly bringing the Dharma into all aspects of our lives, for individual and social transformation. The Order was founded in 1967 by Sangharakshita, an Englishman who spent sixteen years in India as a Buddhist monk. When he returned to the West, Sangharakshita created ways that Buddhist practice could be lived fully in the modern world, without watering down the core teachings.

When I was twenty-nine and living in San Francisco, the basic life components that still characterize my path were already apparent. I was working for social justice, plunging into meditation's depths, sitting silent retreats, studying Dharma, and building a sangha. I was also learning about the heart in a relationship (now a marriage), and enjoying the city and the surrounding natural beauty. I smile as I look back at this young woman, enamored with Dharma practice and life. She was a playful and fearless ball of energy who wanted to live as a bodhisattva and work to end suffering. With a straight face she said that her deepest desire was to awaken as a buddha in this lifetime.

Sometimes I joke that if my ascetic preceptor Sanghadevi had seen all the sequins in my closet, she might not have ordained me. Unlike the woman in the story, I did not give up wearing jewels and ornaments. But my preceptor knew me very well, and she recognized my sincerity and diligence. In the ordination ceremony, my readiness to go forth into the Dharma life was witnessed. My preceptor gave me the name Viveka, meaning "clarity and the seclusion of meditation," and exhorted me to "be in the world, but not of it." The cells in my body quivered for days after the ordination.

The woman in the story and I both undertook the koan of "being in the world but not of it" by practicing the Dharma while maintaining social responsibilities. But unlike my predecessor, I was both empowered and encumbered by the modern myth that as a woman I could do it all! I could "cook curry" and also practice as an ordained woman transforming the world I lived in through teaching Dharma and working for social justice. My predecessor had no choice but to continue as a housewife, despite boldly wishing to go forth as a shaven-headed renunciate. Impressively, she proceeded undeterred and practiced as best she could in her circumstances, until at last her husband saw her sincerity and they both joined Buddha's sangha.

Regardless of lifestyle, we *are* in the world. In this world, anything can and does happen. Going about my full days, I meet situations and people that sometimes appear as "helpful," sometimes as "obstacles." And sometimes I am able to recognize that the obstacles themselves are helpful.

The responsibility for endless daily cooking for a large family could be viewed as an obstacle. But one day your dinner might catch on fire and you could have such deep insight into impermanence that you'll awaken in this lifetime. That's food for thought.

The truths the Buddha revealed are precisely about this endlessly effulgent, messy, and wonderful world that we are and inhabit. The unexpected burning curries and unwelcome obstacles that catch us off guard are so often what catalyze awakening. Zen master Dogen said, "If you cannot find the truth right where you are, where else do you expect to find it?"

When your life burns up completely, is there anything left? Is it selfish to give up the life of a householder in order to join a monastery, or to leave your family to go on retreat?

17. The Woman in Samadhi

CHINA, THIRTEENTH CENTURY ··

L ONG AGO, Manjushri, the bodhisattva of wisdom, went to a gathering of buddhas. By the time he arrived, all had departed except for Shakyamuni Buddha and a woman who was seated in a place of highest honor next to the Buddha, deep in meditation. Manjushri asked the Buddha, "Why can a woman sit beside the Buddha when I cannot?"

The Buddha replied, "Just bring her out of samadhi and ask her yourself."

Manjushri circled the woman three times, snapped his fingers, raised her up to the Brahma heaven, and employed all his supernatural powers, but he was unable to bring her out of samadhi.

The Buddha then said, "Even a hundred thousand Manjushris wouldn't be able to bring this woman out of samadhi. But down below, past twelve hundred million lands as innumerable as the sands of the Ganges River, there is a bodhisattva called Delusive Wisdom who will be able to awaken her." At that very moment Delusive Wisdom emerged from the ground and paid homage to the Buddha. Then he went before the woman and snapped his fingers once. At this the woman emerged from samadhi.

Natalie Goldberg and Miriam Sagan's Reflection

This reflection is written by two women, rather than one; two women working together is not the traditional way of addressing a koan. Such collaboration breaks the structure of student-teacher hierarchy and the duality of the right-or-wrong answer.

In this koan, Manjushri, one of the senior bodhisattvas of the sangha, shows up late to the gathering and is horrified to find a low-status person, an unknown woman, in the honored spot beside the Buddha where Manjushri usually sits. He is jealous and asks why she's there. This question gets the ball rolling—we have to give Manjushri credit for this. But all the powers at his disposal can't awaken her.

The bodhisattva of delusive wisdom—far away and yet available in an instant—knows exactly what to do to wake this woman out of her samadhi, her meditative concentration. He is not identical with delusion; he knows enough to pay homage to the Buddha before he snaps his fingers. With that, the woman springs to life.

NATALIE GOLDBERG: I like the koans that show real human beings, with their camaraderie and willingness to challenge each other. If they can do it, I can too. I backed into this koan, seduced like Manjushri by the immovable woman next to the Buddha and by the unusual mention of delusive wisdom. Wisdom and delusion, interchangeable, inseparable, like pouring milk into milk or melting three squares of chocolate in one cooking pot. Help comes not from the heavens but by yanking up the bodhisattva from the roots of the earth.

What makes the earth turn? Desire, poison, need, aggression, stupidity. Not running from these for a change, but letting them come close, and letting a woman finally be in on this play. If we can't call up all the dimensions of being human, how can we transform that energy into wisdom?

I understand this koan. I, too, have been stuck in samadhi. To be stuck any place is to be impotent, no matter how grand the place, how big and clear. Stuck is stuck. Stuck doesn't know when it's time to leave a celebration, or bend down and help an old man who just tripped and fell on his face. All the meditating in the world doesn't stop a rape in the Congo. Some effort needs to be made; we must be willing to get our white clothes dirty. We don't need more wisdom poured into an empty vessel. We need to be willing to hear about horror, broken bones, economic collapse, betrayal. Such willingness moves the spokes, enlivens us.

MIRIAM SAGAN: The woman in samadhi worked hard to get next to the Buddha. She had to leave her family, go against societal expectations, and follow a path that seemed closed to her.

But sitting in samadhi next to the Buddha was just a first step. When everyone else went home, the woman, convinced she wasn't home, sat still.

Wisdom cannot wake her up. She needs to know about sex and money, about how to change the oil in a car, how to cut a radish, how to make a living. She needs to know the names of her neighbors. I am worried about this woman, cool and peaceful in samadhi.

The sticky trap in this koan is the apparent split between wisdom and ordinary life. Can everyday life wake us up by itself, or do we first need to leave home to sit next to the Buddha? In my own life, I suspect that if I'd stayed in a New Jersey suburb I'd be less awake than I am for having run off to San Francisco as a young woman. The act of simply leaving home makes a spiritual path a possibility.

Delusive wisdom is motherly, always accommodating, always available. Daily life goes on with or without my impetus—there is always soup to be made, a baby to pick up, a phone to be answered.

Let delusive wisdom wake you up!

The woman is not the only one trapped. What wakes us up?

> Curve of a blue door
> Gray wet wall on a gray day
> When you call and tell me your suffering
> When I tell you mine
> Vanilla smell of ponderosa
> Corn tortilla crack in my mouth

Sudden light at day's end
Open highway
The word "Paris"
Coca-Cola
Putting a large condolence card in the neighbor's
    mailbox in the rain
Drinking tea with a friend as dusk falls and the chatter
    around us fades away
The sight of my naked feet
Overheard gossip from the next table
The right song on the car radio
Biting into a jelly doughnut
Sweeping dust

"A woman sits by the Buddha in the place of highest honor."
What do you feel when you think of her there? Have you ever
had trouble coming back to your ordinary life after a time
of retreat or deep concentration?

18. Yu Uses Her Full Strength

THE LAYWOMAN Yu Daopo made doughnuts for a living. She also studied Chan—Chinese Zen—with Master Langye Huijue, who told her to contemplate Linji's phrase, "the true person of no rank." One day she and her husband were delivering doughnuts, and as they walked through the street, they met a beggar who was singing "Happiness in the Lotus Land." Yu was suddenly enlightened and she threw the tray of doughnuts to the ground.

Her husband scolded her: "Have you gone crazy?"

Yu slapped him, saying, "This is not a realm you understand." She then went to see Langye, who immediately verified her awakening.

One day after this, Langye asked the assembly, "Which one is 'the true person of no rank'?"

Yu shouted out this verse:

> There is a true person of no rank, who has six arms and
>   three heads.
> When she uses her full strength to cut, Mount Hua is split
>   into two.
> Her strength is like the ever-flowing water,
> not caring about the coming of spring.

KOKYO MEG PORTER ALEXANDER'S REFLECTION

Thirty-five years ago, when I put on my black robe and headed to the mountain monastery of Tassajara, stories like this—though always of men—were an entry to Zen practice for me; stories made enlightenment something personal and embodied and radical.

Most of us who came to Zen in the 1970s were young and sincere. We were desperate to be comfortable with ourselves and, at the same time, determined to make a difference in the world. We brought all forms of suffering with us to the cushion, to the embrace of Suzuki Roshi's teaching. And with practice, through practice, something in us was transformed. The intensity of practice opened our senses, allowed us to hold our difficulties and cultivate our strength.

When I read the story of Yu, I imagine a woman I might have known or been, someone needing to break open, someone prepared for the effort this would take. A woman whose heart/mind responded deeply to a generous teacher, a teacher whose vision of sangha was wide and inclusive.

The turning phrase, or koan, that Yu contemplated has a timeless ring: "the true person of no rank." The practice of Zen includes living with a phrase, returning to it over and over, not only during meditation but throughout the day's activities. I drew my koan for those early years of practice from words of Tozan in *Zen Mind, Beginner's Mind*, and I rephrased them in the feminine: "The blue mountain is the mother of the white cloud. The white cloud is the daughter of the blue mountain. All day long they depend on each other, without being dependent on each other. The white cloud is always the white cloud. The blue mountain is always the blue mountain. Completely independent, completely dependent." The blue mountain and white cloud moved me to tears.

These koans push us beyond our ideas of "self"—the complicated, emotional self that is faceted by roles and fractured with desire and grief. Fiercely explored, the world can shift and open into a pure and luminous reality right before our eyes. For Yu it happened in the marketplace in the middle of the workday. For me, it was in the pure presence of the Tassajara garden at night, illuminated by the moon, washed in the freshness of the mountain creek.

Yu's teacher could see the "person of no rank" in her when she couldn't see it for herself. And by her efforts, she became that person of "no rank," that person whose sense of herself was deeply rooted and radically expansive.

Our teachers wait for us. I imagine Master Langye, with the pride of a parent barely concealed, offering his respect to Yu by presenting the question to the assembly of monks and lay folks: "Which one is the person of no rank?" Perhaps he had done this before. Perhaps it was the tradition to acknowledge publicly these breakthrough encounters.

I imagine Yu, trepidatious but fully ready, fully attuned, shouting out in response. Shouting! Why not? Her words, full of strength, full of flowing, of arms and heads, a sword that penetrates with ease the solid, the deep, and the vast, like water springing from her own depths. Yu's imagery invokes the power of Manjushri's wisdom sword and Kuan Yin's elixir of compassion. She invokes the power of earth and water, feminine images of the deep and boundless source.

I met my husband at Tassajara. We had a daughter and eventually made our way back into the world as householders, carrying with us a combined practice life of twenty-five years at San Francisco Zen Center. When my daughter left home, I resumed a formal practice, rooted in lay life, and took priest ordination.

Now, as I enter my eighth decade, the story of Yu's enlightenment evokes something nuanced and personal. There is gratitude and tenderness for the ordinary, as well as the difficult and inspired. The Tassajara creek still sings in the background for me, though my life is more like the water I live by now—the Russian River, running wider, smoother, deeper, before emptying into the Pacific Ocean. Step by step by step—for each of us, the only way.

I keep in view these words I found in a hospital's simple meditation room while working as a chaplain:

These many beautiful days cannot be lived again.
But they are compounded in my own flesh and spirit,
and I take them in full measure toward whatever lives ahead.

—Daniel Berrigan

What happens when we deeply see something and are thereby taken beyond the cultural norms and expectations of others? Where do we stand then?

19. The Flower Hall on Buddha's Birthday

HE NUNS of Tokeiji were famous for their beautiful and elaborate flower decorations on Buddha's birthday. Master Yodo, the abbess of Tokeiji and a former imperial princess, wrote a verse for this occasion:

> Decorate the heart of the beholder,
> for the Buddha of the flower hall
> is nowhere else.

Her attendants also wrote verses. Ika, a former court lady, wrote:

> Throw away into the street the years of the past.
> What is born now on the flower dais—
> let it raise its newborn cry.

AMALA WRIGHTSON'S REFLECTION

A quick glance at these verses and you might dismiss them as merely picturesque—aristocratic ladies writing elegant verses about their flower-arranging and devotions in honor of the baby Buddha. How quaint and feminine! But look a little more closely and you'll find direct and powerful teachings about the Great Matter of birth and death.

Whether you are at a Chinese, Korean, Japanese, or American Zen temple, the central ritual of the Buddha's birthday celebrations is the same. A small sculpture of the infant Buddha, one hand pointing skyward and the other to the earth, is decorated with flowers, placed on a dais (often in the form of the white six-tusked elephant that Queen Maya dreamed of at Siddhartha's conception), and then bathed in sweet tea. The sculpture depicts Siddhartha Gautama the moment after he emerged from his mother's womb. He took seven steps in each of the four directions and declared, "Above the heavens, below the heavens, I alone am the Honored One. I shall dispel the suffering of the world!" The bathing ritual reenacts what happened right after that, when the nagas, great chthonic serpent deities, washed the newborn in warm rain.

As the nuns are decorating the flower hall, Master Yodo reminds them that no Buddha exists outside of their own heart. In our ceremonies and devotions we are honoring this One, the Beholder who is born afresh in each moment. Each of us is the only one who can dispel suffering. No one else can do it for us. In the *Dhammapada* the Buddha says, "We are our own protection; we are indeed our own secure abiding; how could it be otherwise? So with due care we attend to ourselves."

The Buddha's birthday is celebrated during the springtime in the northern hemisphere. I grew up in subtropical Auckland where the differences between the seasons are not pronounced. So when I trained in western New York, I was unprepared for the effect that spring had on me after the long, hard winters. When spring finally began its slow procession of blooms (crocuses, daffodils, tulips, magnolias, cherry and crab apple blossoms, peonies . . .) I'd feel an acute tenderness mixed with joy, relief, and gratitude. I could now fully appreciate Master Huangbo's words:

Without a whole spell of cold that bites into your bones,
how could the plum blossoms regale you with their piercing
fragrance?

Huangbo is also writing here about what happens after the "winter" of letting go of all our notions about ourselves and the world, and the wonderful springtime that follows. Lady Ika's verse suggests this birth too:

> Throw away into the street the years of the past
> What is born now on the flower dais—
> let it raise its newborn cry.

We don't know anything about Lady Ika, but her poem suggests hard-won freedom from her past. Certainly many of the women from Tokeiji whose stories we know suffered terribly before entering the monastery. Lady Ika seems ready to meet whatever comes her way, even defiant. Many of us carry heavy burdens from the past. We draw conclusions about ourselves based on what happened to us (we're flawed, unlovable, entitled to more, etc.) and react to people and situations out of these stories. We get criticized or ignored and find ourselves arguing with our long-dead father, or raging against the partner who has left us.

Last year, toward the end of a long retreat, I noticed that despite weeks of sustained sitting, I was still holding back. I asked myself why, and immediately an image of a small child flashed into consciousness. She was huddled in a corner, arms clasped tightly around her legs, head buried between her knees. Here was the one I had been attempting to hold at bay! Was she really so fearsome? Actually she *was* fear. For months after "meeting" her I experienced bouts of acute anxiety and panic. Though the fears that woke me at 2 AM came convincingly clad in present concerns, they were both personal history, connected to my being separated from my mother soon after birth, and at the same time impersonal *dukkha*—the angst that comes from believing we are separate.

Often to throw away the years of the past we must first let in their pain. Let the pain come, let it be, and on its own it goes, because that is its nature. Eventually the fear dissolved and in its place came intense gratitude and joy. "What is born now on the flower dais—let it raise its newborn cry!"

Where is the flower hall of your life? If our spirits are already beautiful, why do we adorn ourselves? And how do you keep family photo albums without clinging to the past?

20. Sonin's Shadeless Tree

ASTER KEIZAN JOKIN asked the nun Mokufu Sonin, "The winter is coming to an end and the springtime is arriving. There is an order to this. What is your understanding?"

Sonin replied, "In the branches of a tree without shade, how could there be any seasons?"

Keizan asked her, "What about right now?"

Sonin bowed. Keizan then transmitted the Dharma robe to her.

ANITA FENG'S REFLECTION

"Winter is coming to an end and the springtime is arriving." Coming and going is our fragile and precious human route. The passing of time and the passing on of a lineage—a koan to last a lifetime. Just consider the old man and the baby who appear in New Year's Day parades all over the United States, the bent old man passing the baton to an infant swaddled in diapers. Good luck, kid! Consider a Zen teacher testing her students to gauge their understanding, so that mind-to-mind transmission will continue into the next generation. This is one view of time, in the relative sense of the word and world.

But consider, also, that there is more to time than this limited view of winter, spring, summer, fall, in orderly progression. What is being exchanged here between these two, Master Keizan Jokin and his disciple, Mokufu Sonin? Their dialogue goes beyond the idea that for everything there is a season.

Every spring I watch the juices of the earth stir and open up to fistfuls of blossoms while the old leaves of autumn disappear into the soil. My father, at eighty-eight, is entering the final phase of his life. Recently his health took a turn for the worse. His lungs weakened suddenly, and he had difficulty breathing or walking on his own. At his age the deterioration of the body is something to be expected. But our family had grown up in the sheltering shade of his tree, and it was a most startling event to find him so incapacitated. All of us who were able came to be with him. Sitting around the kitchen table, we gazed at his weakening figure, our hearts twisted with love and pain.

There is, however, another aspect to time, one which goes beyond the relative world. Master Keizan Jokin invites Sonin to present this, asking, "What is your understanding?" She responds with a demonstration of timelessness, of emptiness, of the absolute world. Like her tree without shade, all phenomena from the microscopic to the galactic are without self-nature. Why? Because inter-being and constant change are our true reality—so how can we possibly pin down *anything* to a fixed point?

Even though our stories of selfhood are limiting, I think that for most people the concept of no-self sounds rather terrifying. But I suggest that you view this impermanence as a mark of freedom, true freedom, already and always at the cusp of *being*. This is a springtime of another order! Before I slap words on the transitory nature of things ("my father is dying"), I can take refuge in this timeless universe of no self-nature.

There was a moment at the kitchen table, one I'm sure you would recognize, when I met my father's eye and we both smiled. Something shimmering happened; you might call it mind-to-mind transmission in Zen language. But it was beyond language—a place of no mind, no tree, no branches, no light or shade.

Here, in this story, Sonin takes up timeless residence with complete assurance and offers this to her master: "In the branches of a tree without shade, how could there be any seasons?"

Master Keizan Jokin then inquires, gauging Sonin's final and complete understanding of time, "What about right now?"

Here, in this momentary and most perfect of all possible worlds, laughter and tears become one. Sitting across from me, my father scolds me, in his usual way: "Now Anita, I don't want you dropping everything and flying across the country every time I sneeze. Okay?"

"Okay," I say, and give him a sloppy kiss, the kind he likes best.

Do you understand Sonin's wordless reply? What is it?

A poem to chew on at *your* kitchen table:

> Yes, there is a remedy for illness—
> it is received by saying into each shaded name and form
> one indivisible word. What is it?
> > (It is just now, as we talk to each other that the medicine
> > begins. Do you hear it?)

> Furthermore, there is a remedy for aging—
> it is attained by stepping off the edge of time and space
> on a single breath.
> > (It is just now, as we turn to each other, that we extend
> > ourselves. Do you see it?)

> And there is a remedy for dying too—
> it is realized by letting the heart out of its cage, turning cause
> and effect to shimmering dust.
> > (It is just now, as a smile lights from one face to another
> > that renewal begins. How will you catch it?)

Can we ever meet the present without the past or the future? When have you and another person truly met each other?

21. Linji Meets the Old Woman Driving the Ox

CHINA, NINTH CENTURY ···

ASTER LINJI YIXUAN went to see Master Bingdian An. On the way he met an old woman driving an ox in a field. Linji asked her, "Which way is the road to Bingdian?"

The woman hit the ox with her stick and said, "This animal. It walks all over the place without even recognizing the road."

He repeated, "I asked you. Which way is the road to Bingdian?"

The woman said, "This beast! It's five years old and still can't be put to use."

Linji said to himself, "If you want to learn something from the person in front of you, first observe what the person does." And he had the feeling his sticking point had been removed.

Then when he reached Master An, An asked him, "Have you seen my sister-in-law?"

Linji said, "Yes, I've already been taken in tow."

MYOKAKU JANE SCHNEIDER'S REFLECTION

In Linji's time monks traveled by foot, and it could take days, weeks, or even months to arrive at their destination. When Linji arrived in the area of An's temple he came to a crossroads, and there saw an older woman driving an ox in a field. It was a familiar sight, and he stopped and asked her for directions.

He was confounded by the woman's answer to his simple question. He no doubt reasoned, "She's old. I guess she didn't hear me." In fact, she had hit the ox, the symbol of practice, to draw his attention to the way that he was looking for answers everywhere except in the most obvious place, himself. Confused by discrimination, he ignored the startling creativity of the moment. Not yet giving her his full attention, he pressed his question further.

The woman answered him again in her unique way: *Wake up. Who are you talking to? What are you doing? Why are you sleeping now?* His confusion suddenly cleared and he looked more closely at their conversation.

Discrimination fell away and he realized that this ordinary woman was someone of strong practice. Linji didn't expect to find a master in a woman driving an ox in a field. By ignoring the unconditioned present, he had been wandering in a dreamlike state looking for what was already there.

Later, when Master An asked whether he had met his sister-in-law, Linji said, "Yes, I've already been taken in tow." By being "taken in tow" he probably meant the meeting between master (the old woman) and student, in which the student, Linji, had found his own ground. Through the old woman's compassionate teaching he realized that wherever he stood, there was the perfect teaching and the perfect teacher. He was expressing gratitude and warm appreciation for their meeting.

I like this image of the older woman with the ox because of my twenty-two years of experiences with a Shingon Buddhist lay-ordained teacher, Kojun Chiba. She was in her early sixties when Peter and I met her in Kyoto in 1973. She had raised four children and her home was a designated part of Mount Koya, the home temple of Shingon Buddhism. She rose at 3:30 AM every day to do her practices. Her altar Buddha was Benzaiten, an eight-armed female figure that had been hand-carved for her by a priest friend.

Benzaiten is very popular in Japan as one of the seven gods of good fortune (the only female) and also as a many-armed figure in Tendai and Shingon Buddhism. She is associated with eloquence and creativity. Chiba-sensei once went with us on an overnight sailboat trip to the island in Lake Biwa where one of the oldest statues of Benzaiten is enshrined. The only picture Chiba-sensei ever allowed us to take of her is the group picture at the end of the trip.

Chiba-sensei's way of teaching through everyday affairs was natural and compassionate. She encouraged me to nurture creativity, and many of our meetings dealt with painting as Buddhist practice. With her encouragement I went to school to learn *nihonga*, Japanese traditional painting. Once she came to my studio to look at some work. She sat for a long time in front of a large painting and finally said, "I like it." Then she went home.

This koan reminds me of one of Chiba-sensei's primary teachings: "Take full responsibility for your life in the world as-it-is." In gratitude I offer my words:

> Cutting off the north,
> east, and west,
> and rolling up the
> south behind me,
> I take a step
> and then another
> and another.

Is it possible to train the wayward mind to stay on the Dharma path? What is the name of your inner ox? When you meet a stranger, how do you know whether she is your teacher?

22. Jiyu-Kennett's Not Bigger, Not Smaller

A PERSON ASKED, "What is a minor enlightenment?"
Master Jiyu-Kennett said, "A what?"
The person continued, "A minor *kensho*, a minor *satori*?"

Jiyu-Kennett replied, "Enlightenment is enlightenment. Sometimes the glimpses are big and sometimes they are small, but it is still one and the same thing. Don't think that the enlightenment is bigger or smaller."

The questioner continued, "I had the impression that once you got enlightenment, you got it."

Jiyu-Kennett said, "Once you have realized it, you will always know it. But if you don't keep your training up, heaven help you; you'll be worse off than you were before. It's not something that you 'get'; it's not something that you 'keep' for eternity. Training, as Dogen says, is enlightenment. This is why Shakyamuni Buddha always carried his begging bowl and always wore his robe. A lot of people think, 'Why didn't he just sit back and enjoy it?' Enlightenment isn't something you have; it's something you are, something you do."

Heila Downey's Reflection

The simplicity and directness of Jiyu-Kennett's answer to this questioner reminds me of my own struggles with similar questions, as well as my teachers' ongoing and compassionate encouragement, sesshin after sesshin. Perhaps I might not have used the exact same phraseology—still, I remained perplexed about what "enlightenment" was. How would I know if I had "it"?

My very early years of Zen practice were punctuated by pre- and post-sesshin whisperings centered around kensho, satori, and answering koans. Though the question of "bigger" or "smaller" did not arise, I wanted to know: What is kensho? What is satori? And ultimately what is enlightenment?

Within the realms of perceived mystery and secrecy surrounding these words, it eventually became clear that no other person could provide answers to these perplexing questions. So what was I missing? Why did I not get it? Then one day after an interview with Kapleau Roshi, adrenalin pumping, I rushed down some stairs back to the Dharma hall and bashed head-on into a rather large bell—*boooooom*—ouch! It was immediately clear that the answers to these questions are in action and doing, not explanations and words!

Despite this insight, my discomfort in not understanding eased only marginally as I had to admit that satori and kensho still remained totally incomprehensible, while the more explicable "enlightenment," another frequently used word, felt more familiar and thus became my companion and mantra. To "enlighten," or "bring light to," denotes casting light upon "what is," enabling one to perceive it more clearly.

Now I would say that kensho, satori, and enlightenment are a doing, a way of life, not things or states, and can be likened to looking through a pinprick hole in a rice paper screen, when all at once we see that which was previously hidden. But unless we continue to meticulously clear the viewing hole, through sustained and ongoing practice and the deepening of our insight, eventually this view will diminish, returning us to a state of darkness, hunger, thirst, and attachments caused by our deluded thinking. With deep gratitude I have to admit that Roshi continuously admonished us with the words, "Less thinking, much less thinking, more hard training!" which concurs with Jiyu-Kennett's "if you do not keep up the training, heaven help you."

Some years after I received *inka*, or Dharma transmission, an older student who had attended retreats regularly came to an interview with me. I asked him, "Do you have any questions?"

He replied, "No!" Then quickly added, "But I want something."

I asked, "What can I do for you?"

He said, "As I am of an advanced age, I am sure not to have many years left in this current form and I would like to attain enlightenment before I die! Can you help me please?"

While not doubting his commitment and sincerity, it was clear to me that his request was born out of delusion, out of "I want." After pointing this out to him and encouraging him to relinquish all "I want" by returning to before-thinking-mind, I poured him a cup of tea, saying, "Remember, in the Lankavatara Sutra the Buddha urges us to just drink the tea, no attainment, with nothing to attain. So, please have some of this hot, sweet, amber-colored tea. Just drink tea!"

After some moments he reached for the tea *very* hesitatingly, all the while looking at me. He sipped, and sipped again. More silence ensued. Then he exclaimed: "I just didn't get it, did I?"

I then said, "The tea was indeed amber colored, but neither *hot* nor *sweet*! Caught up in words and 'I want,' you were unable to taste what is." His "I want" mind prevented him from attaining his true nature and becoming one with what is—in this case: cool, unsweetened tea.

Any glimmer of insight, not bigger, not smaller—even "I just didn't get it, did I?"—has the potential to break the mold of conditioned behavior, benefiting our lives and the world.

As Sengcan, the Third Zen Patriarch, wrote in the *Xinxin Ming*:

> Not only here, not only there,
> truth's right before your very eyes.

> Distinctions such as large and small
> have relevance for you no more.

> The largest is the smallest too—
> here limitations have no place.

What is the smallest experience of enlightenment you have ever had?
Is it possible that you missed it altogether? What would change in
your heart if "enlightenment" wasn't a noun, after all?

23. Jiaoan's Sand in the Eye

CHINA, TENTH–ELEVENTH CENTURIES ·······································

JIAOAN WAS the niece of a high official of the Song dynasty. When she was young, she decided not to marry or bear children and she set her heart on the way of Chan. She experienced a clear awakening at the words of Master Yuanwu Keqin as he spoke to the assembly.

Later, Yuanwu said to her, "You should go on to erase your views—then you will finally be free."

She answered in verse:

> The pillar pulls out the bone sideways;
> the void shows its claws and fangs;
> even if one profoundly understands,
> there is still sand in the eye.

ZENKI MARY MOCINE'S REFLECTION

I would like to have known Jiaoan Roshi. I don't know if she would agree with my understanding of her verse, but I think she would support me in offering my own interpretation. In this koan, she stands up to her teacher and effectively disagrees with his instruction. He tells her to erase her views. She says there will still be "sand in the eye." I understand her to be saying, "I will still be a human being."

When I began practice I struggled with what I took to be the instruction to suppress emotions. I heard that I would find equanimity by not having views, or emotions, and it seemed to me that I was being asked to give up my humanity and my personality. There may have been some such flavor to the teachings I heard, but I think I exaggerated it out of my own fear of the teaching of "no-self" and my own need to do it "right."

Eventually, I took ownership of my own practice, as Jiaoan does, and came to an understanding of liberation that includes my own emotions, views, and personality. In her verse, Jiaoan tells Yuanwu that one may struggle like hell, fight with the fearsome beast that emptiness (the void) can represent, and arrive at a profound understanding—and yet there is still sand in the eye.

What is this sand? I think it represents our small self, our humanity. We must include this small self within our profound understanding of the "Big Self" that includes everyone, or we fall off into one-sided practice. So we must practice everyday life, but with the mind of emptiness. We need to include our emotions and views in our practice so as to see their emptiness.

I have found that my life works when I do not try to suppress emotions or deny that I have views. When I deny them, they just sneak up on me later and cause problems.

Years ago, when I was first at Tassajara Zen Mountain Monastery, I had a friend from Mexico. He taught me to make *budin azteca*, an enchilada casserole. Not long after, he died of AIDS. That summer, I made budin azteca for the Tassajara guests. As I cooked, I thought of my departed friend. I felt heavy, as if I were moving through molasses, but I just kept going. Guest dinner must be served at 7:00, no matter what! I suffered all afternoon. Had I allowed myself to feel the pain, to really physically experience it, I would have been able to let it go rather quickly. This is the emptiness of emotions. They arise, abide, and pass away, but only if we allow them to arise in the first place.

It is human to have emotions. However, it is our practice to not let them have us. In the years since that experience at Tassajara, I have learned to pay attention to my breath and my body. When I'm suppressing something, my body feels heavy and my belly feels tense. Then I know to stop, breathe, and ask myself, "What is this?"

Sometimes an answer is readily apparent, sometimes not, but simply noticing and breathing always helps me to find some equanimity.

We need to understand that we are hard-wired to process our direct experience with words and concepts. We cannot get rid of this "sand" in our eyes.

I need the mediation that words and concepts provide. This is necessary "sand" that must come between me and my direct experience in order for me to function in the world. All is indeed "One," and sometimes I may have an unmediated experience of this oneness, but still, for practical purposes, I must separate my "self" from the table and see the table as an object, in order to avoid stubbing my toe on its leg.

Jiaoan reminds us, then, to accept the koan of our lives. We do need to engage in the profound struggle to realize emptiness. She says the pillar pulls out the bone sideways. Difficult! A drastic removal of our usual support!

At the same time, we live in the realm of emotions, views, and concepts. But—we do not need to be caught by them. Let us meet Jiaoan right here.

Is it possible to get rid of all thoughts and views? If so, how can you decide what to make for dinner without them? Can tears be an expression of deep understanding? Did the Buddha cry at the sight of suffering?

24. Punnika and the Brahman's Purification

THE SLAVE PUNNIKA was a follower of the Buddha and attained the first stage of awakening while carrying water from the river to her master's house. Sometime later she was again bringing water from the river when she saw the Brahman Udakasuddhika taking a ritual bath. She said to him, "I must come down to the river even on cold days like today because I am a water carrier and a slave. But why do you come to the river, even when it makes you shiver with the cold? What are you afraid of?"

"You know the laws of karma," he said. "I am washing away my past evil acts."

"Who told you that would work?" she asked. "If this were true, frogs, turtles, and water snakes would all go to heaven. And evildoers like pork butchers, thieves, and executioners could all be cleansed with a bath. Besides, doesn't water wash away your merit too? It would be better to avoid doing evil in the first place. So spare yourself from this freezing water and go home."

The Brahman saw the truth of her words and tried to give her his robe in gratitude, but she refused. Instead she suggested that he should take refuge in the Buddha, Dharma, and Sangha, and train in the precepts. He took refuge, and said to her, "Your words have washed me clean."

DIANA WINSTON'S REFLECTION

Let's imagine it's 500 BCE, and not only are you a woman but you're a slave. So you probably are about as low as it gets in a highly stratified culture where rules of caste, gender, and class are everything. And then let's imagine that you have the incredible good fortune of hearing a discourse of the Buddha, and in a nanosecond, like most people back in Buddha's time, you get enlightened. Okay, maybe not full-on, final-stage, zipped-bam-boom to nirvana, but a fairly do-able, in-this-lifetime awakening. One that's so profound it transforms you to the core.

So let's say then that you're still you. In spite of your transformation, you have to now go back to being a slave (although, thankfully, years later Punnika was freed from slavery). And let's stop here for a moment to notice that no matter what your spiritual awakening is, no matter how profound, you're still you and you still have to go back to your day job (unless you become a guru or something).

I used to spend a lot of time in long meditation retreats, and when you spend a lot of time meditating, something wakes up. I sat and sat and saw deeply into my own mind and body and experienced all sorts of letting-go's, from the mundane to the profound. But no matter what happened in all those years on cushions and in and out of monasteries, I now spend a good deal of time washing dishes, responding to email, and thanklessly wiping my two-year-old's (soon to be potty-trained, I hope) bottom. But that's just how life is—how mine is, anyway—and if I think my deep spiritual practice makes me special, I'm asking for trouble.

That's half of what I love about Punnika's koan. She's just herself, fetching water in chilly weather, evidently, and hardly special.

Except she's pretty special.

Now imagine that you're a slave fetching water and you notice a Brahman—a member of the highest caste in India—doing his purification rites, which to you seem utterly inane, based on your own waked-up knowledge. So you see the Brahman shivering and you take pity on him and decide to break all barriers of caste and class and profession and gender, just about everything that could be broken, in order to tell him that he's a moron. When he hears your words, well, he gets transformed and tries to turn you into a guru, but you just pass the buck to the real guru—the triple gem.

What ovaries! What chutzpah! Talking to a Brahman, contradicting him, telling him he's got it wrong. Wow. But she does it from a place of very little self. "Yes, I know a truth, but it's the Dharma that holds me. Go check it out."

Punnika has no fear of singing her song of liberation. She has no fear of breaking rank and shouting with a loud and clear voice her truth of awakening.

It is way easier to hem and haw and say *yeah, I know a little something and I did a lot of practice, um,* but it's not easy to loudly proclaim, like Punnika, and to speak from our deepest knowledge of liberation, without fear. Many times I have spoken in public, sharing the Dharma in hundreds of contexts and hoping I embody it, but I've been vague about my own experience. Is this courageous?

Punnika was a revolutionary. For us she's a model. There have always been so many pressures, especially for women, to hide our truth, to not be as big as we know we can be, or as we secretly dream of being. We hide our light and our deepest realizations, and the world isn't better because of it. Nobody benefits by our hiddenness.

And we don't need to crow our realizations in arrogance or to be somebody special or to get gurufied or adored. We do it with humility and no-self-ness. We speak our Dharma from the place of Dharma. But we don't shy away.

And I say all this to you and I say this to me because the time is now to speak out, loudly, with a clear true voice—just like Punnika—that liberation is possible, and that we've done it, and countless women have done it throughout time, and of course there's more to go, but please, please don't hide your awakening.

As an ordinary person, do you have a responsibility to help someone who seems more confused than you are?

25. Nyozen's Pale Moon of Dawn

HE NUN Nyozen of Tokeiji used to meditate on the enlightenment poem of Chiyono as her theme for realization:

> With this and that I tried to keep the bucket together,
> and then the bottom fell out.
> Where water does not collect
> the moon does not dwell.

Later, Nyozen grasped the essence of Zen, and she presented this poem to her teacher:

> The bottom fell out of the bucket
> of that woman of humble birth;
> the pale moon of dawn
> is caught in the rain puddles.

KUYA MINOGUE'S REFLECTION

Nyozen trained at the nunnery of Tokeiji at a time when Tokeiji served as a refuge for women who were escaping violent or unhappy marriages and families; she studied Zen in a safe house. Did she arrive there looking for shelter from violence as I did, when I first appeared at the Eugene Buddhist Priory in 1986, seeking sanctuary from the threatening fists of my ex-husband? It is quite possible. If so, I can see that she would connect with Chiyono's poem about the bottom falling out of a water bucket. That's how it feels when a marriage ends for any reason. But when a marriage ends because safety has been violated, the bottom falls out of a container that was constructed to hold trust and faith in the durability of love. When a marriage ends, a conditioned self dissolves.

Chiyono was the first Zen woman to receive Dharma transmission in Japan. A century later, Nyozen practiced by meditating on Chiyono's enlightenment poem. It is extremely rare in Zen literature to have an account of Dharma realization in one woman leading to the awakening of another. As a teacher who works primarily with women, this koan inspires me.

It is important to notice that Chiyono's realization of buddha nature comes when she is engaged in the daily work of fetching water. Enlightenment does not erupt while she is sitting zazen; it doesn't arrive while she is chanting, and it isn't shocked into her during Dharma combat with a brilliant Zen master. Chiyono's awakening arrives when she is doing *samu*, simple manual labour. I like to imagine that Nyozen penetrated Chiyono's poem as she filled her own water bucket at Tokeiji's well.

In Zen literature, the moon has traditionally been used as a metaphor for Buddha, buddha nature, or enlightenment. In Chiyono's poem, when the bottom falls out of the bucket, the moon no longer shines. Something is lost; something is gone. But in Nyozen's poem nothing is lost; nothing is gone. Instead, the moon has multiplied, and it reflects in every puddle. It is neither created nor destroyed by the disintegration of the bucket. The illusion of separation, of containment, has dropped off.

When the self is deflated or dismantled, buddha nature appears in the ten thousand things. It appears in radish seeds as they sink roots into warming soil, in compost that emanates heat, in raindrops that ripple tiny moons that have settled into puddles, and in full moon reflections that line up from moon-edge to moon-edge to create the illusion of a path of light on a windless lake. Nothing is permanent. There is nothing to grasp after and nothing to grasp with. And there is no one to do the grasping.

When the conditions that have defined the boundaries of self dissolve we no longer need to guard against threats; we no longer need to grasp after rewards. Free of threats and objects of desire, we can drop worry and dissatisfaction, and relax completely. And in that relaxed state we realize our natural state, the enlightened state. We are no longer confined to the space within our skulls, or to a water bucket.

In the fall of 2011, the awakening of Chiyono and Nyozen sparked the process of awakening in five women students who attended a three-day writing workshop at the Creston Zendo where I am the teacher. We studied the centuries-old poems and wrote our own in response. To witness the birth of insight in my students as they worked with these poems was to witness the transmission of women's Dharma from Chiyono in the thirteenth century, through Nyozen in the fourteenth century, to the women I train with in the twenty-first century. I wrote the poem below during that workshop.

Nyozen's Moon
Ice crunches on the garden path.
The pale moon of dawn
opens the zendo doors.
Snowflakes melt in the heat.

When your body no longer holds together, where will your buddha
nature go? How can the moon be caught in a rain puddle?
And how can one person's enlightenment light another's?

Bring Me a Mustard Seed

Being Human

26. The Old Woman Burns Down the Hermitage

CHINA, PERIOD UNKNOWN ··

 N OLD woman in China supported a monk for many years. She built him a hermitage and provided him with food and clothing.

After twenty years, she wondered what he had attained and resolved to test him. She summoned a beautiful girl from the village and sent her to the hermit with instructions to embrace him and then ask him how he felt.

The girl caressed the monk and asked, "How do you feel just now?"

"A withered tree on a cold boulder has no warmth in winter," replied the monk.

The girl returned to the old woman and told her what had happened.

"What!?" the old woman said. "To think I've been supporting an impostor for all these years!" She grabbed a stick, hurried to the hermitage, and beat the monk, shouting, "Get out of here!" Then she burned the hermitage to the ground.

Zenkei Blanche Hartman's Reflection

I think that the monk in this koan was totally off-base in his attempt to squelch his human feelings, in his efforts to shut down rather than celebrate his human feelings. Eihei Dogen describes enlightened beings as "having few desires," but I don't think that "having few desires" means suppressing feeling; for me it means just being aware of all that we have to be grateful for and thereby knowing that we don't need anything more.

Through Zen practice we develop a greater and greater appreciation of everything around us; we don't become an old withered stump! I'm much more alive than I was when I started this practice, and much more appreciative, and that's true of most Zen people I know. The practice is not about suppressing desire or destroying our humanity but about allowing it to flow out to everything rather than to a particular object.

I met Zen practice through Suzuki Roshi, Katagiri Roshi, and Sojun Mel Weitsman, and these were not withered trees; these were very lively people. In every photo I have of Suzuki Roshi—and I have a lot of them—he's laughing or smiling. My teachers and my practice have never taught me not to enjoy life. The deeply seasoned teachers I've had the opportunity to meet have all been supportive to people who are suffering, but they have also been very playful and lighthearted.

I understand the precepts not as rules to follow, but more as, "Be very careful in this area of human life because there's a lot of suffering there, so pay attention to what you're doing." Like a sign on a frozen pond that says, "Danger, thin ice," rather than, "Shame on you!" Our vow is to help people end suffering, not to add to their suffering. I feel that there is a way to live without objectifying anyone as a sexual object, while still appreciating their beauty. This is living by the precepts.

In the case of the monk and the young girl, was she going to be hurt by any show of affection on his part? I don't know the circumstances of her life, but I get the impression that the girl was a willing participant, and as such likely to have her feelings hurt by rejection. But the monk had used the practice to shut down all feeling, so as not to be disturbed by it. That's a misunderstanding of the teaching, which is about the ending of suffering. The monk could have responded to the young woman kindly, saying to her, for instance, "You're young and beautiful and very attractive, but I'm a celibate monk so I'm really sorry, I can't accommodate you." Responding in the way he did, he wasn't being compassionate.

I love to teach the Brahma Viharas (practices of loving-kindness and compassion) and the Metta Sutta. In the Metta Sutta we chant, "Suffusing love over the entire world, above, below, and all around without limit, cultivating an infinite goodwill toward the whole world." I find this a sublime vision, considering all the discord and enmity that seems to be happening in our world.

I exchange a lot of hugs with students in the dokusan (Dharma interview) room. I know it's not orthodox, and perhaps some people might brand it as inappropriate, but since I'm old enough to be most people's grandmother, I hope it's all right. If someone is suffering, I might get up at the end of the interview and give someone a hug. Sometimes, of course, I realize that a hug would be an encroachment, so I don't hug the person. So far, people seem to have found it comforting, rather than distressing or confusing.

One time Brother David Steindl-Rast, a Benedictine monk who practiced with Suzuki Roshi, was giving a talk at Tassajara Zen Monastery, and someone asked him about his vow of celibacy. Brother David said in response, "But if I want to love everyone the same, I have to be either celibate or very promiscuous!" I love that image of loving everyone the same. That's something I've taken on myself, to love everyone the same, to love everyone completely. It's not about withering our perception or appreciation of the world around us; it's about becoming more and more appreciative of the world around us: its beauty, all it has to offer us, and our total connection with it.

Can the pain of desire be meditated away? What can you do with desire that you can neither fulfill nor eliminate?

27. Zhaozhou's Deeply Secret Mind

··

NUN ASKED Master Zhaozhou Congshen, "What is the deeply secret mind?"

Zhaozhou squeezed her hand.

The nun said, "Do you still have this?"

Zhaozhou said, "You are the one who has this."

IKUSHIN DANA VELDEN'S REFLECTION

Koans often delight me. They play with my heart and mind like a schoolyard full of boisterous children. There are so many intrigues and distractions, so many games to join in on and tangents to follow. This koan is no exception. It runs up, full of energy and mischief, and playfully tosses a ball in my direction: "What is the deeply secret mind?"

The word "secret" snags at something inside of me and I fumble. The ball bounces out into a busy street and I follow after it. What is a secret? Perhaps the nun meant "hidden"? Is that a better way to understand this? I duck and dodge and flail about, looking for safety and some way out. Thinking about secrets has led me to a dangerous place, as secrets often do, and I freeze.

Zhaozhou squeezes my hand.

I turn to another translation, one that gives the question as, "What is the innermost mind?" The question finds a shape inside of me and fills it completely. I sit with it for a while and settle down some.

There's less pursuit and more exploration; less trying to know and more experiencing. Time passes. I grow quiet and still, like an open field on a snowy night. More time passes.

And again, Zhaozhou's squeeze.

In Zen, and indeed in much of life, a gesture can speak more powerfully, and perhaps more truthfully, than words. So I turn away from the question and toward the gesture. I think of all the times someone has squeezed my hand. I remember walking with my father as a small child in the woods out in front of our house, his large hand completely engulfing mine. And the final squeeze on his deathbed, just minutes before he died, when there were no longer any words. And the squeezes from other people that have said, "Pay attention!" or, "Hello!" Hands offered in sympathy, in guidance, in warning, in comfort, in anger, in emphasis, in fear, in love, in friendship.

I think about connection and acknowledgment. How a squeeze is a reminder, of sorts, a message that cannot be said or heard but can be known and trusted. Maybe this is the path on which the innermost mind, the deeply secret understanding, travels.

And once again, Zhaozhou squeezes my hand.

In the end I have no answer to this koan, at least not in words. The nun and Zhaozhou continue on. I feel their ease and intimacy, and how together they create an understanding that is deeper than if they were separate. The river that flows through everything is understood to flow through everything. And so it does, back and forth; boundless waters, endless sky. Dragon play.

So these aren't secrets, but perhaps they are mysteries, to be discovered over and over again. Innermost, but not hidden, they flow from warm hand to warm hand. The plain and courageous intimacy of one human life intersecting with another, beyond words, beyond comprehension, and yet fully and completely received.

Wherever you are, you are one with the clouds and one with the sun and the stars that you see. You are still one with everything. This is more true than I can say, and more true than you can hear.

—Shunryu Suzuki

When you hold a precious secret that can't be spoken,
how can you share it?

28. Miaozong's Dharma Interview

EFORE MIAOZONG became a nun, she used to visit Master Dahui Zonggao's monastery to study with him, and he gave her a room in the abbot's quarters. The senior monk, Wanan, did not approve.

Dahui said to him, "Although she's a woman, she has outstanding merits."

Wanan still disapproved, so Dahui urged him to have an interview with Miaozong. Wanan reluctantly agreed, and requested an interview.

Miaozong said, "Do you want a Dharma interview or a worldly interview?"

"A Dharma interview," replied Wanan.

Miaozong said, "Then send your attendants away." She went into the room first and after a few moments she called, "Please come in."

When Wanan entered he saw Miaozong lying naked on her back on the bed. He pointed at her genitals, saying, "What is this place?"

Miaozong replied, "All the buddhas of the three worlds, the six patriarchs, and all great monks everywhere come out of this place."

Wanan said, "And may I enter?"

Miaozong replied, "Horses may cross; asses may not."

Wanan was unable to reply. Miaozong declared: "I have met you, Senior Monk. The interview is over. " She turned her back to him.

Wanan left, ashamed.

Later Dahui said to him, "The old dragon has some wisdom, doesn't she?"

Hoka Chris Fortin's Reflection

I have practiced as a Zen Buddhist priest for many years. Practice is the source and foundation of my life, and the bodhisattva vow is the root of my daily activity. I cherish the teachings and I practice with wonderful Dharma brothers and sisters in the Everyday Zen Sangha in Northern California.

The women of our sangha met last year for our seventh annual women's retreat. This koan seemed perfect to investigate together as a vehicle to enliven and deepen our Dharma conversation with one another. The theme of "Authentic Meeting: Ferocious Vulnerability and Vulnerable Ferocity" guided the weekend.

We performed a skit of this koan on the opening evening, and I volunteered to be Miaozong. I wore a flesh-colored full-body stocking, and I was deeply moved and even jolted by the experience of entering into Miaozong's skin and enacting her fearless and compassionate activity. Here was direct body-to-body, heart-to-heart transmission, across time and space, from a full-blooded woman who had no shame about her body, and who was a deeply realized practitioner, to me, now, a woman practitioner more than a thousand years later.

Zen teachings have been traditionally conveyed through a predomi-nately male lineage, a lineage that I have entered and that I honor. But prior to entering Miaozong's skin, I had never before been consciously aware of how some part of me was subtly and perpetually changing from a woman's body into a man's body in order to fully engage with the teachings. As I lay on my back on the floor, my knees apart, calling out, "All beings everywhere come out of this place!" I became aware that this womb that bled rich red blood every month in my youth, and that had given birth to a son, was timeless, the womb of every woman. Miaozong's unbounded confidence in the pure Dharma body of practice, and her embodied faith in the sacredness of a woman's body, resonated through me like a dragon's roar.

Zazen is the practice of intimately entering into the naked vulnera-bility of being human. Alone on our cushion, we become one with our particular life and the comings and goings of breath, thoughts, feelings, and sensations. Offering ourselves with wholehearted devotion, we connect with the spacious nature of who we really are. What arises is a deep trust that is rooted in this human body, enabling us to respond with freedom to what is before us.

Miaozong fearlessly turns toward sexuality and human confusion. She meets Wanan's discriminative attitude and desire as she bares her most vulnerable part, her vagina—the passage to her dark womb, the gateway of creation, the source of birth and death. She invokes beautiful images of the feminine that are at the heart of Buddhist nondual teachings, as found in the Prajnaparamita sutras and the Tathagatagarbha sutras. The womb is the source of all the buddhas, of awakening, and of buddha nature. The womb is the birthplace of compassion!

She tells Wanan, and she tell us, that this all-inclusive Way includes clear limits. Views that discriminate against women are not a bridge to enlightenment.

Although in the Ultimate there is no separate self, no female or male, we become true human beings through embodied relationship. The heart awakens to compassion when we are able to open ourselves to one another. We embrace the truth of our interconnection through the poignant beauty and vulnerability of revealed and intimate meeting with another.

All beings are our teachers. The whole world is singing the Dharma. But there is an invaluable mirroring that only women can offer to other women. Miaozong of ancient China continues to teach me of a fierce strength born of vulnerability and of an ease with body and mind that resounds through me, awakening me to our shared heart.

We need to continue to cultivate and nurture many good, strong, women Dharma teachers who are not afraid to be women, and who are not afraid to be vulnerable. We need mirrors that help us remember the ancient lineage of women, a lineage that asks us not to turn from suffering. The words "That old dragon has some wisdom, doesn't she!" resonate in our own time.

We need this for our children and for our grandchildren. We need this to free all women and all beings everywhere who suffer under the yoke of oppression. May we all awaken together to the joy of a free heart and the boundless love and kindness of our true nature.

What is the difference between going in and coming out?
If someone you knew was deeply mistaken, how far would you go
to try to teach them something? Would you take
your clothes off, if that's what it took?

29. Zhaozhou and the Old Woman's Obstacles

N OLD WOMAN asked Master Zhaozhou Congshan, "I have a body that contains the five obstacles. How can I be free of the world of suffering?"

Zhaozhou said, "Pray that all beings are born in heaven and that you yourself suffer forever in a sea of hardships."

DIANE ESHIN RIZZETTO'S REFLECTION

This exchange between Zhaozhou and the old woman can be a bit of a shocker if we take it on face value. Can it be that all Zhaozhou can offer this old woman is to pray for the liberation of others while, for herself, only praying that she drown in a sea of suffering? And where's her voice? Does she just sit back and swallow those words without a "Hey, wait a minute!"?

The old woman has a body, she laments, that contains the five obstacles. There are several ways to view these "obstacles." One is that they refer to the traditional list of five hindrances common to all practitioners (desire, anger, sloth, restlessness, and doubt). Another is that they refer to an early Buddhist teaching that no woman could become the god Brahma, the god Sakra, the tempter Mara, a wheel-turning king, or a buddha. Finally, the reference could be to the five obstacles particular to women: the necessity of leaving her own family to be married into another's, menstruation, pregnancy, childbirth, and the obligation to wait on a man.

But whichever way you slice it, from this old woman's perspective, these obstacles are causing her pain and, she believes, are preventing her from moving on in her spiritual journey. I hear a desperation stemming from the belief that she is entrapped in such a body. But Zhaozhou won't have any part of such thinking. He picks up the old woman's lament and turns it on its heels, offering her, instead, liberation now, in this life and through this female body.

It's the third day into a long Zen retreat. A young woman sits in stillness facing the wall; her hands rest softly on the full belly of a nine-month pregnancy. The wind shifts gently through the window, and on another side of the room, a gray-haired woman moves slightly to pick up some relief from a hot flash and red face. I ask myself: Hindrance? Obstacle? What are these many hindrances and obstacles women are supposed to have?

Who is this *you, yourself* Zhaozhou speaks of? Can he be asking who is this self that has obstacles? He challenges the old woman, and all of us, into the marrow of Zen practice. He says, allow yourself to suffer in the very ways you see as obstacles, and by entering deeply that very suffering, through the suffering of a woman's body, the suffering of a mother, the suffering of giving birth, you will find a way to help others. Don't waste one hot flash, one pang of childbirth, one tear of sadness, one wonderful opportunity in this woman's body.

It's my first of many visits to St. Peter's Basilica in Rome, Italy. As I enter the front door of this vast space, I am drawn slightly to the right, and I am stopped dead in my tracks as I face Michelangelo's sculpture, the *Pieta*. This magnificent sculpture shows Mary holding in her arms the body of Jesus just after he was taken down off the cross. Art historians say the piece lacks proportion because a full-grown man seems dwarfed in the lap of a woman almost twice his size. But to me, the proportion is exactly as it should be. Mary sits firmly planted, supporting all the weight of her dead son. Her hands are large and strong and I can almost feel the calluses from hard work on her palms. Her large feet are planted firmly on the ground and her arms, as they cradle her son, are spread in both tenderness and strength. Beyond hindrance, she offers fortitude and strength not in spite of but through grief, through loss, through every cell in the body of a mother.

Is it possible to relieve the suffering of others by taking that suffering into yourself? Can you imagine taking the medicine that Zhaozhou offered to the old woman?

30. Eshun's Deep Thing

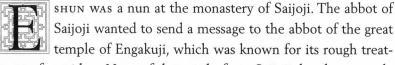

ESHUN WAS a nun at the monastery of Saijoji. The abbot of Saijoji wanted to send a message to the abbot of the great temple of Engakuji, which was known for its rough treatment of outsiders. None of the monks from Saijoji dared to go; only Eshun was willing to volunteer. When the Engakuji monks saw her walk through the main gate, one of them rushed forward, raised his robes to expose himself, and said: "This monk's thing is three feet long. How about it?"

Eshun calmly lifted her robes, spread her legs and said, "This nun's thing is infinitely deep." She dropped her robes and continued down the corridor, unaccosted.

KAREN SUNDHEIM'S REFLECTION

Eshun's understanding was immeasurable and deep. So the monk boasted of a three-foot member? She didn't fall prey to comparison, shock, or provocation. What is a three-foot organ when her mind and body held everything? Who has practiced the Dharma who didn't emerge from a woman's vagina? Didn't the monk realize he, too, had come into the world from a woman's womb? Eshun's response to the monk was calm and assured. The monk may have thought he could measure himself in inches or feet, yet Eshun knew her uterus to be without boundaries. The monk expressed the mind of domination; Eshun held firm. When he threatened to penetrate her, she pulled up her robe to show that what she had was everything and nothing. She presented her nakedness, dispelling fantasy in the mind of the monk, who turned away in shame. The monk is the mind of habit, of avarice; Eshun is the mind of Buddha.

When I was twenty, I left college in search of wisdom. I set off to travel around the world with a small pack on my back and my thumb for transportation. After many months I made my way to Fez, in Morocco. I was drawn to the chaos, the robed figures passing through the labyrinthian streets of the old city, the music, the sweet smell of hashish, the *muezzin's* call to prayer from the minaret before dawn. Later I went to live with the Berbers in the Atlas Mountains, four hours by bus along a winding road from Marrakech. One dollar bought a night in a hut under a starry sky. The terraced hillsides were lit only by a single candle carried by a barefoot shepherd. While living in this cluster of baked earth houses I traded my fine hiking boots for some embroidered slippers, the local footgear. It was hard to walk far in them but I imagined I had sacrificed my greed.

After about a month, it was time to leave this small village. I waited several hours with local people in the frosty early morning for the bus. Buses had no defined schedule and waiting was an accepted daily life activity. An old man with deep creases in his face and a torn robe was muttering to himself and mingling with the crowd of men, women, children, sheep, and chickens. He demanded money from me and angrily rebuked me as I continued to refuse him. I had been in Morocco long enough to observe that most people gave money to beggars, but I was determined to make my small savings last for years. Didn't the acquisition of wisdom take a lifetime? I battled my shame by telling myself that my tightly held coins served a higher purpose. At last the beggar turned away.

As I complained to myself about the cold, all the more bitter without my insulated boots, I noticed that the old man was making a small fire with sticks and heating water in a turquoise teapot. He was making the most popular local drink, sweet mint tea. I smiled to myself and entered a reverie. Wasn't it wonderful that at least he had the means to make tea and to enjoy a most integral national pastime? But then I felt the cold wind bite my neck. I longed for my warm boots. A gravelly voice interrupted my thoughts and I saw the beggar standing in front of me. He was holding a clear glass of steaming tea and moving it toward my hand.

I had not only counted my change but measured my time, believing that the more time I spent wandering the world the more wisdom I would attain. Those measurements in my own mind were overturned in less than a second as a stranger I had stubbornly rebuffed gave me the gift I needed the most. He gave me sweet tea on a cold morning—the only possession he had. And as he did so, he showed me the impermanent nature of my self, as resentment dissolved into kindness. Generosity is immeasurable.

My sangha chants the three refuges after a long day of zazen. We say, "May all living beings deeply enter the sutras, wisdom like an ocean." Wisdom takes the form of its container, infinite and empty. How do you penetrate an ocean? The monk could not penetrate Eshun, as her womb already contained his member and all other things with it. I measured my nickels and dimes but the beggar gave me gold.

How does a bodhisattva respond to lewd overtures? What would you have done, in Eshun's place? And what was it about her —or you—that could be infinitely deep?

31. Ryonen Scars Her Face

S A YOUNG WOMAN, Ryonen Genso was an attendant to the empress and was known for her beauty and intelligence. When the empress died, she felt the impermanence of life, and she decided to become a nun.

Ryonen traveled to the city of Edo in search of a Zen teacher. The first teacher refused her because of her beauty. Then she asked Master Hakuo Dotai, who also refused her. He could see her sincere intention, but he too said that her womanly appearance would cause problems for the monks in his monastery.

Afterward, she saw some women pressing fabric, and she took up a hot iron and held it against her face, scarring herself. Then she wrote this poem on the back of a small mirror:

> To serve my empress, I burned incense to perfume my
>   exquisite clothes.
> Now as a homeless mendicant I burn my face to enter
>   a Zen temple.
> The four seasons flow naturally like this,
> who is this now in the midst of these changes?

She returned to Hakuo and gave him the poem. Hakuo immediately accepted her as a disciple. She became abbess of his temple when he died and later founded her own temple. Before her death she wrote the following poem:

This is the sixty-sixth autumn I have seen.
The moon still lights my face.
Don't ask me about the meaning of Zen teachings—
just listen to what the pines and cedars say on a windless night.

WENDY EGYOKU NAKAO'S REFLECTION

When my sangha members pay homage to our Buddhist women ancestors during morning offerings, among the names we chant is that of "Ryonen Genso, who sacrificed her beauty." Whenever I hear her name, I feel the hot iron singe the skin in the early dawn.

Aiiiiiiieeeeeeeeeeee!

What is this that awakens so powerfully within that it compels you to act—as only you can—to know the truth of your unique life?

When I was in my mid-twenties, I experienced a profound stirring within. It came unexpectedly while I was attending my first Zen sesshin on a dare that I could not be quiet and sit still for an entire week. Sometime during those days, there arose within me a powerful force seeking to know itself. In a short time, I had left my marriage, career, and home and instinctively followed the call to fulfill this longing that is blood in the veins.

What is it that slumbers and then stirs so powerfully within us that the "little me" that we so often identify with is rendered helpless and insignificant? What is it that awakens to and then heeds the call to return home? As Ryonen herself asked, "Who is this now in the midst of these changes?"

Ryonen sacrificed her beauty so that what was most important to her, her spiritual quest into the Great Matter of life and death, would be taken seriously in the male-dominated Zen world of her day. In the West today, a woman need not take the extreme measure of disfigurement in response to sexism. Ryonen's horrifying action expresses the depth of her commitment; she enters an endless lifegiving stream of women courageously claiming our rightful inheritance as buddhas.

Each of us as women today has sacrificed in order to pursue this call. What have you as a woman given up in order to practice? Perhaps you gave up having a child, or a special relationship, or time with your partner and children, or becoming financially secure in your old age. Perhaps your so-called sacrifice is not seen as sacrifice at all, or is at least mitigated by the wisdom that "the four seasons flow naturally like this."

Ryonen's act of burning and scarring, not unheard of in her time, also reverberates in the spiritual quest of women today, in questions like these: How do we find our voice in traditions that value silence and are bound by historical and cultural imperatives to ignore the voice of women? How do we women claim our sense of personal power and a healthy sense of self in traditions that confirm the truth of selflessness? How do we women affirm our bodies in traditions that emphasize abstaining from desire? How do we find freedom within the forms that were born out of male domination?

Today, the vibrant quest of women into the Great Matter is reshaping how Zen is practiced in the West. Women intuitively bring forth relational and horizontal forms, such as councils, circles, and shared stewarding, as skillful means that manifest the truth of inter-relatedness. These forms of cocreating do not depend on hierarchical domination and, at the same time, affirm the life of all without compromising its depth.

Zen Buddhism speaks to liberation, to fully realizing and freely living this journey wherever we are, however we are, in whatever circumstances we find ourselves, including relationships, family life, and work. There is much laid out for us in the tradition on how to awaken and ripen in the depths of this transient life—as we are living it. Ryonen herself plumbed these depths and implores us to just listen to what the pines and cedars say on a windless night.

And there is no doubt that the deeper we plunge into this awakening, the more expansive is our awareness and our caring, and the more we are called to address the conditions in which awakening can arise. Ryonen had her own temple and built bridges and schools in service to her community. Today, the moon still lights our faces in the here and now, and we all must work to be of service on behalf of the well-being of others. So how about for you? In what ways is your practice broadening the heart? Serving others? Helping to transform your home, your community and organizations, and the world?

Aiiiiiiieeeeeeeeeee!

What would you be willing to sacrifice in order to awaken and find freedom? What would be too great a barrier?

32. Vasumitra Teaches Freedom from Passion

INDIA, SECOND CENTURY ···

N THE *Flower Ornament Scripture*, a nun encouraged the pilgrim Sudhana to meet the courtesan Vasumitra. When he arrived in Vasumitra's city, people said, "Why would you want to meet her? You should not be under the power of such a woman; you should not enter the realm of temptation." Others, though, knowing of her virtues and wisdom, directed him to her house.

Vasumitra was more beautiful than a goddess. She had golden skin and black hair, and her body was decorated with jewels and emanated light. She knew every language and had mastered all possible ways to help others awaken.

Sudhana went up to her respectfully and asked for her teaching on how to practice as a bodhisattva.

She said, "I have attained an enlightening liberation called 'ultimately dispassionate,' and I appear in the form of a female of splendor and perfection. People come to me with minds full of passion, and I teach them freedom from passion. Some attain freedom from passion as soon as they see me, some merely by talking with me, some by holding my hand, some by staying with me, some by gazing at me, some by embracing me, some by kissing me. They enter various concentration states, including 'light of freedom from bondage' and 'womb receiving all beings without rejection,' and all experience this liberation."

She then directed Sudhana onward on his journey.

ANNE SEISEN SAUNDERS'S REFLECTION

"Without going into the ocean of passions, it is impossible
to obtain the mind of omniscience."
—Vimalakirti Sutra

In this story, the bodhisattva Vasumitra takes the form of a woman. She
teaches Sudhana freedom from passion through sexual or near-sexual
contact. But how does this relate to Buddha's teaching that the end
of suffering is through the cessation of passion?

Many of us see our sexuality as an impediment to enlightenment.
Certainly our unfulfilled desire for people or things creates unhappi-
ness. Is the kind of ecstatic oneness that we experience during physical
love different from samadhi or the experience of oneness that happens
during meditation? Through her great compassion, Vasumitra teaches
true intimacy, which is to be one with our lives. Every aspect of our
life is sacred.

This is the teaching of nonduality. Vasumitra is Sudhana, and
Sudhana is Vasumitra, and they are both us. This intimacy is right
here in our lives. When we make the bodhisattva vow, we choose to
live in our world and to practice intimately with it, as Vasumitra does.
When we realize our true nature we realize that every aspect of our
life is sacred. Our sexuality is our spirituality.

I think that spiritual people can fall into two different kinds of
traps. One is the belief that being spiritual means separating myself
from the joys and pain of everyday life. In this story, Vasumitra
challenges the assumption that physical passion is separate from
enlightenment. The other trap is believing that, since everything is
one, I can behave any way I want. Too often these days we hear of
teachers abusing their position and harming students through their
self-centered sexuality.

I have to see this story as a metaphor for waking up rather than
a defense of teacher-student sex. Students of the Way are harmed
when the teacher uses the student for the teacher's emotional

needs. Vasumitra's great compassion means that her actions are not self-serving.

Being free from passion means waking up to the fact that I am not separate from all that is. That feeling is joyous and not dependent on other people. There is no yearning for another because there is no other. One way to realize that fact is to meditate in the midst of craving—not rejecting or rising above it, and especially not acting out. This transformational practice is to focus on the yearning while letting go of the object of desire.

A few years ago, there was an incident of sexual misconduct in my lineage and I found myself enraged at the teacher who was the perpetrator. The anger was so big that I realized that something in me had been triggered by the incident. I began to get in touch with my own sexual predator. I became aware of sexual desire that was all-encompassing and extremely painful.

I decided to practice with it in the same way that I had learned to practice with a koan. I decided to be one with my desire. Before, I had used the power of zazen to ignore my feelings. Now I opened up to the feelings of desire without trying to satisfy them with externals. It was terrifying and physically painful. I had to maintain the faith that others had done this kind of practice and I could too. Rather than satisfying my desire through sex or fantasy, I let go of the object and embraced the yearning. Finally, I found my sexual desire to be a gateway to freedom, by being one with it.

This story seems to me to be a metaphor for the practice of using lust as a gateway to awakening. Vasumitra is a bodhisattva. A bodhisattva is almost completely enlightened. She has dropped off body and mind and dwells almost without self. However, as a bodhisattva, she holds on to a little bit of self to save others from delusion. And that little bit of self seduces Sudhana for the sake of his awakening. When Sudhana embraces Vasumitra, he doesn't embrace a woman separate from himself. He embraces his own passion. Being one with lust, he realizes that it is empty, and he becomes free. This freedom is also available to us.

Can passion be liberatory? A courtesan sells her body and her
embrace for financial support. What exchange does
a bodhisattva make, if any?

33. Zongchi and Bodhidharma's Flesh

CHINA, FIFTH CENTURY ···

ASTER BODHIDHARMA had four senior students: three monks and the nun Zongchi. When the time came for him to return to India, he gathered them together. He said to them, "The time has come. Please express your understanding."

Daofu said, "The path transcends language and words and yet is not separated from language and words."

Bodhidharma said, "You have attained my skin."

The nun Zongchi said, "It is like the joy of seeing Akshobhya Buddha's paradise just once and not again."

"You have attained my flesh," said Bodhidharma.

Daoyu said, "The four elements are originally empty and the five aggregates are nonexistent. I see nothing to be attained."

"You have attained my bone," said Bodhidharma.

Finally Huike made a bow to the teacher and stood aside in silence. Bodhidharma said, "You have attained my marrow."

SHOSAN VICTORIA AUSTIN'S REFLECTION

The great Zen teacher Bodhidharma was the founder of Zen in China. Some sources say that he was Persian, and some sources say Indian. In any event, his teaching was simple and direct—direct enough to survive to the present day.

In Zen, we usually think of Bodhidharma's disciple Huike as the one who had it right and became Bodhidharma's successor, while the others had a lesser understanding. But actually, Eihei Dogen, the founder of our Zen school in Japan, takes great pains in his commentary on this story to say that all the disciples were right. Any one of them could have been Bodhidharma's successor.

The nun Zongchi's answer is the one that was most maligned by later commentators. They suggested that she was merely repeating something that she had heard. But Bodhidharma said, "You have my flesh." This is acknowledgment of Zongchi's understanding. So what is this paradise that comes just once and not again? Why would Bodhidharma refer to it as flesh? What's important about flesh to Bodhidharma?

At that time, women were thought of as creatures of the flesh, and a woman's flesh was thought of as tainted. Women had to be reborn in the body of a man in order to awaken. This was the common understanding in the culture. But Bodhidharma did not say, "You have a woman's flesh and have to be reborn." He said, "You have *my* flesh."

So what did flesh, or the body, mean to Bodhidharma? Why would he say, "You have my flesh," or my body, to his woman disciple, and not to one of the men?

Elsewhere Bodhidharma said, "The Buddha is your real body, your original mind. This mind has no form, no characteristics, no cause, no effect, no tendons, and no bones. It's like space. You can't hold it. Except for one who's fully realized, no one—no mortal, no deluded being—can fathom it."

So when Bodhidharma says to Zongchi, "You have my flesh," he means that this thigh, this body—go ahead, slap your thigh!—can't be fathomed. But nonetheless, when you slap your thigh it feels like there's something solid there, doesn't it? How can it not really be there? This is what is called the great mystery, or the great matter. And when we sit zazen, we find reality. There is something solid and we can feel that. And, at the same time, we can feel that nothing is ultimately solid. That's what zazen does.

Because we can directly experience this in our meditation practice, we can help people. For instance, a dental hygienist I knew, whose name was Kitty Armel and who died yesterday, was a deeply gentle person. She would bring her dog Shay to the dental office to keep people company when they had their teeth cleaned. Sometimes I would feel her kind hands doing the work through the instruments. The kindness of her hands would transmit something about compassion while cleaning teeth. This is one way to help others.

It's not that we have something called "buddha nature" or "awakened nature." The entire body, one hundred percent, is awakened buddha nature. Manifesting our buddha nature is the essence of all the rituals that we do, all the jobs that we do, all the activity in a Zen temple. It is all just for the transmission of awakeness. I think this is what Bodhidharma was saying. He was saying, "Zongchi, you're a woman. In our society, women can't be awakened. But I'm going to acknowledge your very flesh as the same as mine—as one body of awakening that manifests just like mine. It's a mystery how, as a woman, you have a particular story about yourself in this life. And how, as a man and a monk, I have a different story about myself. And yet, although you manifest in the body of a woman and I manifest in the body of a man, each of us manifests the truth, one hundred percent." I can hear him saying all that with "You have my flesh."

Can we ever see paradise for more than a moment?
And, if not, is a moment enough?

34. The Zen Mirror of Tokeiji

JAPAN, PROBABLY THIRTEENTH CENTURY ·····································

T HE CONVENT of Tokeiji had a great mirror. The founding abbess, Kakuzan Shido, would meditate before it in order to "see into her own nature." Later generations of nuns would practice zazen in front of the mirror, concentrating on the question, "Where is a single feeling, a single thought, in the mirror image at which I gaze?" Each abbess of Tokeiji wrote a verse in response to the mirror practice. The following verse was composed by the fifth abbess, Princess Yodo:

> Heart unclouded, heart clouded;
> standing or falling, it is still the same body.

ZENJU EARTHLYN MANUEL'S REFLECTION

"Where is a single feeling, a single thought, in the mirror image at which I gaze?" When we ask this question at once we enter the purpose of our lives, which is to look upon our lives and discover who we are as living beings. We enter a dark abyss in which we encounter our heart-mind and body. On the journey of discovery we fall through the sky. At times the sky is clouded and at other times it is unclouded. On the earth we plant our feet and still we stumble. What are the clouds and what takes them away? What makes us stand or fall?

Looking into a mirror may seem easy, but being honest with what we see is difficult. A few days before my fifty-ninth birthday I looked into the mirror to see if I looked old. I asked, "Am I old? What is old?" I did this exercise for five minutes a day, for seven days.

On the first day, I didn't see anything because I was afraid of seeing an old lady. My eyes constantly turned away.

On the second day, I spent time plucking the hairs from my chin. I could see them clearly: the white hairs against my dark skin. They provided a nice distraction.

On the third day, I thought I should grow my hair longer so that the thinning parts would disappear. I remembered my mother's hair thinning in the same places when she was my age. Still, I didn't want to see my mother in me nor see an old lady in myself.

On the fourth day, as I looked in the mirror, I wondered what an old lady looked like. So I spent much of my day examining women as I walked in the world, deciding who looked old and who didn't.

On the fifth day, I decided I must be old because my neck skin was beginning to sag like I had seen in the so-called old women the day before.

On the sixth day, I cried in front of the mirror. I felt I had no control of my stumbling into old age. I felt my death was closer than ever before.

On the seventh day, I saw fear in the tightness of my lips, confusion in the brow. I thought what a tough journey life was. Then I looked deeper, without an idea in my head, just the question, "What is old?" and I saw a courageous woman willing at least to look at herself.

There are many mirrors. A physical mirror can reveal expressions on our faces. The mirror of *zazen*, of sitting meditation, allows us to look into the heart-and-body mirror.

When I look in a mirror I see a black face. In the past I have responded to being black with painful emotions. However, through zazen, when I see my black face I am awake to the suffering that arises. I see the old pain rising in the moment of looking in the mirror. I wait for my response to pass (as it is guaranteed to do), and in that passing I see more of who I am and not so much how I appear.

When we face the mirror of zazen, our minds tend to face ourselves as objects first—our skin color, age, gender, sexual orientation—all the ways we are embodied and move in the world. We begin to unfold stories about "I." If we are willing to look long enough in the mirror of zazen, past seeing ourselves as objects, we have the potential to see that we are nature itself—we are born and will die, just as the trees, flowers, and animals in the wild do. And sometimes, in zazen, we can see that the mirror is clear. There are no clouds, no dust. The human condition is set aside. I am not old, middle-aged, or young. I am fulfilled in my own spirit. And in this recognition I feel the connection to my ancestors, to those who came before me, or to a life larger than my own. I am returned to an open field in which there are many possibilities.

This open field is my original home, where there is no blackness, no old age. As Princess Yodo wrote: "Heart unclouded, heart clouded; standing or falling, it is still the same body."

I say: In the silence of my open field, face clear or face colorful, dancing or sitting, it is still the same body.

What do you see when you look in the mirror?
Are you there?

35. Yoshihime's "Look, Look!"

YOSHIHIME WAS a nun at Tokeiji and the daughter of a general. She was very strong, and her nickname was "Devil-girl." She wanted to meet with the teacher at the monastery of Engakuji, but the gatekeeper monk barred her way with a shout: "What is it, the gate through which the buddhas come into the world?"

Yoshihime grabbed his head and forced it between her legs, saying, "Look, look!"

The monk said, "In the middle, there is a fragrance of wind and dew."

Yoshihime said, "This monk! He's not fit to keep the gate; he ought to be looking after the garden."

The gatekeeper ran into the temple and reported this to the teacher's attendant, who said, "Let me test her."

So the attendant went to the gate and asked her again, "What is it, the gate through which the buddhas come into the world?"

Yoshihime grabbed his head and held it between her legs, saying, "Look, look!"

The attendant said, "The buddhas of the three worlds come, giving light."

Yoshihime said, "This monk is one with the eye; he saw the eighty-four thousand gates all thrown open."

JUDITH SIMMER-BROWN'S REFLECTION

This koan makes me laugh with delight! All those old monks of Engakuji were so afraid of women in their midst that they were compelled to test the women's Dharma insight in order to allow them entrance. They were no match for our devil-girl Yoshihime!

This classic case asks about the gate through which buddhas come into the world. Immediately women understand the most obvious answer—through the cervix and vagina. Not only buddhas, but all beings enter the world through their mothers' vaginas. Only the most obtuse monk would not think of this. Rather than hiding or ignoring her gender identity, Yoshishime flaunts it by pressing the gatekeeper's head between her legs, flustering him completely. This is all the more potent because of the prevailing views of the unclean, repulsive qualities of women's vaginas. Devil-girl knows how to deal with the misogynist gatekeeper!

Misogyny is not just a distant memory. Years ago, I was the leader of a predominantly male international delegation to Japan. Our Japanese hosts were extremely nervous, as they had never dealt with a woman leader before—they seemed terrified. Every time I tried to work out our schedule and logistics, they looked over my shoulder at the men, asking them questions meant for me. Later, in a tiny country gift shop, I found a beautiful set of teacups, one large and the other small. Spontaneously I turned to the eldest of our Japanese hosts, asking incredulously, "This couldn't be for a man and woman?" Deeply embarrassed, he reluctantly nodded, and for a moment, we laughed together. Everything changed. Thereafter, our hosts related to me awkwardly but respectfully, and we were able to laugh about the discomfort.

But there is another level of Yoshihime's wordless answer to the gatekeeper's question. The revered *Prajnaparamita*, or "perfect wisdom," the most sublime of Dharma teachings, is sometimes embodied in a female form and called the "Mother of all the Buddhas." Only through realizing her inexpressible teachings of emptiness, which is also suchness, can anyone realize their true nature and become awakened. As the *Prajnaparamita in 8,000 Lines* says:

She is the Perfect Wisdom who gives birthless birth to
all buddhas.

And through the sublimely Awakened Ones,
it is Mother Prajnaparamita alone
who turns the wheel of true teaching.

A woman's body is a central symbol of emptiness in India and Tibet, where she manifests as the elusive and awakened *dakini*, or sky-dancer, the Buddhist goddess-trickster of yogic wisdom, an aspect of the Mother of Wisdom. Her cervix is the symbol of the esoteric sacred mandala of emptiness and suchness, expressed in the renowned diagram of double crossed triangles. For the conventional mind, the dualities of purity and impurity, male and female, awakened and confused are resolved in these symbols of emptiness.

When Yoshihime presses the gatekeeper's face to her crotch, she is testing his own awakening. The gate through which all buddhas come? She turns the question back on him—"Look, look!" She is asking him to investigate the gate from his own experience. In his affected answer, the image "the fragrance of wind and dew" is meant to evoke nonduality between the extremes of her two legs: the resolution of being and nonbeing, form and emptiness, ultimate and provisional truth. However, his response does not meet the direct, earthy, embodied wisdom to which she was pressing his face; it resolves no dualities. Who but a complete fake would comment about wind and dew when pressed into the crotch of a woman?

But the abbot's attendant has a deeper response to Yoshihime's "Look, look!" He does not attempt to change the subject or ignore her earthy wisdom. He proclaims that all the buddhas of the past, present, and future come through this gate of the Mother. When he speaks of "giving light," he is acknowledging the name of the great Dharma hall of Engakuji, known as the Great Light Hall; all the awakened ones of Engakuji have passed through the cervix and vagina of the Mother of all the Buddhas, and so Yoshihime is to be revered and respected. In one flourish, he has flung open the manifold gates that are none other than the single gate of the Mother. We prostrate to Yoshihime, the radiant devil-girl! May we ourselves realize the Dharma gate of the Mother!

"Look, look!" When do you get a chance to look right into
the maw of creation? Can you stand it?

36. The Old Woman, Zhaozhou, and the Tiger

CHINA, NINTH CENTURY ···

NE DAY when Master Zhaozhou Congshen was outside the monastery, he saw an old woman hoeing a field. He asked her, "What would you do if you suddenly met a fierce tiger?"

She replied, "Nothing in this world frightens me," and turned back to her hoeing. Zhaozhou roared like a tiger. She roared back at him. Zhaozhou said, "There's still this."

CHI KWANG SUNIM'S REFLECTION

This is another of those memorable encounters in which an old woman challenges one of the greatest Chan masters of the Tang dynasty. Theirs is a vibrant, dynamic exchange that goes beyond "lips and mouth Zen," or words and phrases. Truth is revealed in yet another everyday life situation.

My first introduction to this powerful koan was about thirty years ago, when I was living in Korea. I was receiving acupuncture from a former Korean monk, when suddenly he blurted out, "What if you meet a hungry tiger on a dark night?" He, like me, had studied with the late Master Kusan, and this encounter was an unexpected inheritance, challenging me to deepen my faith, effort, and courage in befriending this tiger. Why did that tiger Zhaozhou roar, shout, hiss, and spit at an old girl hovering over her hoe as she tilled the soil? What's going on?

I recall that it was old women bodhisattvas who taught me everything in Korea. A one-eyed cook taught me a Korean dialect and how to make kimchi. Another taught me the movement of the hand when slashing the tall grass. The mother of four generations of Zen masters taught me the art of robe-making. Then there were all those wise, inspiring, magical old nuns, who just knew! So it was common to see old monks chatting, laughing, and debating with these natural inheritors of insight.

Zhaozhou's far-reaching, observant eye would have noticed this age-humbled figure in her fields, whether she was known to him or not. He would have heard her hoe's rhythmic tap-tap-tap in the fertile soil. I wonder why he needs to confront her fearlessness with fear-mongering words? Look how she wields her tools! Moment by moment her life is completely devoured; she isn't concerned with untimely death.

After Zhaozhou questions her, the solitary old woman holds his glare steadily in her own and retorts, "Nothing in this world frightens me." Yet beware! An unclear gaze and you may end up in the mouth of the tiger. She returns her attention to cultivating both field and mind, sowing seeds of virtue and compassion, the very foundation of the Buddha's teachings. So too our ordinary, everyday actions require our minds to remain present and clear.

Zhaozhou roars like a tiger—*Grrrr!*—pointing directly to the Great Way. The urgency of the matter is made clear, just as Third Zen Patriarch Jianzhi Sengcan exhorted his students in his "Faith in Mind" poem: "Live neither in the entanglements of outer things, nor in inner feelings of emptiness."

Grrrr! The old woman bellows back her courageous roar, from the belly of her inner spaciousness, instantly freeing infinite generations of her ancestors who had labored and perished on that very spot. After her earth-shattering roar, this boundless woman returns to cultivating her field.

In 2009, such an unforgettable deafening roar shook the very ground of my own reality, awakening a fearless courage within me. I was alone in my forest retreat on "Black Saturday," the day of Australia's worst bush-fire. As the smoke-filled blackness descended, a penetrating silence sliced through all my discriminations, leaving a profound sense of the insignificance of "me." This silence manifested in clarity and precise lifesaving action. Perhaps for me, as for the old woman, there was a distilling of life's purpose in those timeless moments, as the shadowy grip of the fear of death faded in me.

Zhaozhou has pointed out the dangers, and the old woman clearly stands her ground, but is it enough to show one's fearlessness when penetrating into the heart of all things? Zhaozhou's last words on the matter are: "There's still this." Though both the great Zen master and the old cultivator are poised and snarling, neither really pounces and Zhaozhou walks away with "this."

"This" what? This magnificent, joyous moment in life, or this fearful thing bringing us grief? Don't smother reality or this-ness with such impressions! What is this tiger in my life, or this fearless old woman in me? What is that great timeless, inner roar of no sound and where does it come from? Such inquiry points to a deep spacious stillness within, yet demands we act now. Only through the cultivation of "this" within Zen action may Zhaozhou's last words be grasped.

> Compared to a nonvirtuous
> human heart
> the tiger is very kind,
> but to speak one word
> or even create
> a single Dharma
> you're devoured!

What do you say to your fear? Did Zhaozhou and that old woman have the same roar? Where is the tiger right now?

37. Shotaku's Paper Sword

SHOTAKU WAS the third abbess of the Tokeiji convent. One evening she was returning to Tokeiji from a nearby monastery when a man armed with a sword accosted her and threatened to rape her. She took out a piece of paper and rolled it up, then thrust it like a sword at the man's eyes. He was completely overcome by her spiritual strength and was unable to strike her. He turned to run and she gave him a Zen shout, hitting him and knocking him down with her "sword." He fled.

NANCY MUJO BAKER'S REFLECTION

This story about Shotaku reminds me of a news item that came out of Somalia last year about a remarkable woman doctor, Dr. Hawa Abdi, who runs a small hospital that she built on her own land. It's the only hospital for miles around. One day she heard gunshots. A group of warlords had surrounded the hospital with guns drawn. They belonged to one of Somalia's most fearsome militant groups, notorious for chopping off hands and stoning adulterers. "Why are you running this hospital?" they demanded. "You are old and you are a woman." She was held at gunpoint while the hospital was ransacked and severely damaged by the warlords' underlings. She was then put under house arrest for five days while the hospital was shut down. In that time, two dozen malnourished children from the hospital died.

But then something extraordinary happened. Hundreds of women from the sprawling refugee camp on Dr. Abdi's property dared to protest, adding to a flood of condemnation from Somalis abroad that forced the gunmen to back down. Because of so much publicity about their misdeeds they agreed to open the hospital again. But Dr. Abdi refused until the warlords *apologized in writing!* They did—in both English and Somali. In their document they apologized to Dr. Abdi, to the NGOs helping in the camp, to the camp's staff, and to the Somali people around the area who had lost loved ones.

Here are two marvelous examples of "spiritual strength" many centuries apart. What exactly is spiritual strength? In this Zen story with the Zen shout and a would-be rapist being overcome by Shotaku, it is easy to romanticize or idealize some mysterious Zen thing called "spiritual strength" as if it is possessed only by the "enlightened" ones, whoever they are. But Dr. Abdi's story brings this idea down to earth, here and now, and challenges us in a realistic way to ask if we could do what she did.

Actually, we all have that strength. It's the same strength we use whenever we commit ourselves to something completely. An example would be skiing downhill with one's whole body and mind, one hundred percent. It is, on many ski slopes, the only way to avoid breaking a leg. If I ever had to have brain surgery, I would hope that my surgeon could be one-hundred-percent present in this way. It is hard for us to do something—anything—one hundred percent, especially when it involves others. We are usually worried about making a mistake: do we look right, will we be approved of, will we offend someone? And in this koan and the story from Somalia, we might also be worried about whether we would be killed. We are completely tied to others for reference points to assure us that we are solid, separate, and permanent. We resist doing anything one hundred percent because it involves giving up those reference points and thus our "self," something we are very reluctant to do.

Master Linji said, "Just be autonomous!" That means to give up everything, to take a stand, not over or against something, but rather fully expressing oneself without any self-consciousness—in these two cases with a powerful "*No!*" This story makes me think of the eighth

Zen precept about not being stingy. We are stingy when we hold back part of ourselves for what we imagine is safety's sake. If it's not my life that is at stake, then it's my reputation, or apparent likeableness, or even just being right. Shotaku married young, but after her husband died she became a nun and eventually abbess of her convent, which was known as a "sanctuary temple," one of only two places in Japan where women could obtain a divorce. She was obviously used to taking a stand, even against powerful social norms.

Thank you, Shotaku and Dr. Abdi, for showing us the way of spiritual strength—warrior women with your paper swords!

A Zen teacher once said that even if you weren't a bodhisattva yet,
you could pretend to be one. What is the significance
of imagination on the spiritual path?
Can you overcome fear by pretending to be brave?

38. Dipa Ma's Fearless Daughters

INDIA / UNITED STATES, TWENTIETH CENTURY ·······························

 IPA MA was on an airplane with a woman student. It was very turbulent, and the woman screamed. Dipa Ma was sitting across the aisle and took her hand and held it. Then she whispered, "The daughters of the Buddha are fearless."

AMITA SCHMIDT'S REFLECTION

The first time I heard this story I thought, "Wait a minute, the Buddha never had a daughter." Dipa Ma, however, is pointing to a truth here that is deeper than historical facts. First of all she is teaching her student that as Buddhist practitioners each one of us belongs to the Buddha's family. No one is left out, not by gender, nor by time or history. We all belong to the lineage and the awakening of the Buddha, right here, right now.

Dipa Ma is also emphasizing the fearlessness needed on this path of the Dharma. To know the truth one must be fearless, no matter what is happening. Whether there is airplane turbulence, or physical injury, can you have a heart and mind that are unshakeable? Waking up is not a part-time job for the faint-hearted. It is the intention to meet every moment continually without flinching. As a daughter of the Buddha, are you an example to all beings of the willingness to face what is, right now, without fear or argument?

A few months ago I had a lesson in being a fearless daughter of the Buddha. On a balmy sunny morning I decided to go out for a solo swim in the ocean in Hawaii where I live. There were some colorful fish where I was swimming and I became preoccupied with follow-ing some of them. Unfortunately I didn't notice until it was too late that I had drifted out with an ocean current about one mile from the shore. To make matters worse a strong wind suddenly arose, and as I tried to swim to shore, the whitecaps pushed me back for every stroke I took. When I realized I was a long way out, alone, in shark territory, and unable to make much progress against the wind, I had a moment of panic. It was similar to the scream of Dipa Ma's student on the airplane.

But then my Dharma practice kicked in. It was as if the power of my intention from years of practice came forward, on its own, to help. It labeled the feeling, "This is just panic. Panic is not going to help you. Don't believe panic." Then my daughter-of-the-Buddha mind said, "Just do what you can do, stay focused on right now, one thing at a time. Start with one kick and one arm movement at a time. You can do that. Don't worry about anything else." I put a concentrated focus on the body and stayed out of the mind. I paid attention to the movement of my arms in the swimming motion, one breath at a time, and the kicking of my legs. I noticed that despite the wind I was able to move a tiny bit forward with each stroke. I focused on this small amount of forward motion, rather than the feeling of being pushed back. A spontaneous resolve arose to not give up no matter how long it took. This protective Dharma of the present moment, along with the resolve of the Buddha, eventually brought me back, exhausted, to the shore.

Whether we are experiencing a bumpy flight, a difficult ocean swim, or a turbulent life, our practice is the same. We are given the chance to meet this moment with openness and fearlessness. It doesn't matter how long it takes or how much the wind pushes us back. If there is a willingness not to give up and a resolve to keep taking that one next step, then it is inevitable that each one of us will find lasting freedom. As women, our lives are a message to each other. When we live from the intuitive truth that anything is possible, then this message of fearlessness can be passed on through generations of women. This is the true legacy of a daughter of the Buddha.

When you are afraid, where do you find Buddha? How do you find fearlessness within fear? How do you find freedom within fear?

39. Maylie Scott Meets Loneliness

UNITED STATES, TWENTIETH CENTURY ·····································

RYING IN despair, an earnest student asked her teacher, Seisho Maylie Scott, "I've worked so hard to transform this crippling loneliness. I can neither shake it nor live with it. Can you help me?"

Holding the student in a steady gaze and offering her confident smile, Maylie ended the conversation with, "Please don't ever think anything is out of place."

DIANE MUSHO HAMILTON'S REFLECTION

"Don't ever think anything is out of place." Hmmm . . . What is the teacher saying here? Is she empathizing with the student's feeling, her bodily ache, her lament? Does the teacher fully feel the serious plight of a heart filled with longing? Why doesn't she comfort her student, promising that everything will be OK?

Instead she says, "Don't ever think that anything is out of place." Her words seem strangely impersonal for such a question. They invoke an image not of a person but of a dinner table before the meal is served. The way white plates are evenly spaced, folded napkins to one side, wine glasses above. Forks line up, then spoons; one knife for cutting, another for spreading. Flowers bend out from the center, candlelight glints off silver and glass. Everything in its place.

How can loneliness have an appropriate place? Loneliness is the essential human cry that something is wrong. The word *loneliness* evokes to me an image of the dinner table *after* the meal is over and the guests have all gone home. The table is cluttered with dirty plates and a smattering of silverware; wine and candle wax stain the table-cloth. Suddenly, you find yourself all alone in a silent house, with no one to help you clean up.

Loneliness, by its very nature, is out of place. It is not orderly or aligned. It has the messy dimensions all bad feelings do. It hurts. It is the baby crying for its mother, the lover reaching out in the night for the one who has left. Loneliness yearns for someone to come; it pines for something to change. Yet the teacher tells us, "Don't ever think anything is out of place." What happens when we just allow loneliness to be as it is?

I have spent a great deal of my life working with loneliness. I am one of those people whose main strategy to secure myself in life is through connecting with others—making friends and creating a sense of belonging. I went one step further in my work and became a mediator, a professional in bringing people together. I worked to help people understand one another, to exchange points of view, and to solve problems together.

One night, after a long day of communication training in New York City, I was sitting in the bathtub when a profound loneliness overcame me. I had just spent the day with many open-hearted, com-municative people, and yet, just a few hours later, I was feeling alone in a way I had never felt before. For a moment, I panicked. There is no place like New York City to really feel existential loneliness when it comes knocking. Such a strong feeling won't go away by recalling a comforting memory or by reaching for the phone. It demands to be felt—felt beyond the boundaries of self-concept, beyond the limits of belonging, beyond any other source of security. It's scary. Primordial loneliness puts us on notice that in many ways, including dying, we are completely on our own.

With nowhere else to go, I allowed this loneliness in. As I sank deeper into the feeling and into the tub, something surprising hap-pened. I felt the warmth of the water surround my skin and saw the steam rising and fading. The tub showed up vivid and white, and the walls stood out in their dingy hotel yellow. Soon the pipes, the faucets, the toilet, and the sink were all there. Nothing was out of place, and I couldn't have felt more at home.

Seishi Maylie Scott was right. When we make room for loneliness, we allow for everything. We experience directly the pain of the separate self, and we can see beyond its limits to everything as it is. Nothing can ever be out of place. The one true heart that embraces all things reveals itself to us.

As the great Sufi poet Rumi wrote: "A joy, a depression, a meanness, some momentary awareness comes as an unexpected visitor. Welcome and entertain them all."

The cry of our loneliness has a place at the table, and so does our tenderness. Our troubling questions are good company. And the teacher's response is a smiling welcome to all of our life: "Don't ever think that anything is out of place." Include all of the unexpected visitors, and entertain them all.

How do you accept the unacceptable?
If nothing is out of place, is there anything we need to change?
How does the lonely body feel?

40. Yasodhara's Path

INDIA, SIXTH CENTURY BCE ···

ASODHARA WAS Siddhartha Gautama's wife. In one of the less well-known stories told about her life, Yasodhara ("The Glorious One") and Siddhartha had been married in many previous lifetimes. The night that Siddhartha left home, Yasodhara had eight dreams that foretold his awakening, and so she allowed him to leave her. They made love before he left, and their son, Rahula, was conceived.

For the next six years, Yasodhara remained pregnant with Rahula, and although she did not leave home, she traveled the same spiritual path and experienced the same difficulties as her husband Siddhartha. She gave birth to Rahula ("Moon God" in this particular story) on the full moon night of the Buddha's enlightenment. She prophesied that Siddhartha had awakened and that he would return in six years. Later, she and her son Rahula both became part of the Buddhist sangha.

BYAKUREN JUDITH RAGIR'S REFLECTION

Oh yes! Yes! What a relief. I smiled as I read this newly excavated version of Buddha's home-leaving found in the Sarvastivadin literature. I immediately felt a relaxation in my body, the release of a stress I didn't even know I was holding.

Every time I had to tell Buddha's early story in my teaching life, I gulped. In the postfeminist world of the twenty-first century, can we continue to tell stories from the past in which the women are invisible or rejected?

What needs to be renounced as we enter into a spiritual path? In the West, Buddhist practice is often an odd combination of monastic visits and householder lives. When I was ordained, I was already married and had two children. I did not leave my family, but I learned to practice with my story-filled life by transforming the basis of operation in my mind. I have had to work with my egocentricity; my attachments and clinging; and my greed, anger, and delusion right in the middle of the mess of household life and an urban zendo. After forty years of practice, I'm still practicing home-leaving within the boundaries of a home, as Yasodhara did. I take heart from the story of a Tibetan teacher's mother who got enlightened, as she tells it, by "practicing in the gaps" of her everyday life. Or as my root teacher, Katagiri Roshi, would encourage us by saying, "In every moment, merge subject and object into the very activity that is arising."

The idea that Dharma practice requires the renunciation of attachments of ordinary life, family, and work seems to come out of the privileged and one-sided point of view of the all-male founding fathers of Buddhism. Women simply can't afford to abandon the manifested world while we still are raising our children. It seems that in renouncing the world, the early Buddhists made women the so-called "enemies" of practice by making them the symbol of the "form world." Our "allure" was considered dangerous to monks. Women, with our blood, birth, noisy children, families, earthly bodies, life, creativity, love, and sexuality, were what needed to be renounced. Can this hold up in the evolution of twenty-first-century Buddhism?

There are some telling details in the two myths of Buddha's leaving the palace. The translation of the name "Rahula," Siddhartha and Yasodhara's son, is quite different in different versions. In the Theravadin school, Rahula means "fetter," implying that a child is one of the ties that bind us, like a chain or shackle, to the illusory world. But in the Sarvastivadin version, Rahula means "moon god," reflecting simply that he was born on the night of the full moon, when the Buddha himself awakened.

In the Sarvastivadin version of the story, the separation of Buddha and Yasodhara was a sorrowful event. They loved each other, but they knew that there must be a separation. Yasodhara saw in her dreams the possibility of Siddhartha's greatness. Out of love, and for the sake of the liberation of all beings, she let Siddhartha go. This inevitable separation may have been a heart-breaking truth for both of them. This is a great example of how a devastating loss can often initiate the spiritual journey, as many of us have experienced.

What I love about this version of the story is that it honors the spiritual path of the home. Yasodhara, the one who stayed home, dug into her own spiritual life right where she was. When I first had my babies, I laughed and told all my friends, "Child rearing is just like going into a monastery. Everything you do is for the 'other' and there is hardly a moment to think of yourself." Another Buddhist teacher who is a father commented, "It's like my heart is running around outside my body." Becoming a mother completely connected me to the mystery of life. I could no longer be self-centered, and my heart burst open.

Yasodhara's separation from her husband and the pregnancy she went through without him meant that she was practicing against all odds. But our ordinary suffering can transform into wisdom and compassion. Years later, she and her son reunited with Buddha and joined his sangha.

All birth is magic. In this legend, Yasodhara giving birth on the same full-moon night as Buddha's enlightenment under the bodhi tree is a miraculous honoring of nonduality—the dynamic dance of man and woman, enlightenment and delusion, ordinary and sacred, birth and death.

Sometimes a hero's journey is made without ever leaving home. What invisible journeys have you made? Does this story change how you feel about the Buddha?

41. Bhadda Kapilani and Mahakassapa

HEN BHADDA KAPILANI was a child, she witnessed the suffering of insects being eaten by crows and vowed never to marry, but to live as a spiritual renunciate.

On the same day, far away, a boy named Mahakassapa saw worms being eaten by birds in a freshly plowed field. He was overcome with pity and vowed to become a monk one day. He, too, vowed that he would never marry. This upset his parents, so he made an agreement with them. He made a golden statue of a beautiful woman and he promised his parents that if a woman could be found who was exactly like the statue, he would marry her. Messengers were sent far and wide, searching for a living match, and Bhadda was found.

Before the marriage, Bhadda and Mahakassapa agreed that they would live a celibate life and renounce the world together. After they were married, they cut off each other's hair, put on robes, and set off into homelessness.

Mahakassapa encountered the Buddha and ordained, later becoming an arahant and leader in the sangha. Five years later, when Mahapajapati established the order of nuns, Bhadda ordained, also becoming an arahant.

Bhadda wrote a poem:

> Seeing the world's deep misery, we both went forth
> and are now both free of mind's obsessions.
> Cooled of passions, we have found deliverance;
> cooled of passions, we have found our freedom.

JACQUELINE MANDELL'S REFLECTION

My first three-year journey around the world began in 1971, shortly after college. I traveled overland from Europe through Central Asia to India on rickety buses and overnight trains, through unknown cultures, languages, and customs. Seeking freedom, I did not know of the deep inner adventure that lay before me. Wisdom ancestors of Buddhism would soon guide my way.

I walked through the gates of my first Buddhist meditation retreat in Bodh Gaya, India, prepared only with this advice from a friend: "Follow the teachers' instructions, wake up early, participate in all meditation sessions, follow the retreat schedule, and don't pay attention to anyone else. Be single-minded and diligent."

Early on the first day, with the moon still shining in the sky, I sat on my mat in the silent hall meditating into the morning while the soft mist rose outside. Later, on a full-moon night, I sat until dawn at the Bodhi Temple under the bodhi tree, while the quiet presence of the land of enlightenment glimmered with a new way of being.

I started a new life with many new spiritual ancestors, among them Bhaddha Kapilani and Mahakassapa. I appreciated that they took controversial risks in their pursuit of enlightenment. Actualizing full awakening as their highest priority, these close disciples of the Buddha, with their unwavering faith, have inspired multitudes of practitioners through the generations. Bhadda Kapilani and Mahakassapa chose, from the time they were very young, to orient their lives toward the pursuit of the third noble truth of Buddhism: the cessation of suffering. I learned on my first retreat that this aspiration gives us the courage to walk the path of liberation from suffering, which is the fourth noble truth.

Bhaddha Kapilani and Mahakassapa are two of the most prominent enlightened Buddhist ancestors. At a time of fixed societal codes, people from their class were expected to continue the tradition of family responsibility, civic duty, and land management. Instead, they each chose to follow a path different from their parents'.

What inspired the couple? At the exact moment of the Buddha's enlightenment under the bodhi tree, two small sensitive children, living in different regions, simultaneously saw deeply into the unsatisfactory nature of life. Later, the two would empower each other, side by side, to renounce home and land holdings. Unwavering intentionality compelled these two ancient leaders onto their path of true freedom.

The rare occurrence of receiving teachings from a buddha, combined with strong personal intention, created the perfect condition for Bhaddha Kapilani and Mahakassapa to become arahants. Mahakassapa received awakened mind-to-mind transmission when the Buddha held up a flower in front of the assembly, without speaking. At the moment of awakening, Mahakassapa smiled.

Bhaddha Kapilani became a fully ordained nun, arahant, and enlightened teacher. She possessed visionary powers—her ability to see into the karma of her own past lives echoed the Buddha's experience during the night of his enlightenment. Bhadda Kapilani's noted abilities to subsequently see into her students' past lives as well allowed her to guide these disciples with unusual skill.

The histories of Bhadda Kapilani and Mahakassapa remind me of an aspiration I made early in life. One of my earliest memories was standing on the warm beach of the Atlantic Ocean, gazing toward the horizon. Watching ocean liners traverse the thin line between sea and sky, I heard myself say, "One day I will travel to freedom." As I grew up, I always had an underlying feeling that "this couldn't be all that life is about." I didn't know that these feelings had a name: dissatisfaction, the first noble truth of Buddhism. As a young woman I set out on the journey toward ultimate freedom.

Bhadda Kapilani and Mahakassapa had the fortitude and creative thinking to change their circumstances and travel the path to enlightenment. Today their journey is like a timeless spark that continues to ignite our hearts, urging us toward the rich fulfillment of freedom: our common thread.

Were Bhadda and her husband still married even as they went into homelessness and awakened? What is their kind of marriage? The first of the four bodhisattva vows is to save all sentient beings. How does it change that vow if you take it with another person?

42. Ikkyu and Kannon's Messenger

KKYU Sojun was a twenty-one-year-old monk when his beloved teacher died. He was distraught and wandered aimlessly, praying to Kannon, the bodhisattva of compassion. His mother was so worried about him that she assigned a servant to surreptitiously follow him.

One day Ikkyu came to a bridge and thought, "I will throw myself into the water. If my life is spared, it will be proof of the bodhisattva Kannon's protection. And if not, at least I will be good fish food. In either case, Kannon will not fail me."

Just as he was about to leap off, the servant appeared, caught his arm, and gave him a message from his mother: "It would be unfilial to harm your body. Enlightenment will have its proper day; please persevere."

Ikkyu did not jump off the bridge; instead he returned to the capitol to pay his respects to his mother.

MUSHIM PATRICIA IKEDA'S REFLECTION

"We're standing in a very safe place," my host said approvingly. He was the owner of the property, and we were standing in front of his trailer, watching my son's dad, who was perched atop a tall eucalyptus tree, wielding a chain saw to trim off a huge limb. He was cutting it so that it would fall away from us. My toddler, Josh, was playing on the lawn in front of me, and we were quite a distance from the tree.

It seemed like a relaxed way to spend a Sunday afternoon, hanging out in a eucalyptus grove and helping a friend.

I remember distinctly how my body moved suddenly and purposefully without my willing it. In one fluid movement I lunged forward, grabbed my son, and moved backward, just as the tree-sized limb torqued hard, changed direction, and crashed onto the exact spot where my son had been. Its top fell on our friend's Airstream trailer, damaging the roof.

Raising children is a risky business. I could have lost my son that day, and my life would be very different. As it is, Josh is twenty-three now, interning as a quality assurance computer technician. Monday through Friday, he gets up early, puts on a tie, and takes the commuter train into San Francisco from our home in Oakland.

Thus, when we consider the case of Ikkyu and Kannon's messenger, we may ask: "Was the servant really Kannon, the bodhisattva of great compassion, in disguise? Did Kannon propel my body forward to save my son? Is Kannon a powerful metaphor for our instinctual desire to protect our beloved children, or is she 'real'?"

The classic Zen Buddhist answer to all such questions, is, of course, "Yes."

Kannon is Avalokiteshvara Bodhisattva, the One Who Hears the Cries of the World. In Mahayana lore, this great being has thousands of arms and hands, holding thousands of implements and utensils, like frying pans and cell phones and wisdom swords, through which the work of compassion is performed daily, often invisibly. Compassion has many names: Kannon in Japan, Kuan Yin in China, Kwan Seum Posal in Korea, Quan The Am Botat in Vietnam, you, me, our family members, our friends, and sometimes complete strangers, animals, and plants. If we are alert to it, compassion falls from the sky.

I remember talking years ago to Ho, a Vietnamese man in Albuquerque who had escaped from Vietnam in the late seventies with his young son, leaving his wife and other children behind. The family had never been reunited. Lighting a cigarette and staring into his coffee cup, Ho talked about how frightening it had been to be at sea in a small boat. He said that, during a thunderstorm, a friend thought to spread out a nylon windbreaker and use it to collect rainwater for Ho's child, who otherwise would have died of thirst. Since then, I have heard of Vietnamese boat people, floating on the open ocean without food or water, who saw visions of Kannon, or Quan The Am Botat, in the air above them. These visions gave them hope that they would eventually reach a safe shore.

Through the mercy of Kannon, his mother's concern, and the servant messenger's skillful intervention, Ikkyu got through his crisis of grief and went on to be a famously eccentric Zen monk, poet, calligrapher, master of the tea ceremony, and frequenter of brothels. His body did not become food for the fish in Lake Biwa that day.

I discussed all this over lunch in a Korean restaurant in Oakland with my Dharma friend Jim Willems, who practices deeply with chronic pain, and who has had wide exposure to Dharma and other spiritual lineages. This was much more relaxing than going head-to-head in a tiny room with a Zen master waving a stick, as has happened in my past.

"The koan implies this question," Jim said, "*How were the fishes fed?*"

Perhaps the waters of Lake Biwa were cold and dark that day, and the fishes remained hungry. Or maybe it was sunny, and they rose cheerfully to the surface to gulp down mosquitoes. I was not there and I do not know. But I am glad that Ikkyu didn't jump, and I am happy he went instead to see his mother, and I imagine that she hugged him with two of Kannon's one thousand arms.

What would it be like if we saw a possible Kannon in every person we met, in every relative, in every dog or cat? Or in your own mother?

43. Senjo and Her Soul Are Separated

CHINA, FOLKTALE ···

ENJO WAS the beloved daughter of Chokan. In childhood she played with her cousin Ochu, and Senjo's father jokingly told them they were betrothed. They believed him and later fell in love. When her father told her she would marry another man, they were heartbroken.

Ochu left the village in a boat before the marriage. As he left, he saw a figure running along the riverbank, calling to him. It was Senjo. Joyfully, she joined him, and they traveled far away, where they married and had two children.

Five years went by, and Senjo longed to see her parents and ask their forgiveness. They traveled back to their village and Ochu went to her father, told him the story, and apologized for them both.

Chokan, astonished, asked Ochu, "What girl are you talking about?"

"Your daughter Senjo," replied Ochu.

Chokan said, "My daughter Senjo? Ever since you left, she's been sick in bed, unable to speak."

Then Ochu brought Senjo up from the boat. As they approached her parents' door, the Senjo who had been sick got up from her bed, smiling. When the two Senjos met, they merged into one.

Senjo said, "I saw Ochu going away, and that night I dreamed that I ran after his boat. But now I cannot tell which was really me—the one that went away in the boat, or the one that stayed at home."

Later, Zen Master Wuzu asked, "Senjo was separated from her soul. Which was the real Senjo?"

Eijun Linda Ruth Cutts's Reflection

"Senjo and Her Soul Are Separated" is a beloved Zen story from *The Gateless Gate* (Case 35). Every time I have brought this case up in a Dharma talk it seems to fully resonate with practitioners, especially with women. The listeners seem to be enthralled with this account of what happened to Senjo. What is it about this Tang dynasty folk tale, brought into the koan literature, that speaks to our life—that allows us to study ourselves and our practice more vividly, and to realize the teachings more intimately?

The conventional elements of the story mirror many of the situations that brought me and many women to practice. Like Senjo we may have grown up in circumstances in which we had little agency; where familial, religious, cultural, gender, and social pressures were strong and where meeting the prevailing expectations was conveyed as more important than anything else. Like Senjo, whose older sister had died, we may have been born into a family ecology with many challenges and intense karmic patterns. Like Senjo, we may have experienced great love, great loss, and deep disappointment. Conditioned by this difficult environment we try to relieve our pain in unskillful ways, resulting in feeling divided and distanced from our once lively self. Like the two Senjos unaware of each other—one drained of energy, sick in bed without speech; the other an active wife and mother, yet riven by contradiction and separation—eventually we begin longing to be whole—for something real, for our true home. Which one is the true Senjo?

The poem commentary on Case 35 by Wumen (Mumon) is:

> The moon above the clouds is ever the same;
> valleys and mountains are separate from each other.
> All are blessed, all are blessed;
> are they one or are they two?

The Dharma teachings on the nature of self pervade this story. Actions of body, speech, and mind that are based on ignorance, or the belief in a separate self, create more and more causes and conditions for suffering. When one practices, especially sitting still, one can reunite not only with a lost self of flowing energy, buoyancy, and active compassionate concern for oneself and others, but also with a fuller acknowledgment of shadow and delusion. The fruit of our practice and of integrating all parts of ourselves may be experienced as a blessing and a reprieve after a ghost-like existence. And yet, right from the start one hears the teachings of the emptiness of a separate self, an ungraspable nonabiding self—the compassionate clear-seeing of which relieves all suffering. Which is the true self?

Senjo, after five years living with her husband and children, found she was not at peace and longed for home. Her decision to leave her home, though understandable, had not been wholehearted, not complete. After following after our desires again and again, we find that this way of life does not satisfy. Understanding how samsara (the world of suffering and rebirth) works, coming back home, taking refuge in the practice of just sitting down and stopping, is itself peace. Senjo's longing to return and reunite with her family expresses the innermost longing to find true contentment, which comes only through realizing our true self.

The big surprise at the end is the discovery that there appear to be two Senjos. The koan asks us, "Which is the real Senjo?" When the two saw each other face to face, they smiled. And with that smile, closer and closer they moved toward each other and became one. This smile of recognition is the same as Buddha's successor Mahakassapa's smile when the World-Honored One on Vulture Peak held up a flower and winked. This was their transmission ceremony of nothing-to-transmit. Mahakassapa understood that the Buddha and he himself were not actually separated. Though we appear in different forms and colors, mountains and valleys, all phenomena are equal in the moonlight of their dependent coarising. Senjo's smiling and realizing "not one, not two" in her practice body is the way it has always been. Even if she doesn't know it she is intimately living it. Even if we have not realized it we must practice it as realization itself.

The longing to be good, the longing to be true, the longing to come home, the longing to be whole . . . What longings call you now? And what is this "self" that can be so insistent, shimmering like a rainbow, arcing between the boundless sky and our tremendous passions? Are there times when life requires you to divide yourself in parts?

44. Iron Grindstone Liu's Feast

IRON GRINDSTONE LIU went to Master Guishan Lingyou. Guishan said, "Old cow, so you've come?"
The Iron Grinder said, "Tomorrow on Mount Wutai there's a big gathering and feast—are you going, teacher?"
Guishan lay down and sprawled out. The Iron Grinder immediately left.

PAT ENKYO O'HARA'S REFLECTION

A perfect *pas de deux*: This jewel of a koan reveals the intimacy and playfulness possible between two Zen masters, in this case a man and a woman. Iron Grindstone Liu, or "The Grinder," left home at an early age, entered a convent, and was ordained. After a few years, she left and wandered through China, seeking a teacher and challenging those who would engage her about the Dharma. She had encounters with various Zen teachers and eventually gained a reputation as a brilliant and devastating opponent in Dharma combat: she was said to be a steely stone who could grind up—and also sharpen—the wits of those whom she encountered.

Eventually, she studied with the revered Zen master Guishan and became his Dharma heir. At the time of this encounter, she had completed formal study and had settled on a mountain nearby. We can assume that she would visit her old teacher from time to time. The koan itself, appearing in the *Blue Cliff Record* (Case 24) and in the *Book of Serenity* (Case 60), reads like a classic *pas de deux*, with *entrée*, *adagio*, *variation*, and *coda*. It is satisfyingly complete and heartbreakingly intimate.

The first thing to note is that she is visiting him—she is physically entering his space—and in a related verse to this koan, her entrance is described as "Riding an iron horse, she entered the fortress." So while she may be making a social visit, we can also see that she is strong and ready for any challenge. Guishan, by now somewhat old, sees her enter and says, "Old cow, so you've come?" Now "cow" may not be an endearing term in contemporary English, but it's said that Guishan had a particular affection for buffalos; he was quoted as saying that after his death he would return as a buffalo. The key word, and the first volley, arrives subtly, *adagio*, "you've come." Old Guishan is very simply lifting up the question of how one can come and go from the ultimate view, where there is no coming and no going, where there is the single pristine point of here, now.

How is she to respond to this sweetly delivered trap? Without a moment's hesitation (the verse says she is still "gripping the golden whip"), the Grinder responds by asking him if tomorrow he is going to attend a feast that is being held six hundred miles away—a physical impossibility in those days. She matches Guishan's gesture of the ultimate by questioning its implication—if all is one point, are you going to this impossibly far away place? A *variation*, a check!

Guishan, looking up at this clear-eyed woman, lazily sprawls out and relaxes his body, as if to say, "Ah, you got me! Where is 'here' or 'there' in the Way?" This vulnerable body, releasing, expresses a remarkable intimacy and connection between these two Zen adepts, as well as being a direct response to her; his bluff called, he admits it is right here, where there is no coming and going. Another *variation*, a check of a different kind!

And at that, without a word, she leaves! A final *coda* in this incredible dance in which the Grindstone shows what cannot be said and demonstrates the shifting truth of boundlessness penetrated by ordinary space and time. She leaves with her body much as Guishan sprawls with his. Form is emptiness, emptiness form.

What does this koan teach us today? Is it not that New York melts the arctic ice; that karmic threads of colonialism have woven twenty-first century violence; that restitution across the globe rests in our hearts, here at home?

Beyond that, what a privilege for us to witness through koan the meeting of these two delightful old masters, playfully displaying their insight while engaging the most precarious of truths: the balance of ultimate and relative. A perfectly balanced *pas de deux*! One can imagine the Grindstone's laugh as she left and the smile on old Guishan's face as he sprawled, at his ease, having been visited by the great Grinder!

Why go to a festival far away, or even travel to visit your teacher, when you can study the Way in your own kitchen?

45. The Old Woman Recognizes Mazu

WHEN MASTER MAZU DAOYI returned to his native place for a short visit, he was warmly welcomed by his countrymen. But an old woman, who used to be his next-door neighbor, said, "I thought that all the commotion was caused by the visit of some extraordinary personage. In fact, it's none other than that little chap who is the son of Ma, the garbage collector."

On hearing this, Mazu improvised the following poem:

> I advise you not to return to your native place
> for no one can be a sage in his own home.
> This old woman by the side of the brook
> still calls me the garbage man's son!

EIDO FRANCES CARNEY'S REFLECTION

This is a sweet story of the famous Master Mazu returning to his childhood home, where he's warmly greeted by locals. Whom should he encounter but a next-door neighbor who remembers him as a boy. She doesn't acknowledge Mazu as Zen master in the great lineage of Bodhidharma and Huineng. No, she remembers him as the son of the garbage collector! So, Mazu writes a little poem in response that essentially says: true liberation is far beyond a constricted identity.

What pivotal role does the old woman play in this narrative? She isn't given a name, and because of that we have to pay close attention to how essential she is to the story. She is an archetypal ghost who hovers over the scene, reminding us to be authentic. Such old women appear throughout literature, serving as foils for other characters to realize themselves and saving us from arrogance.

In this story we might think the woman is the old biddy who knows everyone's business, the one who hangs out on her doorstep and watches everyone's coming and going. It's a trick to throw us off guard. Her presence, after all, brings about Mazu's insight. She had witnessed the formative part of his life. She makes us ask: Which part of life can we ignore or just toss into the garbage? When Mazu says, "I advise you not to return to your native place," perhaps he means that our true buddha nature cannot be found in a particular place. It can't be found in any geography. We can't go back to our first residence and expect to find something special. All we will find is a shadow of the wisdom that is walking alongside us.

The old woman didn't go elsewhere—she remained at home. She is a metaphor for the true nature of home; she doesn't have to travel or be promoted in order to be authentic. And it is Mazu who brings this point forward. He says, "No one can be a sage in his own home." He is saying there is no deeper place other than mind, our true home. In that home which is not a state, or a space, we are beyond any identity at all, even beyond being called "sage." So Mazu writes, "no one can be a sage in his own home." There is no personal identity in the home of true self.

When Mazu says, "The old woman still calls me the garbage man's son!" I might think he's rebuking the old woman for being a small-minded busybody. But I have to think more of both of them. After all, the story is there for my growth, and how I see it is who I am. I am all the characters of the story—no separation between the old woman, Mazu, and me.

We have to *be* buddha nature to *see* buddha nature, to allow goodness to appear. When Mazu says, "She still calls me the garbage man's son!" he is also celebrating his father's life. "Hurrah," he is saying, "she remembers both of us!" He is awash in gratitude. He has grown in modesty, accepting the totality of his life. His humanness is apparent. The old woman succeeds!

During my training at a very large monastery in Japan, a high-ranking old priest from the district came to the temple for an important annual ceremony. Red carpets were spread from the entry gate to the temple door. The priest walked through a pathway of deeply bowing monks.

Along with the other training monks, I helped serve the celebration dinner. The visiting dignitary was seated in a place of honor. It was more than he could do to eat the huge meal put in front of him, but he couldn't be rude and not touch it at all. When I came close and served tea, I saw that his nose was running and there was some food caught on the edge of his lips. I offered him a tissue and motioned to where he should wipe. He did so without embarrassment. In that moment I saw that this high official had not taken his position so seriously that he was beyond being human. His eyes revealed a true person, warm and present, far beyond the constricted identity of his title. He seemed to be saying, "We are all made of the patchwork robe, of fabric rescued from the garbage; we are all children of the Buddha."

What did you leave behind in your native place?
Who is your old woman, and what does she see in you?

46. Satsujo Overthrows Hakuin

ASTER HAKUIN explained a koan to his student, the young laywoman Satsujo. Then he asked her, "How do you understand this?"

She replied, "Would you please go over it again?"

As soon as he opened his mouth to speak, she put her hands to the floor and bowed. "Thank you for your trouble," she said, and walked out, leaving Hakuin with his mouth open.

Hakuin exclaimed, "Oh dear! I've been trounced by this terrible little woman!"

CAITRIONA REED'S REFLECTION

I've always imagined that the best sort of kindness is the one that holds people absolutely accountable. I am thinking of the kindness that does not tolerate any sort of victimhood or hesitation, and will always look you straight in the eye. It will push the student ahead of the teacher without thought of form or mere propriety. Satsujo had learned well from her teacher. I wonder if Hakuin deliberately set himself up and let himself fall for her ruse. This would mean an altogether deeper sort of kindness, and isn't kindness one of those things that has no limits?

I once found myself at a three-day seminar with my partner. Neither of us knew what we were getting into or what we wanted out of the experience, but we both felt we needed "a kick in the butt," as my partner had said.

My partner and I sat near the back, aloof to the speakers and events. After all, we'd been teaching the Dharma for years. We knew a thing or two about change and helping people bring out the best in themselves—or so we thought.

Late in the day the speaker said, "There are some of you, no doubt, sitting in the back, who think you're way too cool for this. But you aren't getting what you want out of life. You're not contributing all you know you could." That was the first of many well-aimed kicks in the butt.

The kindness of the speaker was not something that came to mind at that moment. I was confused by his approach. Now I realize that before that day, I had often mistaken gentleness for kindness. How often had I listened patiently, sensitive to the vulnerability of my student, or client, or friend, when what would have been far more effective was one of those proverbial kicks to the backside? And how often had I found mentors who listened rather than challenged me? I didn't know it yet, but that was about to change.

During a break, I happened to fall into conversation with one of the presenters. I was nervous and looking for reassurance. She seemed sympathetic. I explained how stuck I was, doing what I did, teaching Buddhism, running a meditation center on a shoestring, not making the difference I might, no longer connected to the relevance of it all. She listened patiently.

When I paused she asked, "When did you forget the solution to your problem?"

I was dumbstruck. It was a perfect koan, breaking through all the assumptions that held my story together. Yes, there was a solution. Yes, I did know what it was. Yes, apparently I had forgotten it. She didn't leave me a leg to stand on. Of course, her timing was impeccable. After all, isn't timing what makes the koan? And in some mysterious way isn't that where the kindness is, in the easy flow, the synchronicity, of a well-aimed blow to a cherished presupposition?

And isn't it the job of the student, ultimately, to trounce the teacher? If Hakuin had, in fact, allowed himself to fall for Satsujo's ruse, wasn't he giving her the opportunity to express the same fierce kindness that he had, no doubt, shown to her in the past?

The woman I had spoken to during the break became my mentor for a while. Then, after a couple of years, we reversed roles, and I mentored her. Both of us were thoroughly trounced on numerous occasions, with calls for clarity, accountability, and action. We were driven, as Hakuin was, by kindness of the fiercest sort, one that will risk anything to further the student's awakening.

Is it possible to explain the Dharma to another person? When is it helpful to repeat a teaching, and when is it like kicking a dead horse?

47. The Old Woman Steals Zhaozhou's Bamboo Shoots

NE DAY Master Zhaozhou Congshen was outside the monastery and an old woman came along carrying a basket. He asked her, "Where are you going?"

The old woman said, "I'm going to steal Zhaozhou's bamboo shoots."

Zhaozhou asked, "What will you do if you run into Zhaozhou?"

The old woman walked up to Zhaozhou and slapped him.

FURYU NANCY SCHROEDER'S REFLECTION

I must confess to finding secret delight in this story. How daring of a woman, and an old woman at that, to assault not only a full grown man, but a full-blown Zen master to boot. It certainly goes against our training as women and as disciples of the Buddha to whack our teachers, and yet we also know how tempting it can be, not only to take a poke at the Zen masters who have trained us, but even more so at the entire tradition, which has seen fit through most of its history to leave us, as women, out.

I think of how it hurt me as a child to discover from my parents, my teachers, and even my playground friends how little value there was in being "a girl." And so I made sure I didn't throw like a girl, walk like a girl, or think like a girl, because I had come to believe that to do so would be a great embarrassment for me.

But this story is about a lot more than the failure to take women seriously in Buddhist history. For me this story invites a deeper look at all exchanges between students and teachers of the Dharma, or even deeper still, at how we face the world in each and every moment. Isn't that the reason we got into this Dharma practice in the first place? Didn't we come to the monastery gate to look for answers to great questions?

Every moment, each of us—man, woman, child, dog, beetle, cat—is met and made by vast networks of causes and conditions that sprout up like Zhaozhou's bamboo shoots, which are always lively, fresh, and freely given. And yet the old woman talks of stealing. How curious is that!

And what about that empty basket? How often do each of us move through our day with a list, a wad of cash, and an empty basket that we're longing to fill, enacting the Buddha's first and second noble truths? There is an aching in my heart; the aching is caused by my sincere desire that things be different, but especially, better, than they are. "If only I had a few bamboo shoots to brighten the afternoon meal." "If only my parents would stop quarrelling." "If only I wasn't growing old, getting sick, and about to die." "If only . . ."

To the enlightened eye, myriad things fit perfectly together every moment, as if by magic and without regrets. Like the Big Bang in reverse . . . old woman, old man, empty basket, bamboo shoots, and spring: Kapow!

When Zhaozhou asks, "Where are you going?" I think the old lady is being challenged to respond. So the old lady checks out his humanity with a smack.

This koan is a cliff hanger! Does Zhaozhou meet the old woman freshly and openly, or has he forgotten for a moment who she truly is and that without her, without the bamboo shoots, without the spring, and without the empty basket, he would have no life at all?

Not just this woman, this meeting, at this moment—all meetings, all moments, all women. They've known each other, loved each other, slapped each other before. After all, she must have changed his dirty diapers a hundred million times. And that slap she gave him was a doozy. Maybe she thought that if she hit him really hard his loving heart would open to her once again, as it had those many lifetimes ago: "Mom?" "Sweetheart?" "Darling?" We don't see the word "love" used so often in the Dharma. In fact, there seems to be a fear of it. In particular, the body of it: the lovely body, at every age, of the child, of the woman, and of the man. But if what's happening in this story isn't love, including, dare I say, "sex," then I'm a monkey's uncle.

Do we think he hit her back? I doubt it. I think he laughed his goofy old head off and so did his silly old girlfriend. They, like us, hand in hand, will keep traveling the pathways together, delighting the children and rattling the cages of the frightened young monks. Boo!

How do you steal from someone who is willing to give everything away?
What if someone you respect obstructs your way?

48. The Old Woman's Relatives

 NCE A MONK on pilgrimage met an old woman living alone in a hut. The monk asked, "Do you have any relatives?" She said, "Yes."

The monk asked, "Where are they?"

She answered, "The mountains, rivers, and the whole earth, the plants and trees, are all my relatives."

ZENSHIN FLORENCE CAPLOW'S REFLECTION

I haven't studied koans in the formal Zen way, but as a midwife to this book I have lived and breathed these koans about women for a few years. And this particular old woman and her relatives have accompanied me as I sat in winter retreat, as I worked in the Mojave Desert springtime as a field biologist, as I sit now on a log on the shores of Willapa Bay on the Washington coast, watching the tide move in, listening to the harsh cries of Caspian terns as they wheel and dive out over the water.

Encountering a koan can be like diving into the middle of the ocean. At the surface there is brightness and little waves: my ideas and prior knowledge. Down a few feet things get quieter and dimmer, and there's more room for the unexpected. Deeper still and anything at all could appear: sharks, whales, or even the Buddha him/herself, rising up from the depths with that eighteen-foot golden body glimmering in the dark.

When I first dove into this koan, I was struck by ". . . an old woman living alone in a hut." In all the stories of old Chinese Buddhist hermits, this is the only one I know where the hermit is a woman. A woman in China under Confucian law was subject, from birth to death, to the absolute will of male family members: father, husband, brother, son. It was neither safe nor sanctioned for a woman to live alone. So who was this old woman, anyway? The monk wasn't sure either, perhaps even a little uneasy. Didn't this woman have relatives nearby? How else would she survive?

Like her, I have chosen to live alone—and often without a fixed home at all—these last few years, and I've met people like this monk, who need to fit me into something they can understand. Even now a woman alone by choice is suspect. Maybe for us in the West there is an old resonance with witches in the woods—a woman alone is perhaps a woman with powers, or a woman too unpleasant for company, or a woman crazed.

But when the old woman turns the monk's question on its head, we know immediately that she is a Zen adept, a teacher. Oh yes, he needn't worry, she has relatives: "Just look around, monk, and show me one thing that is not a relative!" She's not alone after all; she isn't unsupported. None of us are, however we may feel.

"Alone." What a word. Am I alone or unsupported, as I sit here on this log in the twilight? Maybe, maybe not. There is no one who will make dinner for me tonight; on the other hand, the food in my belly was grown for me by many human hands, by earth, by sunlight. This log grew for a hundred years or more, upright in the rain, and is now home to countless creatures other than the one who sits here for a while. I have felt more alone in a crowded room than I feel here now.

But there is another kind of aloneness, a more pernicious sense of separation that comes from ideas of "here" and "there," "I" and "not-I." Were the old woman's relatives "out there" beyond her skin, or somewhere closer by? With this question I enter the ocean's depths, the place where anything can appear. And I realize that I need to ask my question to that old hermit, that ancient sister.

The Zen stories are quite clear: if you want to truly meet a teacher, you have to ask a question, a real soul-shivering Dharma question. And we *can* ask. Any teacher, alive or dead, has vowed to answer. So I close my eyes and say to her, across the years, "How distant are these relatives of yours?"

She says, "Come closer."

I lean forward. "Even closer." And we are face to face.

In that moment of meeting I understand that relatives are not just "out there," they are through and through—mountains and rivers and faces and eyebrows and guts and the very subtlest stirrings of mind.

But you must understand that it is the *asking* that matters, not the answer. Because every real asking, every real meeting comes from the place where the Buddha glimmers in the depths. In the asking is the answerer; in the answer is the asker. And in the meeting of the two, there are mountains, rivers, and the whole earth.

Dogen says rocks and walls teach the Dharma too. If trees are our relatives, what about the trash in the gutter, the mice under the floor? What do they teach us?

49. Kisagotami's Mustard Seed

KISAGOTAMI CAME from a poor family, but the son of a wealthy family loved her and married her. Her in-laws treated her unkindly because of her background, but when she gave birth to a son, they finally respected her. Then, when the child was a toddler, he died, and Kisagotami went mad with grief.

She carried the dead child from house to house, begging for medicine to make him well, and everyone sent her away, saying, "The child is dead. No medicine can help him." At last a kind man directed her to the Buddha.

The Buddha said, "I will give you medicine to revive your child if you bring me a mustard seed from a house where no one has died."

With renewed hope, Kisagotami went forth to get the mustard seed, but at every house she learned that someone had died. And so, still carrying her child's body in her arms, she returned to the Buddha.

"Did you bring me a mustard seed?" he asked her.

"I thought that death had happened only to my little son, but now I understand that it happens to everyone. Impermanence is the universal law."

She buried her child in the forest and returned to the Buddha to receive ordination.

CHRISTINA FELDMAN'S REFLECTION

Kisagotami's story is the story of every mother who loses a child, the story of every human being who knows in their heart that to love, cherish, and care for another is to risk heartache and loss. As women we hold in our lives a timeless human dilemma—to know how to love, wholeheartedly and deeply, and to know how to lose that which we love with compassion and wisdom.

The Buddha did not admonish Kisagotami for her grief and distress, nor did he lecture her on the inarguable laws of impermanence. Instead he sent her into the village to find even one person who did not know the barren landscape of grief, the deep painfulness of being separated from those one holds most dear. Every home she went to, every person she spoke to, only revealed to her how vast is the landscape of loss.

Each of us holds within us a personal story and a universal story. Our personal story, born of all that we have experienced and felt in this life, is unique to us. Our families; our joys and sorrows; our values, aspirations, and hopes; our disappointments; the countless events of our lives have shaped who we are and how we see in ways that no single other human being can know. But when we understand that our personal story holds within it the universal story of all human beings, then we have the radical possibility of dissolving the boundaries of "I" and "you," "us" and "them."

Kisagotami's realization that all mothers could experience just the same pain as she experienced did not necessarily diminish her grief, but she came to understand she was not alone. She began to accept that which had felt so deeply unacceptable. By acknowledging this she embarked upon a path of seeking an unshakeable inner freedom.

So much of the path of liberation is woven into the story of Kisagotami. Some of the most profound insights that liberate our hearts from struggle are found within the most deeply challenging moments of our lives. When our worlds crumble and our certainties dissolve we face a choice—to turn toward those moments with compassion, or to flee. Our own experience tells us again and again that flight will almost certainly ensure we find neither healing nor freedom.

Impermanence is the law that governs all experience. We live with our feet on shifting sands that can crumble beneath us in a moment.

Loss, death, and separation reveal to us, so poignantly, that as long as we are misaligned with this core truth we will live in a state of argument with our lives. To embrace this truth of impermanence wholeheartedly, deeply, and unshakeably will not save us from grief but will perhaps teach us to embrace the moments of deepest pain in our lives without dispute. I do not imagine that Kisagotami's embracing of a nun's life meant an end to her grieving. The memory of her son must have lived on in her heart and very bones, but perhaps the pain could be borne.

The Buddha's teachings of impermanence and equanimity show us how to live in this world of uncertainty without being shattered. None of us can control the world of conditions that are intrinsically unstable. We can learn to cultivate an inner poise that allows us to be a conscious participant in this life without our hearts being hostage to conditions. A few lines from a Sri Lankan text on equanimity tell us:

> Life is a play of joy and sorrow.
> May I remain unshaken by life's rise and fall.
> I care for you deeply,
> but sadly, I cannot protect you from distress.

What is the difference between suffering alone and suffering with others? And why did the Buddha ask for a mustard seed, of all things?

50. Satsujo Weeps

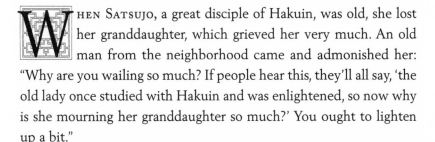HEN SATSUJO, a great disciple of Hakuin, was old, she lost her granddaughter, which grieved her very much. An old man from the neighborhood came and admonished her: "Why are you wailing so much? If people hear this, they'll all say, 'the old lady once studied with Hakuin and was enlightened, so now why is she mourning her granddaughter so much?' You ought to lighten up a bit."

Satsujo glared at her neighbor and scolded him: "You baldheaded fool, what do you know? My tears and weeping are better for my granddaughter than incense, flowers, and lamps!"

The old man left without a word.

REIGETSU SUSAN MOON'S REFLECTION

This koan comforts me because Satsujo is being completely human, weeping and wailing over the death of her granddaughter, and this is not quite what I expect from a Dharma story. Aren't we supposed to let go of attachment?

Embedded in the story of Satsujo's tears are the well-known stories of Buddha's disciples, Patacara and Kisagotami, who each came to Buddha crazed with grief after the death of their children. Buddha's response to Patacara was, "Sister, recover your presence of mind." Both women did, after he helped them understand that every family knows the death of loved ones.

As a mother and a grandmother, I can't imagine any suffering greater than the death of a child. That's why the stories of Patacara, Kisagotami, and Satsujo are so powerful. They are archetypal.

When I was two years old, in the midst of World War II, my mother had a baby boy. My father came back to Chicago from the army base in Columbus, Ohio, where he was in training to visit the baby, and my parents named him Benjamin. When Benjamin was five days old he died because he had a hole in his stomach that they didn't know how to fix. My father got leave to come again, and they buried the baby. Soon after, my father was sent overseas.

Many years later my mother told me that as she was folding up the baby clothes and putting them away in our little apartment, she couldn't hold back her tears, and I stood there watching her—two-year-old me—and I said, "Don't cry." *(Please, Mom! Recover your presence of mind!)* Her tears must have been frightening to me—she was my whole world, after all. But would it have been better for me to have a mother who *could* hold back her tears at such a time?

When is it okay to weep? What was the difference between Satsujo's tears and Patacara's? Patacara was completely overwhelmed by grief. She had lost not only her children but her faith, her groundedness, her sense of connection. She needed Buddha's guidance.

Satsujo was wailing too, but she didn't need to be told to stop. I love Satsujo for her tears. She was weeping because something tragic had happened—a beloved child had died—but she had not lost her presence of mind; she was able to snap out of her wailing long enough to call the old man a "bald-headed fool."

I see a pivot point in the koan, when Satsujo says, "My tears and weeping are better for my granddaughter than incense, flowers, and lamps!" *Better for my granddaughter.* What does she mean? If she stayed quiet and burned some incense, she didn't think it would particularly *help* the dead child. She could ask a monk at the local Buddhist temple to light some incense for her granddaughter; that's a good job for a monk. But a grandmother weeps; that's the job of a grandmother. Her tears are not for herself; they are for her granddaughter and, by extension, for all grandchildren. She is expressing what Dogen calls "grandmother mind, the mind of great compassion."

When is it a good idea to tell someone who is suffering to lighten up? The old man was not trying to alleviate Satsujo's suffering. He was worried about her reputation, and perhaps he didn't like her tears because he didn't know what to do. He didn't like the snot, and he didn't have any Kleenex.

When my mother was quite old her feelings could be easily hurt and she would get upset. Then I would say, "Don't worry about it! He didn't mean it. It's not that bad."

And she would shout: "It is *too* that bad! Why won't you believe me?!" And she became even more upset. I was like the bald-headed monk, telling her to cool it, more for my own sake than hers. But finally, in the last year or so of my mother's life, I stopped telling her to lighten up. I learned to listen better. This is a good way to help a person recover her presence of mind.

Satsujo respected her own grief. It was a sign of her deep connection to her granddaughter. She didn't need to be told to recover her presence of mind because she never really lost it. She knew that children need to live in a world where old women weep at the death of a child even if they have studied Zen for many years.

What is this "nonattachment" business we hear so much about? Is there any contradiction between awakening and love? Is there such a thing as letting go of grief? Can you recognize an enlightened person by his or her actions?

51. Ziyong's Last Teaching

ASTER ZIYONG CHENGRU was dying, and her disciple, the nun Jingxuan, was very anxious. Ziyong said to her, "From the beginning there has been neither birth nor death—so what nirvana will there be?"

But Jingxuan's grief continued.

Ziyong then gave a shout, and Jingxuan went into a state of deep meditation. Ziyong called her out of it and asked, "At this moment is there any nirvana, or is there not any nirvana?"

Jingxuan said, "Your disciple from the beginning has experienced neither birth nor death, so what nirvana can there be?"

Ziyong then said, "Since there is no birth or death, how can there be a nirvana?" Jingxuan did not know what to say.

Ziyong said, "This is what it is like before the dream."

Jingxuan asked, "What is it like after the dream?"

Ziyong said, "When you are in a dream, you still speak the language of dreams."

MYOSHIN KATE MCCANDLESS'S REFLECTION

The Buddha taught that sooner or later we will have to part with everything and everyone we love, but as human beings we are creatures of attachment and do not take kindly to such separations. The loss of a beloved spiritual teacher is not easy to bear, even for longtime disciples, as this poignant story illustrates. It recounts the deathbed teaching that the seventeenth-century Chinese nun Ziyong Chengru gave to her personal attendant, Jingxuan.

Jingxuan is distraught at the prospect of her teacher's death. Ziyong admonishes her, "From the beginning there has been neither birth nor death—so what nirvana will there be?" This is a classic Zen statement of nonduality. The Buddha taught that all phenomena are impermanent and have no separate existence apart from all other phenomena. Birth and death, being and nonbeing, unity and difference are all relative constructs of the mind. Vietnamese Zen teacher Thich Nhat Hanh has said, "If we are mindful of the true nature of reality, we never truly lose anyone—even to death."

Nevertheless, I would not recommend offering this philosophy to someone who has recently lost a loved one. It could seem like a Buddhist version of the kind of religious platitude that can be hurtful and offensive. In my years as a hospice bereavement counsellor I often heard complaints about such remarks. One mother who had lost a young daughter told me that when her pastor said, "God wanted her to be with him in heaven," she had to restrain herself from snapping back, "Yeah, well, I want her here!" It's hard to feel "we never truly lose anyone" when we're grieving.

This tactic doesn't work very well with Jingxuan either, initially. She continues to weep. But these two know each other well and can take risks based on a deep trust in their practice. Ziyong gives a shout. (She had a reputation for shouts and blows that matched any male Zen master's.) That prompts Jingxuan to enter a state of deep meditative concentration. Ziyong calls her back and asks, "At this moment, is there still any nirvana, or is there still not any nirvana?" She's saying, "Now tell me. Is there any separation at all?"

Jingxuan tries to find the words. Maybe she's still a bit tentative. Ziyong pushes her once again, and this time Jingxuan is at a loss. "This is what it is like before the dream of our human life," Ziyong tells her. I'm reminded of the classic koan in which Zen Master Huineng asks, "Don't think good; don't think evil. At this very moment what is your original face?"

What is our original face, before our birth, before our parents' birth? Words cannot say, can they?

But Jingxuan wants to know, "What is it like after the dream?" What happens after death? This is the great inquiry of human consciousness. In Zen we call it "the Great Matter of life and death." We want to know!

Ziyong's response? "When you are in a dream, you still speak the language of dreams." In this human life, we speak the language of the phenomenal world, of life and death, coming and going, right and wrong. Here is this powerful teacher's compassion coming forth. Ziyong once wrote:

> The sorrow of parting is meaningful and so hard to dismiss;
> but if the way is in tune with no-mind, it will go as it should.

In the dream of separation we weep, and it is real, but in the very next moment we may awaken to the reality of nonseparation. We release our clinging to what has been or might be and open to all that is, in this moment.

Maybe you've experienced a time when you suddenly felt a sense of connection, of interpenetrating being, with a loved one who has died. It's mysterious, difficult to describe, and usually comes unbidden. I remember, twenty-two years ago, going outside the crematorium and looking up into the sky as my sister's body burned. As the smoke rose and was carried on the west wind, I too was released.

Spiritual teachers are not the only ones who can offer deathbed teachings. My sister, as she was dying, taught me how to keep showing up day after day, with no agenda, not knowing how I'd find her each time I entered the hospital room. Or perhaps it would be better to say the Great Matter taught us both, as it did Ziyong and Jingxuan.

Can you speak a word that is not in the language of dreams?
How can you wake up if you are not asleep?

52. Lingzhao Goes First

···

HEN IT was time for Layman Pang to die, he said to his daughter Lingzhao, "Go look at the sun and tell me when it's exactly noon."

Lingzhao went to the door and looked out, saying, "The sun has reached the zenith, but there's a total eclipse!"

When Layman Pang stepped outside to see this remarkable event, Lingzhao sat down in her father's seat, put her palms together, and passed away.

Layman Pang looked in from the doorway and smiled, saying, "My daughter has gone ahead of me once more."

He waited seven days and then he died.

CATHERINE GENNO PAGÈS'S REFLECTION

When I first read this story, I found it rather puzzling: it seemed to be praising a voluntary death and perhaps a competition between the two over who would die first. But then I saw, with a deep resonance, that these two people had no fear—no fear of death and no fear of life. They were free.

Once in my life I was very close to death. I remember it as a moment of perfect peace such as I had never experienced before: there was no more resistance, just tranquility. Everything was the way it was, the way it should be. It was like going with the flow of a river, merging with the fluid current. Everything was without substance and that was more real than anything I had known before.

I survived, and for some time after I had no fear. I could do every-thing that I had been afraid to do before, and I changed many situa-tions in my life. I had the courage to live fully because I was no longer afraid of death. Then gradually, reality came back as I had known it before: more and more solid. Fear came back too: fear of the disap-pearance of this "I," which is so busy solidifying itself because it is so uncertain of the nature of its existence.

Lingzhao and her father have no fear. They are fully alive until the moment they choose to die, playfully challenging each other, express-ing, in a dance involving even the sun and the moon, their complic-ity, their love for each other, and the unfailing meeting of their two minds/hearts.

Layman Pang was held in high esteem by the different renowned Zen masters of eighth-century China with whom he studied. Ling-zhao traveled on pilgrimages with her father, and they sought teach-ings together and debated with one another.

In this story, Layman Pang is ready to die and wants to choose the exact time of his last breath: noon! In Zen a mark of accomplishment was to choose the time of death and the position in which to die. Layman Pang asks his daughter to go and look at the sun and tell him when it is noon. Lingzhao goes to the door and says that it is noon, but there is an eclipse.

Was there really an eclipse? Was she saying to her father, "Why do you bother with the exact time? It is and it is not! Let go of this last attachment to form!" or was she saying, "Do not be attached to brightness. Here is the other side, the moon, eclipsing the sun, beyond brightness." Whatever happened and whatever she meant, she used the opportunity to take over her father's seat and die there.

Why did she want to die first? Was it to free him from his last attachment, his attachment to her? Was it an ultimate mark of her love for him? What about her father's reaction when he turns around and sees his daughter dead in his chair? He smiles! How can one smile at the death of one's child? Unthinkable! Unless, of course, we see it as the ultimate manifestation of their intimacy and their appreciation and love for each other. And this is what Layman Pang expresses when he says, "My daughter has gone ahead of me once more." During all their journeys together, I imagine that this was his deepest wish, that his child would outgrow him, definitively.

The story says he waited seven days to die. Why did he wait seven days? Was it to honor his daughter's way of dying? Was it also to mourn her as a father mourns his daughter?

The last words he spoke, to someone who had come to inquire about his health, were, "I ask you to regard everything that is as empty and not to give substance to that which has none. Farewell. The world is like reflections and echoes."

He was expressing what Lingzhao had also expressed. But she said it without any words at all.

Why do Zen masters think it's so great to choose the time they die?
Why not let death come when it comes? Dying is generally
a serious business, but these two seem to be playing
a lighthearted game. What's going on?

53. Yuanji Knocks the Body Down

CHINA, EIGHTH CENTURY ···

WHEN MASTER YUANJUE was about to die on Mount Wutai, he said to the monks around him, "I've heard of masters passing away while sitting or lying down, but have any died while standing?"

"Yes, some," they replied.

"What about upside down?" asked Yuanjue.

"No, we have never heard of such a thing," they said.

Yuanjue stood on his head and died, and his robes continued to drape his body in a dignified manner. The monks decided it was time to take his body to be cremated but it was as immoveable as a stone pillar. People from near and far came to marvel at the amazing sight.

Yuanjue's younger sister, the nun Yuanji, came to the place. She scolded: "Older brother! When you were alive you flouted the laws of the Dharma, and even now that you're dead, you're still causing problems and making a nuisance of yourself."

She gave the body a little push and it toppled to the ground. Then the monks took the body to be cremated.

MELISSA MYOZEN BLACKER'S REFLECTION

In Zen practice, we emphasize a delight in paradox and an energetic love of life lived fully. My teachers always encouraged me to be both spacious and suspicious about anything I thought was true, and I continue to encourage my students to go beyond their conventional ideas about the nature of reality. This attitude of freedom from convention can lead to becoming a person who enjoys making trouble, and this koan tells the tale of two excellent Zen troublemakers. In this version of the story they are a sister and a brother, Yuanji and Yuanjue. They are wonderfully fresh and alive in their commitment to playing with ordinary understanding, even in the face of death.

The brother in this story, Yuanjue, is a particular kind of trouble-maker. He wants his death to be special. This is not unusual for us human beings—many of us have a similar desire to stand out from the crowd, to do something no one else has done. We want to be seen and known for our uniqueness. Of course everything each one of us does is completely unique—there is no need to prove this. But insisting on our special qualities can get us into a lot of trouble, making life diffi-cult for everyone, especially ourselves. The brother dies upside down, thumbing his nose at the convention of ordinary death. But Yuanjue is not a simple narcissist. When we look more closely, we can see that this upside-down death is a representation of Yuanjue's insight into the magic of emptiness, where mountains dance and everything is alive with possibility. He had penetrated ordinary reality, and had entered the upside-down kingdom of awakening. But what are we going to do with such an absurd declaration? His body, stuck in emp-tiness, cannot be moved. This creates a real problem for everyone.

When we have had an opening into nonduality, the coming together of opposites, we can get stuck there. Some teachers call this "Zen sick-ness" and it can last for some time. Everything is empty and upside down. There are no consequences to what we do. Wisdom, compas-sion, equanimity, and the precepts, all the long-developed fruits of Zen practice, can go right out the window. We become "Dharma bums" and feel free and wild.

I love this story because it so beautifully illustrates the limitations of opening to emptiness and the danger of getting stuck in that aware-ness. I can remember my early days practicing Zen where everything turned topsy-turvy for me. Nothing was impossible, and I was heady with delight in the magical quality of life. Zhaozhou's "oak tree in the garden" made me giddy with identity with oak trees. I literally went around, for a blessedly brief period, hugging and kissing trees. Standing on my head to die would have been business as usual. It took many more years of practice to get my feet back on the ground.

Even if we have never had such an opening, we can become stuck in theories and ideas about freedom, believing that nothing we do has any consequences. Whether we are stuck in a genuine experience of emptiness, or we are convinced that we know what the awakened life should be like, we can become quite dangerous to others and to ourselves.

Halfway through the koan, when her brother's body becomes "as immovable as a stone pillar," Yuanji takes over. She is not stuck in emptiness but has entered the more mature view, where all apparent dualities are seen through, and life becomes much simpler. Many Zen teachings set us up to compare opposites (form and emptiness, life and death, special and ordinary, male and female, brother and sister) and then topple down our ideas about any separation between them, as Yuanji topples her brother's body down to the ground. The wise sister has no patience with her brother's emptiness-oriented death. His upside-down-ness is playful, but it also demonstrates the limitation of this intoxicating period of opening: no one can move his body. His sister comes along and knows exactly how to rebalance emptiness and form. With a quick shove, she sets things right again, and her brother can be buried. She is the kind of troublemaker who speaks truth to power, who says it like it is. Such clarity and balance save us all.

It's so important, in our own lives, to enjoy the freedom of emptiness, but never to ignore the consequences of form. There is no death, and we all die. There is no male or female, and only women can give birth to a child. Living an awakened life is not so complicated. We get up in the morning, go to the bathroom, get dressed, and do our work. There is nothing special. And in this "nothing special," everything shines with its own light.

What can one learn by looking at the world upside-down?
What can very old friends and relatives offer even to enlightened
people that others cannot offer?

54. Anne Aitken's "Get On and Go"

UNITED STATES, TWENTIETH CENTURY ·······································

NNE AITKEN was a student of Master Yamada Koun. One day he asked her: "What do you think of death?"
She replied: "Why, it's like when a bus stops before you—you get on and go."

NANCY GENSHIN GABRYSCH'S REFLECTION

The great matter of life and death is what Zen is about—or so I was taught. Nowadays, though, I think Zen is more about how you live your life. As for death? Well, as for death—I just don't know. My long years of training, under my teacher Genpo Roshi, have left a rich legacy. The lineage has entered the marrow of my dodgy old bones. And it has been a full-time practice to forget Zen, forget everything I know, and simply live this life. I hope with all my heart that the bus will be slow in coming. Our teacher often told the story of the monk who rapped on a coffin lid and asked his master the great question: "Alive or dead?" The master replied: "Why ask me? I'm not dead yet!"

Every morning I wake up surprised that I am still here. "Am I dead or alive?" I ask myself for a few seconds. For me, stroke-ridden, it becomes a part of my practice.

My primary caregiver, Roxy, sees what needs to be done for me and does it. Without her love and common sense, I would not be able to enjoy this life. She shows compassion and wisdom in all she does. I treasure the times when we go out shopping or to a cafe, because in those times she's as much of a friend as a caregiver. But it's challenging, because wherever we go we always see so many people whom she's taken care of in the past, and they all want to exchange hugs and tell her how they are getting on. She's a master of standing in other people's shoes (or slippers, as the case may be), and knows just what is needed at any given moment. To me she is an example of how to live.

Going back to the koan, the bus had various destinations at different parts of my life. The very early destination was "the arms of Jesus," then it was "the Kingdom of God," and then nirvana. Later it became the bodhisattva bus owned by the Mahayana Company and then, excitingly, rebirth influenced by good karma. And then it became the theory of quantum physics, believed to be the most accurate description of true reality. And on it goes . . . Let's be honest—when all the props of religion fall away, what do we really know?

One thing I often think about is how much our beliefs are said to influence our dying experiences. Anyway, I don't know if the bus is going anywhere or whether it has already reached its terminus. Either way, when it's time to die, it's time to die. We spend much of our lives letting go of our attachments, which I guess comes in handy when we have to let go of that which we value most—our life.

How can you ready yourself for death without wasting time planning for it? Is it even possible to get ready for death?

55. Permanence and Impermanence

UNITED KINGDOM, TWENTY-FIRST CENTURY ·······························

 GRIEVING WOMAN said to Chan Master John Crook (Chuan-deng Jing-di), "Master, truly—presence is impermanent, but absence is permanent."

"Indeed so," he replied.

What did the woman understand?

HILARY RICHARDS'S REFLECTION

In the early morning before meditation my teacher, Chan Master John Crook, would invite us to say the opening lines of a Tibetan verse:

> In our hearts we turn to the Three Jewels of Refuge;
> may we save suffering creatures and place them in bliss,
> may the compassionate spirit of love grow within us,
> so that we may complete the enlightening path.

The koan helps me explore the meaning of this verse. It has particular resonance for me now that John himself is absent. He died in the summer of 2011.

A woman's grief can arise for many reasons. Our bodies hold sorrow as well as joy. Perhaps the woman grieves for the environment: for the loss of her place within nature or the violation of a familiar landscape. Maybe her grief is deeply personal: the loss of a child, parent, or partner; the loss of hope or opportunity. The death of a loved one leaves absence: an empty chair, an empty crib. The loss is permanent.

But while the feeling may be one of emptiness, absence is not the same as emptiness. The teachings tell us emptiness is the impermanence of everything. But emptiness is also form, form becoming empty as part of the universal process of change. Does the Master see that the grieving woman has understood this when he replies, "Indeed so"?

For some practitioners this koan will lead to an exploration of grief. For others, it will lead to a reflection on absence and presence. The koan directs me to explore the space in my heart that holds those close to me, both the living and the dead. I am fortunate to know love, but my heart contains difficult emotions as well—anger, fear, sadness, guilt.

Exploration of the heart is not logical; it requires our rational and educated minds to rediscover and reengage with another way of being. When we are able to explore our hearts we allow expression of an often-neglected part of being human. The heart has a soft, intuitive, intimate voice. For me, meditation on this koan does not generate silence. Instead it disturbs, generating doubt and questions about life. It encourages investigation of both heart and mind, which requires courage. If we persist with this kind of practice we can learn how to be truly human, and compassion can arise. While I meditated with this koan in my heart, the grieving lady became Kuan Yin and the master became the Buddha: Kuan Yin offering compassion to the suffering world and the Buddha emanating wisdom.

After the tears and turmoil of her loss, maybe the woman's heart discovered a new way of being. In his Dharma talks, John would tell his students of a third place that lies above and between all opposites: above and between the absolute and the relative, form and emptiness, subject and object, absence and presence. This place is the middle point where everything is and also, paradoxically, is not. Understanding this is like catching the wind. This cannot be found by searching, and yet it can be discovered.

One early spring day—very cold with blue skies and fluffy white clouds—I was out walking and a gentle, surprising snow shower began to fall, dusting the ground. I felt compelled to catch a snowflake, but I realized that if I actively tried to catch one I would fail, so I held out my arm until a single, perfect snowflake drifted onto my sleeve. As I watched, it melted in the sunlight and was transformed into a single, perfect drop of water. I didn't need to grieve for the snowflake—it had not died. It had simply changed its form.

Our attachment to form, which causes us to experience love and loss, is both noble and grievous. In her grief, the woman may have come to a heartfelt understanding of how life and death express precisely the natural wholeness of the universe. If we are able to let go of our logical minds, our hearts can respond to the universe in an extraordinary way. This opens us to the insights of the teachings and allows us to take refuge in the three jewels: Buddha, Dharma, and Sangha. And when we take refuge, we are on the path; we appreciate suffering and can learn to transform it with wisdom and compassion. Love grows as we continue the enlightening path.

"Indeed so," Chan Master John Crook might have replied.

After people you love die, missing them comes in waves. When you miss them less are they farther away? Have you ever felt that that they didn't die after all? How can absence be permanent?

56. Patacara's Presence of Mind

·······································

N A SINGLE DAY Patacara experienced the deaths of her whole family: her husband was bitten by a poisonous snake, her newborn child was carried off by a hawk, her older child drowned in a river, and her brother, mother, and father were killed when their house collapsed. Mad with grief, she tore off her clothes and wandered naked in circles for a long time, until she stumbled into the place where the Buddha was teaching. The monks wanted to send her away, but the Buddha stopped them and said to her, "Sister, recover your presence of mind."

At his words she regained her sanity and knew she was naked. A man threw her his cloak and she covered herself. She told the Buddha of her tragedies and begged him to help her.

He said, "I can't help you. For countless lives you have wept for loved ones. Your tears could fill the four oceans. But no one can be a secure hiding place from suffering. Knowing this, a wise person walks the path of awakening."

His words eased her mind. She ordained and practiced diligently. One day she saw into the nature of impermanence, and a vision of the Buddha appeared before her. He said, "Patacara, all human beings die. It is better to see the truth of impermanence even for just a moment than to live for a hundred years and not know it."

Patacara awakened and became the greatest of the women teachers in the Buddha's sangha.

Anna Prajna Douglas's Reflection

Patacara's story seems very dramatic, almost mythological—losing her entire family in a swift series of deadly events. Thinking about Patacara the other night, I was startled to see on the nightly news a contemporary version of her story—a woman had lost her three children and her parents in a deadly house fire. The pundits wondered whether the smoke alarm systems were functioning properly and whether a lawsuit would be brought. This is how it is in America; when something deadly occurs we look for who is to blame. But sometimes there is no one to blame. Instead, the event is a teaching on the unpredictability of conditions, and this is the nature of human existence.

It is so easy to feel victimized: "I am suffering and someone or something must be to blame!" The Buddha's view was larger than that. He could see that to adopt the role of victim is to suffer and to perpetuate that suffering. A good therapist or spiritual guide will help traumatized people remember that they are more than their grief or loss or trauma. This is what the Buddha showed Patacara: that although her loss was great, she had not lost everything. She still had something of great value, which could restore her sanity; she had a precious resource—her presence of mind.

One's presence of mind is more fundamental, of course, than simply remembering one's name, address, and social security number. In fact, in the Buddhist tradition it is considered our most precious resource. One translation of the word "mindfulness" is *sati*, which means "remembering." When we practice meditation we are practicing remembering our presence here and now, our wakefulness right here and now. Presence is always with us, no matter whether our experience is good or bad. Our presence of mind was with us when we were born and will stay with us as we grow old, get sick, and die.

Luckily for Patacara, in the midst of devastation she found her way to the Buddha, and he provided the "reminder" she needed in order to come back to herself, to recover her "presence of mind." Coming back to oneself after being lost in the afflictive emotions is a great relief. *I'm alive!* Flowers are blooming, my heart is beating, I taste the air that nourishes me. Life has not forgotten me; it is here to hold me whenever I return.

In the next part of the story Patacara begs the Buddha to help her. He answers, "I can't help you . . . No other person can save you from suffering."

Imagine! We may not commonly think of the Buddha as saying to someone who is suffering, "I can't help you." But he did, and even more surprising is the effect these words had on Patacara: "His words eased her mind." How can that be?

Years ago, I was struggling with a personal problem and I felt that my family and friends didn't hear me or understand what I was saying. So I asked the spiritual teacher Byron Katie to help me. I told her what I was struggling with. She listened intently and then suggested, "I will pretend I am your friends. Now you tell me what you want me to hear."

"Okay," I said, launching into my well-worn tale. Katie listened patiently.

When I was through, she said, with compassion, "Anna, we don't really want to hear it. We don't want to hear about it." That was it. Nothing more.

I was momentarily stunned, and then—my mind cleared! The burden of wanting to be heard lifted and evaporated. Someone was finally telling me the truth! No one actually wanted to hear my sad story! I could accept what Katie told me because I saw with sparkling clarity that it was true. Like Patacara, my mind was eased and liberated. From that day to this I have never had to be heard on the matter again.

This is the effect of truth. When we are told the truth, no matter how painful, it helps us to settle down. We feel heard, seen, responded to accurately. We feel sane, connected.

For Patacara, the truth that no one could help her but herself opened a door for her. She ordained and practiced diligently, coming to a deeper understanding of the truth of impermanence. She was no longer the sorry victim of her fate but a clear-eyed knower of truth.

Can you weep with an awakened mind for those you love?
Is there a place where suffering can't enter?
And if the Buddha can't help you, who can?

57. Asan's Dewdrop

SAN WAS a lay student of the Soto Zen master Tetsumon and was greatly enlightened. Later, she also met with Hakuin. In her old age, Asan became seriously ill and her sons and daughters gathered around her, seeking some last words.

Asan laughed and said: "In this world where not even a drop of dew on a leaf of a word remains, what sort of saying should I leave?" Then she serenely passed away.

Tonen Sara O'Connor's Reflection

As Asan (or "old San"), an enlightened old lady, lies dying, her children ask for some last words and she laughs aloud. Then her last words question whether any last words can be said. What a wonderful paradox! Words vanish with the breath that carries them, yet we speak to say we cannot speak. The Buddha is reputed to have said, "In forty years I have not spoken a single word."

I can't help wondering why her children are begging her for last words. Haven't they had a lifetime of her words? Or is it that they paid too little attention to those words and now at the last moment want her to give them a bit of precious crystal to cherish? Or do they wish to be able to brag about Mom's enlightenment?

But it's not surprising that they are seeking some last words. The death poem has a long tradition within Japanese culture and there are recorded death poems of Zen priests, haiku poets, and samurai warriors. Even today, it is a tradition among Soto priests to have a prepared death poem ready, just in case. So why shouldn't the children of the greatly enlightened Asan seek hers? These poems answer our deep longing to receive something from those departing that we can hold on to when they're gone. Sometimes those words are life changing. My dying mother's last words were, "I've got to figure it out." I feel their impact today.

Unfortunately, some of those brilliantly insightful poems from Japan may have been constructed by devoted followers, rather than uttered by the dying person. Those who are dying may be in the grip of the truth of dying, rather than ready to indulge in a literary exercise. The preface to Yoel Hoffmann's collection of Japanese death poems reports one revealing exchange. In 1837, when Sengai Gibon was asked by one of his students if he had anything to say before passing away, he replied, "I don't want to die."

Astounded, a student exclaimed, "What was that you said?"

"I really don't want to die," repeated Sengai. (He was eighty-eight.) Yet an elaborate death poem was proudly recorded.

I feel a deep affinity with Asan, perhaps because I, too, am old. Or perhaps because for me she represents all the enlightened old ladies who have given so much to their families and communities and have been relied on for a no-nonsense answer to life's mysteries. These are the grandmas who channel their enlightenment into raising babies, cooking meals, cleaning houses, cherishing grandchildren. They go through life without fuss or fanfare, yet their understanding lights up the world around them. They laugh at the absurdity of life's transience and go on baking bread.

Another reason I cherish this story is that Asan so clearly puts her finger on the great dilemma of our existence: How can we express the inexpressible nature of life's ceaseless change and flow? Asan speaks of a drop of dew on a leaf of a word, which evokes for me the image of leaves falling, scattering, blowing on the wind, just as the words from our mouths disperse. If nothing lasts, what should we leave behind? Should it be a name carved on the cornerstone of a building? Or should it be the infinite flow of events put into motion by our life's activity? These will go on forever. Asan's words remain, and through them she offers her enlightenment to us today. An English teacher in a small-town high school altered my life forever when she asked me to read Boswell's *Life of Samuel Johnson*. I'm grateful to them both.

Though nothing in this world remains, Asan nevertheless generously responds to her children with a laugh, giving them, in fact, a good death poem:

> In this world
> where not even a drop of dew
> on a leaf of a word
> remains
> what sort of saying should I leave?

So saying, she serenely passed away, leaving her life to speak for itself.

Asan didn't need to leave anything behind her.
Can you say the same?

Why Do You Call Yourself a Woman?

Words in the Midst of Wordlessness

58. The Goddess's Transformations

INDIA, SECOND CENTURY ··

GODDESS MET the arahant Shariputra, and they began to converse. He was impressed with her great wisdom, but he wondered why she continued to be female, since surely being male would be preferable. He asked, "Why don't you transform yourself out of your female state?"

The goddess said, "I have looked for the innate characteristics of the female form to no avail. How can I change them? If a magician created the illusion of a woman, would you ask her, 'Why don't you transform yourself out of your female state?'"

Shariputra replied, "No. Such a woman would not really exist, so what would there be to transform?"

She said, "Just so. All things do not really exist, so how can you ask something that doesn't exist to change its form?"

Then the goddess, by supernatural power, changed Shariputra into a likeness of herself and changed herself into a likeness of Shariputra and asked, "Why don't you transform yourself out of your female state?"

Shariputra cried, "I no longer appear in the form of a male! My body has changed into woman's body! I don't know what to transform!"

She replied, "Just as you are not really a woman but appear to be female in form, all women appear to be female in form but are not really women. Therefore, Buddha said that all beings are not really men or women."

Then she changed Shariputra back into his own form and asked, "And where is your female form now?"

Jan Chozen Bays's Reflection

Once someone asked me, "In India it is said that you cannot be enlightened if you are a woman. What does Zen say about this?" I answered, "In Zen practice we say that in order to be enlightened, you must become completely a woman, completely a man, both, and neither."

The Buddha stated clearly that women and men are equally capable of attaining enlightenment and he had enlightened women disciples. However, prejudice crept back in after Buddha's time. An example of this is found in a Jizo statue in Japan, which had been commissioned by three nuns in 1228. The statue was carved as a nude image, with ambiguous genitalia, a concrete sign of a truth the nuns must have known well—our essential nature is neither male nor female. And yet, found within the statue was a prayer one of the nuns wrote to Jizo, asking to be reborn as a man.

This nun and Shariputra both knew that it was preferable to be a man in the relative world, the world of their time and their countries, where a woman without father, son, husband, or brother to protect her lived an uncertain and sometimes desperate life, vulnerable to starvation, rape, or servitude. Even if she were married, unless she was wealthy, she would be pregnant, nursing, cooking, cleaning, and sewing almost every minute of her probably short life. For most women, it *would* have been immensely easier to practice and to become enlightened in a male body.

As an arahant Shariputra is well practiced in seeing through mind-made creations, and yet his words, like all words spoken from the point of view of prejudice, give life to prejudice. However, the goddess responds to him with an answer arising from the essential truth underlying all existence. In asking, "If a magician created the illusion of a woman . . ." she is pointing out that we are all constantly creating ourselves out of bits of sound and color; and the glue that holds it all together is the subliminal thought, "I am this, this is mine." The illusion is so powerful that we will defend it to our death. The goddess is poking Shariputra: imagine the astonishment on the arahant's face as he looked down at his curvaceous body.

Zazen allows us to zoom in like a microscope, past skin and hair, sinking into the commonality of bone and flesh, of carbon and hydrogen, all the way down to gluons and quarks dancing in empty space—a field of potential energy filled with forms flashing in and out of existence.

Zazen also allows us to zoom out like a telescope, past city, nation, planet, and solar system, all the way out to pulsars and black holes dancing in empty space—a field of potential energy filled with form flashing in and out of existence.

Our fundamental nature has nothing to do with the chromosomes we have or what parts of us stick out or fold in. It is called our pure nature because it is completely clean of these distinctions.

We have been, are, and will be everything. Our practice helps us at last to let go of all differentiation and sit at ease in the humming maw of potential energy we call emptiness. To let go and to smile, as out of that emptiness arise mischievous goddesses and serious arahants—and you and me.

Sometimes people hope their unborn child will be a boy, and sometimes they hope for a girl. Sometimes a person whose body appears to be one gender transforms into a person whose body appears to be the other. Some people don't want to be labeled as either male or female. Why do gender identities mean so much—having them, changing them, refusing them? What are the differences between our form and our identity?

59. Soma Rebukes Mara

THE NUN Soma was a disciple of the Buddha. One day she was deep in meditation beneath a tree in a forest grove. Mara, the Lord of Delusion, approached her, cloaked in invisibility. He whispered in her ear, "Because a woman has a naturally limited consciousness, and the realm of wisdom is hard to reach, no woman has the ability to attain it."

Soma recognized Mara and rebuked him, saying, "How could a woman's consciousness be a hindrance when her heart is set on liberation? Am I a woman in these matters, or a man? This question has no power over me. Mara, begone!"

And he was gone.

BARBARA JOSHIN O'HARA'S REFLECTION

No one—and certainly not a woman—survives childhood without being imprinted with their culture's ideas of who one is and what one can or cannot do. Growing up in Ireland in the 1950s, I remember my father holding forth with eloquence and conviction on a wide range of topics. When my mother, eager to chip in with her own observations, voiced her opinion, he would inquire with a rhetorical flourish: "My dear, why do you always have to add?" The silence that followed made it clear that his opinion alone mattered.

It was a struggle to find my own voice. Convinced that no one was interested, not only did I not talk about my own experience, I discounted it. Integrating all aspects of my experience was a challenge, as I disowned feelings of need and desire and prided myself on getting by with very little. When I found Zen, I seemed to take very naturally to sitting. I could face the wall without too much difficulty and even fancied that I had less ego to contend with than my peers. But after my mother died, I entered a Zen monastery for three years, and there I had frequent encounters with Mara.

Mara is the internalized voice of conditioning that keeps us in thrall to the familial and cultural messages that maintain the status quo. Mara isn't interested in liberation; it is interested in control. It will argue that its job is to protect us from pain, all the while binding us with reactive patterns of anger, avoidance, or addiction. By keeping us in the grip of our conditioned selves—for example, with a compulsive need to please in order to feel accepted—Mara has all the power, just like any jailer. But when we open to our own experience, whatever it is, and meet it with courage, we have an opportunity to rediscover our inherent wholeness and perfection, and then Mara is a goner.

Over and over, during those three years in the monastery, I had the chance to see how the inner template I brought to inchoate experience reproduced familiar dynamics. Feelings I'd originally turned away from because they were overwhelming—despair over not being heard, seen, or valued—were reawakened, and by dint of endless hours of sesshin during which there was no escape, I was visited by Mara time and again. He would assume different forms and shapes, but often enough he came in the guise of an inner protest at how unfair everything seemed. These reactive emotions of anger, I realized, were hiding deeper layers of older hurt. By bathing in the awareness of this rawness deep at the core, I discovered the salve of compassion.

When the Buddha was sitting with the firm intention to become enlightened, Mara tempted him with all kinds of distractions—power, lust, anger—questioning his capacity for liberation by asking, "What gives you the right to seek awakening?" Shakyamuni responded by pointing to the earth. He simply was, and this being, this presence, was enough, as earth was his witness.

Similarly, Soma's intention to liberate herself is the true measure of her worth. When Mara suggests that she doesn't have what it takes because she's a woman, she asserts: "How can a woman's consciousness be a hindrance when her heart is set on liberation?" When one cultivates the capacity to be present and fully open to one's experience, such categories as "male" or "female," "good" or "bad," "sacred" or "profane" no longer apply, for one discovers in their place a dynamic fluidity of form, the dance of emptiness itself. Soma is telling us that when we meet whatever arises in the field of consciousness with awareness, and can acknowledge but not identify with the contents of our mind, we say "No" to Mara. This is how one is liberated from the constraints of a limited self.

Soma's spiritual genius shows the importance of questioning the imprints of our conditioning, of examining the automatic ways we perpetuate an identity that keeps us feeling inadequate. Soma shows us how a fearless resolve gives the courage to dislodge even the most prevalent beliefs.

My own sense is that Mara is never vanquished, once and for all, just as our human conditioning is never fully overcome. When our practice is strong enough, we can heed our own reactivity and, out of the stillness, reach for what is true in the moment, and from there, respond appropriately.

What do you say to the voice that tells you, "You aren't ready yet?"
What happens to delusion when it's recognized?

60. Ziyong's Ship of Compassion

CHINA, SEVENTEENTH CENTURY ··

 SCHOLAR TRAVELED a long distance to meet with Master Ziyong Chengru. He entered the hall and he and Ziyong looked at each other. Then the scholar said, "I've come to visit this 'Ship of Compassion,' but who would have guessed that the 'Ship of Compassion' would turn out to be nothing but an old crone?"

Ziyong gave an earthshaking roar. "What is this place? Tell me. Is it male? Or is it female?"

When the scholar couldn't reply, she said to him, "Come closer and I'll tell you."

When the scholar was right in front of her she grabbed him and said, "From the day you left Spirit Mountain, there has been no place to seek; from this day on, mother and son are reunited."

The scholar said, "I trust you completely," and bowing to Ziyong, requested ordination from her.

DAIJAKU JUDITH KINST'S REFLECTION

Ziyong Chengru was a vibrant seventeenth-century Dharma successor in the Linji lineage. She was revered for her wisdom, ability to embody and teach the Dharma, and dedication to developing monastic centers for women. She had many students, both women and men, and was given the honorary titles "Ship of Compassion" and "Universal Salvation" by the Kangxi emperor.

Our friend the scholar has traveled far to meet an esteemed teacher on her home turf. He knows full well that the Ship of Compassion is an old crone, yet he challenges her with words designed to provoke her. He is fierce in his desire to find what is trustworthy, what will not be swayed or taken in by his foolishness, what will stand up to his challenge, what is worthy of veneration—in a teacher and in himself.

Like the scholar, we seek that which will not be fooled by the categories we impose on life and our living of it—male, female, old, young, good, bad. We seek the vibrant wisdom that can meet our deep yearning and transform our quest. Like the scholar we must have the courage to enter the hall and risk intimacy with the true nature of our existence.

As a young woman I entered Zen practice a confirmed feminist, wary, critical, and drawn by an affinity I could not explain. Entering the life of practice I found a Way worthy of my testing. I have been taught genuine trust.

Dogen asks us, "What strength can we depend on to rub pieces of ice together and make fire?" What strength can we depend on when we step close and encounter what is most true about ourselves and all beings? The earthshaking roar of Ziyong is in our bones, and this is the strength that animates our days and clarifies our lives. This is what we depend on.

Our deepest wisdom asks us moment by moment, "What is this place? Tell me." Tell me with the posture and breath of your body in zazen, with the kind words you speak to your neighbor, with the dignity you give to all you meet, with your ability to face honestly the life you live without pretense or the need for position or identity.

Every day we have the opportunity to live eye-to-eye with Master Ziyong. Washing dishes, driving to work, caring for elderly parents, chanting, sitting, playing. But to do this we must have the courage, like the scholar, to admit to our foolishness, to bow, and to trust. This is the path of genuine practice.

What keeps us from allowing Ziyong's roar to express itself through us in all our actions? Right here, in this ordinary moment, how do I embody the courage of the scholar and the vigor of Ziyong? How do I step closer, risk it all, become intimate with this life?

This is truly trusting that which sings in our bones, that which carries us day by day. This is what makes our ordinary fierce way the way of enlightenment. Nothing special. Nothing extra. Nothing perfect. Like the scholar, we must leave behind the comfort of constructed understanding—useful, but limited. We pluck up our courage and enter the hall, willing to be grabbed, hauled closer to that from which we often flee.

From the day we set out on our journey there has been no place to seek. How often have you heard that? How deeply has that penetrated your being? Student and master have never been separate, never. And yet we must journey to reunite them. Each day, each act, each moment. Will you allow yourself to be united with that which has never been separate? With this very person in front of you, this task, this breath, this earth that cries out for our care?

With our whole being we must find a way to say each moment, "I trust you completely."

Is it necessary to leave home in search of the truth in order to learn
that you don't have to leave home to search for the truth?
Can mother and son be reunited inside your own heart?
Who is the mother in you and who is the son?

61. Tara's Vow

NCE, LONG AGO, the woman who would become the goddess Tara was a princess whose name was Moon of Wisdom. She was wise, compassionate, and devoted to the Dharma. A monk approached her and said, "Because of your virtuous actions, you have been born in a human body, but unfortunately it is a female body. If you want to attain complete awakening, pray that you will be reborn in a male body."

She replied, "In this life there is no such distinction between 'male' and 'female,' and therefore any attachment to ideas of 'male' and 'female' is a delusion. It is foolish to be caught by such a notion."

Then she made the vow that would carry her through to awakening:

> There are many who wish to gain enlightenment in a man's form, and there are but few who wish to work for the welfare of living beings in a female form. Therefore may I, in a female body, work for the welfare of beings right until samsara has been emptied.

RITA M. GROSS'S REFLECTION

This story takes place in the context of Vajrayana Buddhism, which is quite different from the Chan/Zen context of most koans. It is no less pithy than a Zen koan, but understanding it requires a bit of contextualizing. Vajrayana Buddhists in Tibet believe in rebirth quite literally and most expect to be reborn many more times. They aspire always to be reborn as a bodhisattva, someone who works for the liberation of all beings, rather than for his or her own well-being alone. Most of them understand the bodhisattva vow to mean that because the full enlightenment of buddhahood is very difficult to attain, this vow requires many future rebirths to fulfill it.

Vajrayana Buddhists in Tibet also believe, in common with many Asian Buddhists, that it is impossible to attain full enlightenment in a woman's body and that being born female is unfortunate. That tells us a lot about what women have had to go through! Most Buddhists, acknowledging the reality of male dominance, which they took to be inevitable, saw that women's lives were much more difficult than men's lives. Therefore, by conceding that the female gender role in patriarchal societies is quite unpleasant, traditional Buddhists are halfway to a feminist understanding of Buddhism without even knowing it.

Today, Tara is one of the most beloved of all Vajrayana deities, appearing in many forms and meditated upon virtually universally by Tibetans. In this story, Moon of Wisdom, who became the bodhisattva Tara in a later life, gave the monk a Dharma lesson he should have learned long ago in his studies on emptiness. Beings may appear to be male or female, but in reality, those are just words, just labels, just concepts possessing no underlying, inherent, essential reality. You can make a lot out of those labels if you want to, but that is very foolish—something only weak, stupid, worldly people would do, not something people who have been studying and practicing Buddhism for years should do. This kind of story is very common in Mahayana scriptures: esteemed males think they are better than women and that women can have no dharmic attainment, only to be thoroughly defeated in "Dharma combat" by a woman—sometimes even a girl! But we don't seem to get the message, no matter how many times we encounter such stories in the teachings.

Then Tara went further. She pointed out that, heretofore, few, if any,

218 THE HIDDEN LAMP

beings had fulfilled their bodhisattva vow in female form. Not only were women told that their current physical form was inadequate, but they had hardly any role models to the contrary. Buddhas seem always to appear in male form. Almost all the revered teachers were men. It was and still is difficult for someone appearing in a female body even to become a monastic. Realizing the heartache and discouragement such beliefs about women bring to both male and female practitioners, Moon of Wisdom (Tara) resolved always to appear in female form, "until samsara is emptied."

In most Buddhist belief systems, samsara, the cyclic existence in which we repeat the same unsatisfying patterns over and over, lasts for a long time, so long that it is impossible to imagine its duration. But Moon of Wisdom, or Tara, will ceaselessly appear in female form until confusion, ignorance, and suffering are overcome, for, in truth, samsara is nothing but our own confusion. It lasts as long as we are confused—as long as we cling to our self-imposed prison of gender roles, believing that we should conform to conventions and stereotypes about gender.

This story is a personal favorite of mine, one I often tell when I give talks on Buddhism and gender. Like other contemporary women practitioners of Vajrayana Buddhism, I understand my work as a Buddhist feminist to be part of my bodhisattva activity. If there is such a thing as rebirth, I vow to return in female form because unless women work hard to end patriarchy, it will continue.

Where is Tara today? She appears in each of us. It is up to us to stop being caught by conventional expectations about ourselves and each other. It is up to us, especially us women, to become the female teachers and role models we never had, so that future generations of practitioners, both women and men, will never feel the anguish we did when confronted by Buddhist patriarchy. That is how it is that Tara can always, until samsara is emptied, appear as female, working to benefit all sentient beings.

What is your biggest vow? What does it look like? How does your particular body enable you to help others?

62. Dogen Sets the Record Straight

JAPAN, THIRTEENTH CENTURY ··

MASTER EIHEI DOGEN said to his monks: "There are foolish monks who make a vow never to look at a woman. Is this vow based on the teachings of the buddhas, or on the teachings of the non-Buddhists, or on the teachings of Mara?

"What are the inherent faults of women, and what are the inherent virtues of men? There are unwholesome men, and there are unwholesome women. Hoping to hear the Dharma and leave the household does not depend on being female or male.

"Before becoming free from delusion, men and women are equally not free from delusion. At the time of being free from delusion and realizing the truth, there is no difference between men and women.

"If you vow never to look at a woman, must you then abandon women when you chant, 'Beings are numberless, I vow to save them?' If you do so, you are not a bodhisattva. How can you call it the Buddha's compassion?"

SOBUN KATHERINE THANAS'S REFLECTION

This passage is from "Raihai Tokuzui (Getting the Marrow by Doing Obeisance)," which is part of the *Shobogenzo*, a major work by the thirteenth-century Japanese Zen master Eihei Dogen. "Raihai Tokuzui" is a radical celebration of women's strengths and equality as Zen practitioners and teachers, and a condemnation of the misogynist views of Dogen's contemporaries.

As I was considering this passage, I found a line from Rumi: "There is man and woman and a third thing, too, in us." Maybe that sums up my exploration of this koan about men and women and their prospects for liberation in this life.

Some years ago a student transgendered in our sangha. When she told me about her decision to do this, I did not know what was entailed, but I found resistance inside myself as she started the hormonal changes that made possible her transformation into a man's body. What does it mean to be a woman? A man? Is it an inner or outer thing? I felt grief when my student initially told me about her plans and realized how deeply I had bonded with her as a woman. Although she told me she wasn't going away, I didn't know what might be the outcome of this profound change. Maybe she didn't know either.

She educated me with written material and told me that not infrequently doctors decide which gender to assign to a newborn infant when the genitalia were unclear. This was interesting information at the theoretical level, but I still found myself using *her* instead of *him*, *she* instead of *he*. This felt unintentional, but looking back I wonder if inside I wanted to continue to relate to the woman I had known, not the man she was turning into.

As time passed, she took her place as male in our community and began to express himself straightforwardly in a clear voice, instead of remaining mostly quiet, as she had been before.

Even though I found that his essence remained the same regardless of his outer form, the question of gender continued to feel immutable for me, an essential characteristic. I saw how important the distinction between male and female was for me, and I acknowledged that I engage with male and female students differently, have different expectations of myself with each and different expectations of them as sangha members.

I see how completely Dogen identified the mind of discrimination and exclusion when it comes to Buddhist practice. In the "Raihai Tokuzui" he makes clear that women are equal to men in their capacity for awakening. Perhaps surprisingly, that wasn't an issue for me in my early years at San Francisco Zen Center, especially since Trudy Dixon, one of Suzuki Roshi's first disciples, was deeply recognized by him, and the legacy of her practice in San Francisco was well established by the time I arrived at Bush Street. About half of Suzuki Roshi's students were women.

But for years after Suzuki Roshi's death, the teachers at SFZC were all men. As I think back over my own experiences there, I begin to remember what it was like to study and practice under only male teachers. I wanted to please my teachers and found myself acting with caution around them. Working with women felt freer, less bound by need for approval. It surprises me how persistent this conditioning has been.

I have learned a great deal from my transgendering student. He experienced the process as one continuous transition, discovering how changes in his body and energy brought changes in his relationship with himself as well as with men and women. His masculine and feminine sensibilities merged smoothly and I began to understand that "in transition" was in itself the most meaningful enduring condition for him.

As we are experimenting with gender roles in the twenty-first century, we are finding that opposites include each other: *yes* includes *no* and *no* includes *yes*; males and females include each other, psychologically, emotionally, and sometimes physically as well. I am learning that the single term *male* or *female* is inadequate to express the complexity of our physical, emotional, and behavioral characteristics. As long as we are alive, we are all in transition.

Several women have told me how grateful they are to Dogen for his openness to women's practice in his time. My own gratitude is for the depth and subtlety of his explorations into our unexamined mind. And for his warm encouragement.

Dogen takes a sword and slices right through a whole world of poisonous views. How could one thirteenth-century guy see this so clearly, while everyone else was fooled? How do we help each other leap beyond conditioning without nagging each other?

63. Mahapajapati Opens the Door

MAHAPAJAPATI WAS the aunt and foster mother of the Buddha and a queen of the Shakyas. Many women turned to her for counsel when their husbands and sons left home to join the Buddha's order. She was the first to ask the Buddha if women could also ordain.

The Buddha replied, "Don't set your heart on this."

She asked two more times and received the same answer. She departed in tears.

Later Mahapajapati and five hundred other women cut off their hair, put on saffron-colored robes, and walked barefoot for hundreds of miles to where the Buddha was teaching. Weeping, they stood outside the gates.

Ananda saw them there and asked Mahapajapati, "Why are you crying?"

"Because the Buddha does not permit women to ordain."

Ananda went to the Buddha and said, "Your aunt is standing outside with swollen feet, covered with dust, crying because you do not permit women to ordain. It would be good, Lord, if women had permission to ordain."

The Buddha replied, "Enough, Ananda. Don't set your heart on this."

Ananda asked two more times to no avail. Then he asked, "Are women able, Lord, to realize the full fruits of the way, even arahantship?"

"Yes, Ananda, they are."

"Since women are able to realize perfection, and since Mahapajapati was so kind to you—caring for you and suckling you at her own breast—surely it would be good if women were allowed to ordain."

The Buddha relented, and the sangha of women was born.

THANISSARA'S REFLECTION

What is this story? Why is it so? It's the story of Mahapajapati setting her heart. It's the story of the Buddha's refusal of Mahapajapati and it's the story of the Buddha's acceptance of Mahapajapati. As we engage the story we are invited to fathom this "set heart" of Mahapajapati and in doing so to discover our own "set heart."

"Don't set your heart on this," the Buddha said to Mahapajapati. In the Buddha's reluctant transmission of ordination to Mahapajapati, a flower garland of difficulty fell upon her shoulders. Even so, the moment the Buddha ordained her, she joyfully took the path of the ochre robe, leading the way for others who followed through the centuries with strength beyond telling.

In spite of this ambivalent legacy, we celebrate the Buddha's acceptance of a women's order, thanks to Mahapajapati. We also thank Ananda, who demonstrated that a monk can be a true ally of nuns. However, nuns were only able to follow, not to lead; they were mostly unseen and unacknowledged in recorded Buddhist history. Furthermore, the nuns had to take additional precepts known as the Eight Special Rules, which subordinate all nuns to all monks.

When the Buddha saw that Mahapajapati's heart was indeed set, he gave women entry into the order with the simple refrain, "Come, nun." I don't believe his intent was to submit nuns to the monks' authority. But it seems that as time went on, the aim of these rules was to circumscribe the nuns' order, probably in response to its growing independence and strength. Recent scholastic evidence throws grave doubt onto the legitimacy of the Eight Special Rules, suggesting they were a later imposition on the nun's order. This "garland of flowers" to which Mahapajapati is said to have likened these rules is actually a garland of stones upon the shoulders of the nuns.

As a Theravada nun for twelve years, I too knew this heaviness. This isn't the transmission of the Buddha's radical awakening; rather, it is a silent poison that corrodes the potential of the Buddha's full dispensation. One effect of the Eight Special Rules is the loss of the opportunity for full ordination of women as bhikkhunis, which is necessary to empower nuns as legitimate members of the sangha. For example, in Thailand and Burma nuns tend to be viewed as celibate lay people, which undervalues their role as spiritual leaders in society. Likewise in Tibetan lineages, which also deny full ordination to women, nuns struggle for economic support and equal access to teachings and practices.

For many nuns, the intransigence of an entitled male monastic hierarchy is heartbreaking. However, these days, misogyny within Buddhism that is antagonistic to the empowerment of women is increasingly unviable. Supported by visionary monks and lay supporters who align with the Buddha's acceptance of women, nuns are following Mahapajapati by keeping their "hearts set." Women taking their hearts and lives into their own hands, as Mahapajapati and her Dharma sisters did before us, are vitalizing a beautiful reemergence of bhikkhuni ordination. In the wake of this, there is the opportunity to let go of old erroneous narratives that undermine the potential of all Buddhist women and that no longer serve the true heart of the Buddha's transmission.

I have seen this same heart in South Africa, where my husband and I lived for many years—the same brave determination not to submit to "special rules" but to struggle for equality. Many citizens of South Africa, including Nelson Mandela, manifested tremendous heart to overcome apartheid. We see that same heart in Mahatma Gandhi, Dr. Martin Luther King, and Aung San Suu Kyi. We too know this heart when we align with the imperative of the Dharma in the face of oppression. Ultimately what oppresses all of us is the weight of ignorance. But more powerful than ignorance is the bodhisattava intention, and on that I keep my own heart set.

Let us take courage from Mahapajapati, who was victorious because she kept her "heart set." This is a courageous heart, knowing heart, depth-of-intuition heart, beautiful heart, profoundly listening heart, ancient pulse-of-the-earth heart, devoted heart, radical heart, heart that loves all beings. This is Prajnaparamita heart, which does not waver even though it trembles in the face of unimaginable suffering. This is the heart of staying true to the precious Dharma to the end of all times.

Homage to you, Mahapajapati; we follow your benevolent and wise calling: "Keep your heart set on this."

Mahapajapati was the one who first led women into the Dharma. How do we express our gratitude to her? How far would you go in defiance of social norms in order to seek liberation? What risks would you take? What taboos would you break?

64. Changjingjin's No Obstructions

··

BEFORE CHANGJINGJIN (Ever-Pure Progress) became a nun, she traveled with her mother and family to meet Master Wuzhu. Changjingjin asked, "I am a woman with the three obstructions and five difficulties, and a body that is not free. I am determined to cut off the source of birth and death. Please teach me."

Wuzhu said to her, "If you are capable of such resolution, then you are a 'great hero'; why do you call yourself 'a woman'? No-thought is thus no 'male' and no 'female.' No-thought is thus no-obstruction, no-hindrance, no-birth, no-death. At the time of true no-thought, no-thought itself is not. This is none other than cutting off the source of birth and death."

When Changjingjin heard this, she stood absolutely still and unblinking, and Wuzhu immediately knew that she had a resolute mind. She and her mother ordained as Wuzhu's disciples and became leaders among nuns.

MYOKEI LYNDA CAINE-BARRETT'S REFLECTION

This koan speaks to me on many different levels, touching on challenges I have had as a practitioner. Sometimes it is easy to walk through the world following the Dharma path, not caught up in differences or similarities, just simply involved with being. But as a Japanese/African-American woman, I have often been reminded in myriad large and small ways that my difference from perceived societal norms makes me less desirable and not worthy of respect. Because I straddled two cultures, I often found it difficult to be at "home" anywhere. I simply had no place of belonging. This lack led me to Buddhism as a young teenager.

Changjingjin's statement "I am a woman with the three obstacles and five difficulties . . ." is a poignant reminder of what it means to accept "our limitations" as valid. There were many occasions when I struggled to liberate myself from limiting ideas that suggested I was not good enough in some way. My father told me I could achieve anything, while at the same time teaching me that females were less valuable than males. From teachers and others, I learned that girls should be nice and not make waves. I think we have all had this experience as children: people we love and trust teach us limiting ideas that they themselves were taught and simply pass along to us.

For me, these ideas became mental and emotional habits that caused me to separate myself from life and the beauty of all of its nuances. I could not access joy, and my heart shut down. I had few friends. When I began to study the Dharma, I saw that walking the Dharma path was a means to liberation from limitation as well as a way to encounter profound bliss. Strengthening my faith by applying the principles and concepts learned through study, I was able to awaken to this understanding and work to break free of mental and emotional habits—the attachments I had internalized—that were limiting me. I discovered the sources of rage, hurt, and loneliness in my life and learned to strengthen bonds of relationships with others and myself. I learned to fully accept myself and I began to take my place in the world.

Courage is generally considered a male trait, and Master Wuzhu points this out by calling Changjingjin a "great hero." It is clear that she exhibited great courage in her efforts to seek out the Dharma and develop her practice. Her efforts to find a Dharma teacher indicate that her desire for the Dharma was greater than her fear of confronting her limitations. Master Wuzhu recognized her pure desire and great seeking spirit, and used his words to break the mindset of limitation.

Nothing has a permanently existing identity. Master Wuzhu points out that there is no difference between any two things. There is thus no difference between male or female and also no difference between ourselves and the Buddha. The latter is a huge idea that allows us to understand that we all possess buddha nature and that nirvana can truly be ours.

With this understanding, we can affirm our provisional existence with the recognition expressed in the Lotus Sutra that "All things are from the outset in the state of tranquil extinction." Master Wuzhu is acknowledging that Changjingjin—as she is—is already endowed with buddha nature and need not overcome her gender in order to realize the gifts of Dharma practice. All she needs to do is awaken to the true nature of reality. Understanding this was a key element in my own journey: instead of accepting limitations, I could use them to discover the best of myself. This understanding led me to become the first Western woman to be ordained as a Nichiren Shu priest. I truly know that I have a right to be here. I have purpose, and each day I manifest my liberation and purpose.

This koan is an excellent reminder to all practitioners that we must not be defined or governed by what we believe to be our limitations: in our thinking, in our behavior, in the manner in which we approach our lives and practice. Buddhism provides liberation from suffering; liberation requires boldness and unfettered thinking. Liberation requires that we fly free of old ways of thinking, being, and doing. In this way, we can unlock our joy and celebrate all our encounters with a heart full of bliss.

We are all limited by our conditions—or are we? Was Changjingjin a woman or only an idea of one? When you feel limited by a given condition of your life, like arthritis or several dependent children, can this be experienced as a state of "no limitation"?

65. Moshan's Mountain Summit

THE MONK Guanxi Xian was sent by his teacher, Master Linji Yixuan, to meet Master Moshan Liaoran, a powerful woman teacher. When he arrived at Mount Moshan, where she taught, he refused to bow to her or take off his traveling hat. He asked, "What is Moshan?"

Moshan replied, "The summit cannot be seen."

He then asked, "Who is the master of Mount Moshan?"

She replied, "Without the form of a man or a woman."

He shouted, "Why doesn't she transform herself?"

She replied, "She is not a wild fox spirit, nor a ghost. What would you have her become?"

Guanxi bowed and took off his hat. He became the gardener at her monastery and stayed for three years.

SHINSHU ROBERTS'S REFLECTION

Are you awake? Don't get caught by talk of foxes, ghosts, and gender. Let go of attachment to surface appearances and be present for what is actually happening. Guanxi thinks he's the clever one, only to find that this mountain summit cannot be climbed.

Guanxi unskillfully tries to establish his own understanding and the result is rude posturing. He keeps badgering Moshan about her sex. She'll have none of it. She shows him that he cannot rely on such distinctions to be the basis for the practice of discovering the truth. She says that the master of Moshan is without the form of a man, a woman, or a wild fox. When you read this koan, do not get caught in the male-female dynamic yourself. That is just the surface of the truth.

None of us wants to be put in a box. Yet we often want to pin down and define the other. Unfortunately we get caught in our ideas about who can teach us, based upon fixed notions. Is Moshan less a teacher because she is a woman? Is Guanxi less a student because he is a brash young man? Moshan is an immovable mountain and Guanxi has a lot of spirit. There's a good match here.

Sometimes when we have come from a unique teaching style we do not realize the power of a different way. I had this experience years ago, when I went to do a month-long retreat with Katagiri Roshi at his monastery in Iowa. I came away feeling that Katagiri Roshi's style was better than my home temple's. But it was just different, not better. My inflexibility created a divide that, when I returned home, blocked me from learning what was right in front of me. Guanxi is suffering from the same kind of sickness. He is still living his past, at the home of Linji, and not present for Moshan's hospitality.

Later Guanxi would say, "I got half a dipper at Old Papa Linji's place, and I got half a dipper at Old Mama Moshan's place. Making a dipper with both halves, I have finished drinking, and, having arrived directly at the present, I am completely satisfied." Clearly he came to understand that he must drop his prejudices and attitude in order to deeply enter into Moshan's teaching, that both Linji and Moshan were masters worth following.

The whole world is constantly teaching us. I have noticed that when I am being unskillful, when I need to let go or drop my ideas about what is happening, the world responds with a lesson. Sometimes I don't like the messenger. Sometimes the message is not delivered skillfully. But it is delivered. We must keep our eyes and heart open to this wondrous reality. Can we drop the self? Can we practice the real renunciation of being completely alive to the moment?

Guanxi lets go. He realizes that all of his ideas and reservations are moot in the face of Moshan's deep understanding. Often we are so caught in trying to defend our self-image or ideas about what is right and wrong that we cannot understand that what is right in front of us is the Way. Guanxi had to flail around to drop his delusion and meet Moshan. Our job is to meet our life fully as it presents itself, not as we would like it to present itself. Don't get caught by the container; let your life come to you and meet it with an open and curious mind. Take off your hat, bend a little; stay awhile.

It used to be believed that only someone in the body of a man could be enlightened, and yet history is full of enlightened women. How do you uncover your own hidden assumptions about other people?

66. Miaozong's Disappointment

CHINA, TWELFTH CENTURY ·····································

 ASTER JIANYAN YUAN said, "As a well-brought up lady from a wealthy family, how can you be prepared for the business of a 'great hero'?"

Miaozong replied, "Does the Buddhadharma distinguish between male and female forms?"

Yuan questioned her further. He said, "What is the Buddha? This mind is the Buddha. What about you?"

Miaozong replied, "I've heard of you for a long time. I'm disappointed to find that you still say that kind of thing."

URSULA JARAND'S REFLECTION

Many Zen dialogues start with the master questioning the disciple's capability for enlightenment. For example when Huineng, who later became the Sixth Patriarch of Zen, first met the Fifth Patriarch, the Patriarch called him an illiterate barbarian. This koan also begins with Master Yuan's challenge to Miaozong: how can you, a wealthy woman, become "a great hero"?

By now most of us believe that the possibility of enlightenment is not dependent on gender or class or other social distinctions. But despite this understanding, we may still imagine that the "business of a great hero" is extraordinary and unattainable, beyond our own individual ability or talent. We have a tendency to judge ourselves as lacking.

We perceive everything that is happening as happening to "me"—

234

"my" frustration, "my" sadness, "my" success—and we feel that none of it is enough. The Dharma is completely free to manifest in any form, any color, any taste, any thing, and yet by calling it "me" and "mine" we alienate ourselves from this inherent freedom and get stuck in separation and lack of confidence.

So if the Buddhadharma does not distinguish between forms, could it be that everything is already complete? Could it be that everything arises in openness and does not belong to "me"? Could it be that there is not even a "me" it could belong to? Could it be that I am not limited and lacking but am actually this alive openness itself?

These are questions that matter to us today, and they were also important to students of the Dharma in the past. When Yuan tells Miaozhong, "This mind is the Buddha," he is referring to a quote from one of the Chinese Pure Land sutras that gained fame in Zen circles through Master Mazu. It is said that one day Damei, a disciple of Mazu, came up to Mazu and asked, "What is Buddha?" Mazu answered, "This mind is Buddha." The mind asking the question is already Buddha.

Sometimes koans are described as medicine, but they are medicine for the *belief* that we are ill, though in fact there is no illness whatsoever. We could also call a koan a time bomb. It blows up and destroys the illusion of "me" as an independent self, separate from everything else. In this sense it is a cure for an illness that wasn't there in the first place. And once that which seemed to be so real but never existed drops away, there is no reason to carry the bomb around anymore. In fact if somebody is carrying it around and showing it off, it is quite clear that the explosion has not happened.

So if we read the koan assuming that Master Yuan is still feeling the need for a medicine called "this mind is the Buddha," then Miaozong's disappointment makes sense. As my teacher Soko Morinaga Roshi used to say: "If you use a piece of soap—after lathering up you wash away the soap with the dirt."

It's also possible to read this koan in a slightly different way. Yuan could be offering the saying "this mind is the Buddha" as one more bait for Miaozong. And in this case Miaozong's response would be more along the lines of "Nice try, but no thank you!" and her so-called disappointment would be an acknowledgment of Yuan's sleight of hand.

It doesn't matter which version we prefer. What is pointed out is basically the same: everything, as it is, is already the manifestation of the Buddhadharma. You, as you are reading this, are already it. Whether there is understanding or no understanding, happiness or sadness, male or female, success or failure—it is all the alive, free, and perfect form of Buddha. There is nothing lacking that needs to be filled and nothing that needs to be changed.

After I went to Japan and started practicing with Morinaga Roshi, it became clear that there was a gap between what he was saying and what I was hearing. One thing he repeated again and again was *sono mama*, which could be translated as "as it is" or "this is it." And inevitably my inner response was, "That might be so, but I am not there yet. I don't feel enlightened." It took many years until the message wasn't heard by the "I" but hit home and was simply "as it is." Please consider this while reading the koan.

What authorities, inside or outside your own heart,
tell you that you are not capable of being a great hero?
What authorities tell you "Yes, you can"?

67. The Naga Princess's Enlightenment

INDIA, FIRST CENTURY ··

W HEN THE bodhisattva Manjushri returned to the Buddha's assembly after visiting the nagas, who lived under the ocean, he praised the wisdom of the eight-year-old naga princess. He said that she "loves all beings as herself and is capable of realizing the enlightenment of the buddhas."

Another bodhisattva asked, "The Buddha himself spent thousands of lifetimes of practice before enlightenment. How could an eight-year-old girl realize enlightenment?"

Then the princess appeared before the Buddha and his assembly. The Buddha's disciple Shariputra explained to her that it was not possible for her to realize enlightenment, because she had the body and obstacles of a woman.

The princess had a precious jewel, which she presented to the Buddha. She said, "The jewel which I gave to Lord Buddha was quickly received, wasn't it?" The assembly agreed.

She said, "Now I will attain buddhahood even more quickly." In that very instant she became a male bodhisattva, carried out all the practices of a bodhisattva, walked to the foot of the bodhi tree, was completely enlightened, and began teaching the Dharma to beings throughout the universe.

ANNE CAROLYN KLEIN RIGZIN DROLMA'S REFLECTION

I am fire,
soft and brilliant,

comforting and dangerous.
A fiery wisdom,
precise, passionate, and burning.

I am water,
flowing and dissolving;
I am not afraid of fire.
I am a radiant
wisdom mirror.

I relate especially to the energies of the different elements associated
with the persons in this tale: the warm fire of Manjushri, the cool water
of the naga princess. They suggest that we can integrate the often
wildly different dispositions we find—sometimes simultaneously—
within ourselves.

Manjushri has a compelling incandescence that comforts you with
its warmth and captures you with its spark. Like fire, wisdom feels
intimate, alive, and possibly dangerous. Teachers on the path often
show these qualities too, for good reason. On the path, we need to
be both challenged and supported, as the naga princess was in this
story, and as I was, when I first arrived at the retreat residence of the
legendary Geshe Wangyal. It was a hot summer day and he was outside, watering the garden. As I nervously approached, he shifted the
angle of his wrist and started watering me. The sheer surprise relaxed
my worry and also kept me watchful about what might happen next.

Ocean-like wisdom is both the starting point and resolution of
this story. Manjushri, embodiment of all buddhas' wisdom, begins
by acknowledging the wisdom of a young girl from below the waves.

A vital quality of wisdom is freshness; the Third Dodrupchen (a
Tibetan master and scholar) describes wisdom as "smooth, splendid,
and fresh." Paying attention to these qualities in my mind-body, I can
orient to the feel of wisdom and sense the dissolving of what obstructs
it. Freshness is also a quality of water. Water reflects all things equally,
just as mirrors do, and is instantly responsive, just like compassion.

The youth of the underwater princess suggests not only freshness but another vital Buddhist principle: namely, that the qualities we seek so arduously are already present within us. Right from the start they are waiting to be discovered and to grow.

Shariputra, focused as he is on the eons-long way of sutra practice, cannot understand how such a young girl could be so accomplished. He projects imagined limitations onto her, demonstrating how all of us project our ideas onto others. "You're too old," we say, or "You're too young," but these are just constructs. It's all made up. None of it is given. These overwrought categories stifle the free circulation of our best energies. They are artificial stop signs in our bodies, blocking compassion.

The naga princess knows better. She does not lose her focus. She does not collude in Shariputra's projection. Those of us who have felt our energies helplessly shapeshift to match another person's unconscious projection can respect this wise strength in the naga princess. She knows she is a jewel, and with this knowledge she offers a jewel to the Buddha, who mirrors her real nature. Who can give a jewel worthy of Buddha except another buddha? By demonstrating knowledge of her jewel-like nature, and doing so all the more splendidly in the face of a challenge, the princess encourages us to seek our own jewel light.

The Dzogchen master Adzom Rinpoche, whom I met in Tibet in 1996, is considered a speech emanation of Manjushri and incarnation of the great poet Terton Jigme Lingpa. He is famous for singing beautiful poetry, spontaneously and effortlessly. His poetry flows like a river, unifying the energies of wisdom and water—in formal teaching situations, riding in a car, waiting in a hospital for test results, or just relaxing in someone's living room. Once, sitting with some students in a park under a tree, he began to sing: "You must understand that you can become a buddha in this very life." We all relaxed happily. Then he looked at me. "Can you sing like that?" he asked. I was unnerved by his challenge; yet, at the very same moment, my heart felt a huge permission. He saw me the way Manjushri saw the princess, as fully capable of coming forth with my own heart song, the ultimate love song.

Flowing with the joyous recognition of the true jewel that she is, the princess became instantly capable of teaching others. She did this effortlessly, like water pouring down a mountainside. Wisdom is real, the princess knows; compassion is a feeling that flows, the princess shows; and the path opens the door to our inner jewels. I will practice to see and be like this!

As far as attaining buddhahood goes, what is the difference
between thousands of lifetimes and an instant?
What was the jewel in the princess's hand?

68. Ziyong's Earth

MONK ASKED Master Ziyong Chengru, "Thirty blows—are they the actions of a man or an enlightened being?" Ziyong replied, "Just as long as the fellow isn't beaten to death."

The monk said, "When you speak, the congregation assembles like clouds. In the end, who is the 'great hero' among women?"

Ziyong said, "Each and every person has the sky over their head; each and every one has the earth under their feet."

The monk gave a shout.

Ziyong said, "What is the point of recklessly shouting like that?"

The monk then bowed respectfully and Ziyong said, "The Dharma does not rise up alone—it can't emerge without reliance on the world. If I take up the challenge of speaking I must surely borrow the light and the dark, the form and the emptiness of the mountains and hills and the great earth, the call of the magpies and the cries of the crows. The water flows and the flowers blossom, brilliantly preaching without ceasing. In this way there is no restraint."

EVE MYONEN MARKO'S REFLECTION

In the opening session of the 2011 Global Buddhist Conference in New Delhi, the three large stages were filled with male monks, with not one woman among them. The women in the gigantic hall, mostly nuns, took notice and made it one of the big themes of the conference.

When one questions this discrimination, the answers are variations on the same theme: "In the Way there is no male or female." How many Zen women devotedly chant the traditional Zen lineage every day, never forgetting for a minute that the names are all male? How many of us have tired of male nouns, such as "patriarch," and male pronouns sprinkled around as if women do not exist? How many of us have been told that empowering the woman's voice in Buddhism is a shallow affair, a waste of time for real teachers?

The monk asked about "a great hero among women." Is this the real question? There certainly are great women ancestors whose names we have begun to recite in recent years. In our sangha, the lineage chart for the transmission of precepts now incorporates a wheel of women ancestors. But do we pine for a great hero? Where do we seek inspiration? Ziyong tells the monk, "Each and every person has the sky over their head; each and every one has the earth under their feet." In the end it's up to us. That's what I always remind those who are taking the precepts. Living the precepts calls for each person's response to what spontaneously arises in their lives, not the emulation of a role model, no matter how worthy.

But Ziyong says more than that: "The Dharma does not rise up alone—it can't emerge without reliance on the world." To take up the challenge of speaking, to say the unsayable and express the inexpressible, one can't stay mute. As Ziyong says, one must use everything—the language of dualism and the language of oneness, the smell of water and the sound of flowers, the aliveness of life itself. Everything can be used as skillful means to deal with life's varied situations, as long as one is not attached to one side or the other.

I trained as a liturgy chanter at the Zen Community of New York for a number of years. Once, I left our community for the summer to do a three-month intensive at a Zen monastery. There the liturgy was chanted several times a day by a male priest, not in Japanese singsong as is sometimes done, but certainly in a low voice. On one of the days off, a morning service was held and most people weren't there, including the regular chanter. When they asked for someone to take his place I offered to do so. But after I chanted the title of the Heart Sutra and was a few lines into the sutra itself, the service was stopped.

"Can't you chant in a lower voice?" the person in charge asked me.

"Not if I wish to hit the low notes as well," I replied.

"We can't have that here," he said, and asked someone else—a man—to continue.

My voice is not particularly high, and I had been trained to chant in a pitch that could be followed by most men and women in the service. I felt that here there was a clear preference for something different, something recognizably male.

The forsythia outside is yellow and the new spring leaves are green. Each preaches the Dharma according to its karmic life and condition, at the same time manifesting something timeless and essential. Does one do it better than another? We are not identical; each one of us, in our difference, is uniquely suited to meet life's infinitely different needs. Our individual traits, including our gender, cause us to harmonize with certain situations, or to say the precise word, take the precise action, and laugh the great laugh that expresses the inexpressible. That great laugh can be a hearty guffaw or a high, tinkling giggle, a low-pitched chant or a birdlike song. As Ziyong said, we must borrow everything, use everything. Only in this way is there no restraint.

Have you ever called out in unison with the birds in the evening? Can you feel their song in your throat? Is it possible to speak without the help of the world?

69. Kongshi's Bathhouse

CHINA, TWELFTH CENTURY ··

HEN SHE was quite elderly, but before she became a nun, Kongshi Daoren opened a public bathhouse. On the door to the bath she posted these words:

> Nothing exists, not even dirt, so why are you bathing?
> Even a speck of dust—where would it come from?
> Say something true and then you can enter the bath.
> If the ancient spirits can only scrub your back,
> how could I, the founder, bring purity to your mind?
> If you want to be free from dirt
> you should first make such an effort that your whole body
> sweats.
> It is said that water can wash off dust,
> yet how can people realize that the water itself is also dust?
> Even though you suddenly wipe away the distinction between
> water and dirt,
> you must still wash it all off when you come to this bathhouse.

SALLIE JIKO TISDALE'S REFLECTION

Kongshi Daoren's life is so familiar to me; she is my neighbor, my mother, my friend. Duty to others is a part of life; we are enmeshed in each other's lives, each other's needs. Like so many women, Kongshi found that she could not fulfill her dearest wish—to become a nun—because other people wanted her to do otherwise. I have felt this in my own life, the piercing sorrow of being unable to do what I wanted to do—not because I could not, but because I chose the needs of others over my own.

In Kongshi's time, women needed permission from the male head of the family to ordain. Kongshi's father refused to allow her to become a nun; instead she entered a politically expedient marriage. In time, her husband allowed her to leave the marriage, and she had no place to go but back to her father's home. When he died, her brother became her guardian. She asked for permission again, and again she was refused.

When we suffer, our impulse is to blame. We can look at Kongshi's story as a tragedy—the familiar tale of a woman thwarted by men and society, constrained by someone else's rules. But there is more to her story—and to mine, and yours—than what she was not allowed to do. At that time, all of China was built on the harsh constraints of class; every person's life was defined by the society. Men, too, sometimes could not ordain, because of political and family duties. Many such people led lay lives of study and meditation and were known as *daoren*, "people of the Way." Kongshi lived simply, studying alone.

Kongshi was thwarted by men, but what touches me about her story is how inconsequential that was, in the end. Like all of us, she was mainly thwarted by her own desire. We live in hope and fear, lost in the past and racing to the future, imagining the self we want to be instead of who we are. Kongshi thought she needed ordination robes to be happy; she couldn't have them, so she was unhappy for a long time.

In the end, thwarting was her liberation. Kongshi was deeply moved by a few lines from the *Contemplation of the Dharmadhātu*: "One includes all and enters all. All includes one and enters one; one includes one and enters one; all includes all and enters all. They interpenetrate one another without any obstruction." She must have felt resentment—I certainly have. But she saw how the world braids together, intricate beyond measure, that nothing is really obstructed, and she rose above resentment. She rose above her own point of view: with a small shift in perspective, ordination robes are just clothes. What a great gift she received in not being able to do what she wanted to do! Could she have seen into the nature of interpenetration if she had been given what she wanted?

Like Kongshi, I thought I needed ordination robes. I thought I needed a certain life—but as happens to many of us, my fantasy life was blocked by my real one. And I came to see that only by finding ourselves blocked can we seek a doorway. After her brother died, Kongshi went to study with a gifted teacher. There were no more obstacles; she could do what she wanted. She could ordain if she wanted—and she didn't. Meeting her teacher face to face, she said to him, "I make the universe. I unmake the universe." Knowing that, how could it matter what she wore?

Finally, she left her teacher and built a bathhouse outside another monastery. On the door, she wrote the poem. Her days were spent filling tubs, scrubbing backs, washing out dirty towels and hanging them to dry and folding them up carefully the next morning: a woman's work. But she also wrote poems on the walls and engaged her customers in Dharma combat. Dirt? Water? Self? Other? Show me the difference.

Finally, she moved to a convent and taught anyone who came to see her. Almost as an afterthought, she ordained. There had never been any real obstacles at all. I like to think of her washing and drying her robes and folding them as carefully as she had learned to fold a bath towel, because—isn't it obvious?—they were the same.

In what ways do we think, when we practice, that we are somehow cleaning up our act? Are we cleaning up our act? Does taking a bath or a shower help us clean up our act?

70. Asan Claps Both Hands

··

HEN MASTER HAKUIN was invited to the town of Shinano, an enlightened laywoman by the name of Asan ("Old San") went to see him. Hakuin greeted her by silently holding up one hand.

Asan immediately responded, "Even better than hearing Hakuin's sound of one hand, let's clap both hands and do some real business."

Hakuin replied, "If you can do business by clapping both hands, then there's no need to hear the sound of one." He picked up paper and brush and painted a bamboo broom.

He passed it to Asan, and she wrote:

> This broom
> Sweeps away
> All the impostors in Japan—
> First of all
> Hakuin of Hara!

LAURIE SCHLEY SENAUKE'S REFLECTION

Eighteenth-century Zen master Hakuin Ekaku was (and is) famous for his question, "You know the sound of two hands clapping; tell me, what is the sound of one hand?" For three hundred years Zen students have been waking up at these provocative words.

Less commonly heard is the phrase "enlightened laywoman." These are exciting times, as women ancestors are brought forward from the shadows of Buddhist history; I love the way they emerge—as confident advanced students of well-known Zen masters, as excellent challengers to authority, as "enlightened laywomen." In other words, as many-faceted and fully polished jewels. As the Zen saying goes, "Behind every jewel are three thousand sweating horses." I believe there have always been *lots* of women practicing Buddhism; I know this in my bones.

And so we turn to the story of Hakuin Zenji and Old San. Their easy banter reveals joy and confidence, as they flow from the One to the Many and back again. In zazen, in practice, we settle down, through the middle of the waves of our life, down to the still water below. Our toes reach down through the cross-currents, the riptides, the whirlpools, the tsunamis, down down down till they touch the bottom—the ground of groundlessness. We may be able to hear the sound of one hand. But we don't hunker down there forever; we must learn to swim in the surf and ride the waves.

This story makes me think of the dynamic between my daughter and me, especially in her early years. I am quite introverted, whereas she is highly relational. Before her birth I was one alone, then we were one together, then we became two; when we were two, we were often looking into each other's eyes. Relating so intensely was not easy for me at first—merging and separating, merging and separating; it challenged me in ways that several years of monastic practice had never approached. I often felt like I was waking up to the truth of existence. Not the truth of emptiness—the sound of one hand—which is just one side of the story, but the truth of being face to face with another. My daughter woke me up to the amazing mystery of human life: we must be two to meet each other. She was always ready to meet, ready to play, ready to get down to business, the real business of being alive—encountering each other. And making things together, making something out of nothing.

Reading this story, I wonder what word is being translated as "business." I don't usually think of business and practice in the same breath. Business is related to gain and loss, seller's market, buyer's market, Wall Street, Main Street. Indeed, could the work of bodhisattvas be considered our business? Are bodhisattvas those who get down to business, the real business of being alive?

I am reminded of Dickens's *A Christmas Carol*, where Scrooge encounters the ghost of Jacob Marley. Scrooge tries to console the ghost (and himself), saying, "But you were always a good man of business, Jacob."

> "Business!" cried the Ghost, wringing its hands again. "Mankind was my business. The common welfare was my business; charity, mercy, forbearance, and benevolence, were, all, my business. The dealings of my trade were but a drop of water in the comprehensive ocean of my business!"

At the time I am writing this, we are experiencing the Occupy Wall Street movement, which seems to be about waking up to the ocean of our common business. Coincidentally, the Occupiers actually do at times clap with one hand—we raise an arm and wiggle our fingers. This is so we don't drown out the words of the speaker with applause, but to me it seems to breathe new life into Hakuin's old teaching.

That's part of the joy of our Way—the old words, the old stories, always getting a new spin. Asan did not hesitate to clap her hands and make a game of the revered teacher's wondrous turning words, and he seems happy to play along. Real stories keep changing, being reborn fresh and alive, with nourishment for those who hear them. We must receive that nourishment, digest it completely, and then perhaps our own stories can startle, provoke, inspire—and somehow "meet" the women and men who take up this practice in the future.

Leave it to a woman to cut through even the great Hakuin's cutting-through! When you let go of all attempts to please, what's your real business?

71. Dongshan and the Old Woman's Water Buckets

CHINA, NINTH CENTURY ···

WHEN DONGSHAN Liangjie first set out on pilgrimage, he met an old woman carrying water, and he asked for a drink. The old woman said, "I won't stop you from drinking, but I have a question I must ask you first. Tell me, how dirty is the water?"

"The water is not dirty at all," said Dongshan.

"Go away and don't contaminate my water buckets," replied the old woman.

MITRA BISHOP'S REFLECTION

Dongshan Liangjie lived in Tang-era China, during which Chan flourished and many deeply realized masters came forth. Dongshan was one of them, though at the time of this encounter he was most likely not yet awakened. (How can we tell? There's a clue in his response.) Practicing through pilgrimage was not uncommon in China and Japan, and this is just one of several koans detailing encounters between traveling monks and local folk or roadside vendors. The protagonists were often women, and they usually got the best of the monks, inspiring them to seek further training.

But doesn't it look as if Dongshan has answered the old woman's question appropriately? The water didn't look dirty, so what else could he have said? Why didn't the old woman accept his answer? Furthermore, why did she then tell him to scram and not contaminate her buckets?

Zen teaches us to see beyond the relative, and digging into koans is a terrific way to do this. Traditionally, in the Rinzai school, once we have settled our minds to where our teacher feels we can effectively work on a koan, we are assigned a "breakthrough" koan. Much, much later, when a student is close enough that a "turning word" may tip the balance, sending him or her into a *kensho* (literally, "seeing into" one's true nature), or if that kensho has occurred, the teacher will ask a series of testing questions to plumb the depth, breadth, and stability of the student's kensho. Prior to that, this initial koan is gnawed on and dug into for years. To work on a breakthrough koan for even twenty or thirty years is not unheard of.

Chewing on that koan reveals many ways in which we limit ourselves: boredom, frustration, despair. The challenging work of these years "is cumulative," as a Dharma brother told me when I was discouraged—everyone else was passing their breakthrough koan while I still chewed, seemingly fruitlessly, on mine. And as another Zen friend once said, "This practice is truly bodhisattvic! First it shows you where you're caught—and then it sets you free!" If we start with a solid foundation in faith, determination, and perplexity, we've got all the tools we need for this liberating work. And these tools are essential if we're to fully plumb that koan and free ourselves.

Early in my Zen training, my faith in my teacher and in my potential for liberation was hidden from my view, but without such faith I never would have continued my practice. Moreover, later, on the seventh day of a sesshin, I hit a terribly dry place, a veritable desert. In the next sesshin, it happened again, this time on the sixth day, and in the following sesshin, on the fifth day! The implication was clear: it is not uncommon, particularly as one's practice advances and one nears kensho, to create all manner of obstructions, and this is what I was doing. Upset, I asked for an appointment to see the roshi. To get one, you had to give the reason for the request, then Roshi's secretary would inform him and relay back the answer. The next day, the response came back: no appointment. Ouch. So . . . I'd have to go it alone. Deep breath. As usual I filled out an application for the sesshin that followed. But when the list of people accepted to that subsequent sesshin was posted, my name wasn't on it. At that moment I realized I really did want to get through that koan. Fortunately, I was accepted to the subsequent sesshin and the dry spells ended.

So what was this old woman really asking? And what was it about Dongshan's answer that brought her response about dirtying her buckets? How could Dongshan have dirtied her buckets when he hadn't even drunk out of them? He was an honest, hardworking monk, no slacker. He trained hard, and later became a great Zen master and one of the founders of the Soto sect of Zen, a school of Zen still practiced to this day.

"How dirty is the water?" On the surface, an ordinary—if somewhat odd—response to a request for a drink. But this old woman was tricky! You can bet that all these old women asking questions of monks were pretty advanced in their practice. Having sized up Dongshan, could she be asking a testing question?

How would you answer the old woman? Have a drink of that water!

"Pure" and "impure" are both ideas, as are "nirvana" and "samsara."
Do these ideas do any good at all, or do they just get us in trouble?
And what would a life outside ideas look like? Can you let go
of the duality of pure and impure and still work to stop
the pollution of air and water?

72. Satsujo Sits on the Lotus Sutra

A DEVOUT LAYMAN took his young daughter Satsujo with him whenever he visited Master Hakuin Ekaku. Though only a child, Satsujo was devoted to practicing the Dharma.

When she was sixteen, her parents were concerned that she would not find a husband, and asked her to pray to Kannon, the bodhisattva of compassion. She did this day and night, during all of her activities. Before long she experienced an awakening.

One day her father peeked into her room and saw her sitting on a copy of the Lotus Sutra. "What are you doing, sitting on this precious scripture?" he shouted.

"How is this wonderful sutra different from my ass?" she replied.

RACHEL MANSFIELD-HOWLETT'S REFLECTION

A woman found a bit of the light for herself and said to me: "When we recite from Hakuin's *Song of Zazen* 'All beings by nature are buddhas,' I think we should add, '*This means you!*'" She understood that it's tough to see how intimate this matter really is—that it has to do with you and me. To explain this quandary it is sometimes said, "Because it is so very clear, it takes so long to realize."

Rebuked for sitting on the sutras, Satsujo overthrows thoughts of sacred and profane and comes forth with the tender question, "How is this wonderful sutra different from my ass?" With audacious good humor, Satsujo is intimate with the Great Matter and invites us to see the treasure within the body, even when it is the disreputable and bawdy butt.

If you are the "butt" of the joke, an "asshole," or (my favorite) a "buttinsky," you know you're being dissed. We reveal our misgivings about the body by the use of pejorative terms such as "dick," "cunt," and "butthead." On the other hand, we revere the sutras so much that there is danger that we will regard their words at a distance; the Dharma is worth nothing if it stands so aloof. We long to understand how this life, with all its complexity, and this body of pleasure and pain could contain the teachings of the sutras.

Satsujo is in league with those who found awakening in "three pounds of flax" or "a dried shit stick," or, in a more close-at-hand discovery, "in the heart of the one who asks." Kannon, the many-handed bodhisattva of awakened compassion, finds us on such an occasion, just as she did when Satsujo called upon her.

Zen is well known for holding words and letters in contempt, favoring direct experience over discursive thought. The scholar Deshan famously burned the pages of his beloved Diamond Sutra. Even so, it was considered bad form to sit on the sutras. Satsujo's teaching was this: as long as you think awakening is located somewhere outside yourself, even in a sutra, your understanding will be very limited. Zen is grounded in reality, borne out by the empirical discoveries of the old teachers and, today, through our own practice. We come to see the truth of koans and sutras reflected in our lives and, interestingly, vice versa.

I picture Satsujo slightly bent over, looking directly at her father and pointing to her butt. I'm reminded of the seamstress Rosa Parks's 1955 act of civil disobedience—simply sitting her tired butt down on the seat of an Alabama bus and refusing to give up her place to a white man. Rosa Parks's simple gesture helped set the stage for the repeal of segregation laws and inspired the Freedom Rides. Like Satsujo's frank question, Parks's unassuming act raises us all up together. And we're still in the wonderful process of uncovering the women ancestors who put their butts on the line to point the way for us.

For myself, I honor my mother, now gone for a quarter century, as one of the many women ancestors. Raised in rural Oklahoma in the 1930s, my mother was the eldest daughter of a practical-minded country schoolmistress and a handsome, hard-drinking, rodeo-riding Chickasaw. She taught school in the Chickasaw Nation and later taught in a largely Hispanic school in southern California. Although my mother wasn't familiar with Buddhist ideas, she instilled in me the truth of an inherent buddha nature that resides within all beings and taught me that each of us must show it in whatever way we can. Through her daily actions, she taught me that every person has value, no matter their race, gender, or social status.

Through meditation practice I discovered an even broader truth: that my body is the same as the redwood, the mountains and rivers, oceans and kelp forests, and the great earth itself. We must live as if there is only one precious body, and this body includes yours and mine.

Quickly, before thoughts of sacred and profane arise, how is it that your hands and feet are the same as the Buddha's? How is it that your very own fanny is the source of wisdom, that this too is your original face? You must live these questions for yourself, but please know, without your own ass there is no Buddha.

What might a child or teenager know that adults have forgotten? What do we gain by calling certain objects sacred (a statue of the Buddha, a copy of the Bible, the Torah, or the Koran) and treating them with special respect? What makes an object "sacred"?

73. The Old Woman's Rice Cakes

···

DESHAN XUANJIAN was a great scholar of the Diamond Sutra, but he was not a Chan practitioner. He was traveling south in search of the Dharma, carrying his commentaries on the Diamond Sutra with him. In the course of his travels he came across an old woman on the roadside selling tea and rice cakes. He asked her, "Who are you?"

She responded, "I am an old woman selling rice cakes." When he asked if he could buy some refreshments from her, she inquired, "Venerable priest, what are you carrying in your bag?"

He said, "I am a scholar of the Diamond Sutra, and here I have all my notes and commentaries."

Hearing this, the old woman said, "I have heard that, according to the Diamond Sutra, past mind is ungraspable, present mind is ungraspable, and future mind is ungraspable. So where is the mind that you wish to refresh with rice cakes, oh scholar? If you can answer this, you may buy a rice cake from me. If not, you'll have to go elsewhere for refreshment."

Deshan was unable to reply. The old woman then directed him to a Chan master nearby.

Deshan burned all his notes and commentaries the next day.

JOAN HALIFAX'S REFLECTION

What a wonderful koan! An old nameless woman on the road helps the smarty Deshan get free from his load of conceptual detritus. She is the Diamond Sutra itself, signless and aimless. She is nobody we know, and at the same time, she is an intimate manifestation of some kind of wild and cranky freedom. Through her, there is no abiding, no attachment.

Deshan was from northern China. As a youth, he studied the classical precepts, and he also thoroughly penetrated the Diamond Sutra. At the time, there was sectarian strife between the northern and southern schools of Buddhism. Deshan, being from the northern school, was vehemently critical of the southern school. To make his point, he piled the *Qinglong Commentaries* on his back and made his way south to confront the so-called sudden enlightenment of the southern school.

So here is Deshan hauling around his ideas about the sutra, among other interesting burdens of opinion. He encounters the old woman, who cuts him free from the conceptual mind with the diamond of her mind. The first words in the Diamond Sutra are "Thus I have heard." Thus Deshan heard the old woman, for sure. His mind for a rice cake. And he was a stale rice cake, as he could not reveal his own mind when confronted with her fierce clarity.

This nameless old crone became Deshan's catalyst to awakening, challenging his ego-based confidence, introducing him to an ungraspable moment, a moment of absolute freedom from glosses, commentaries, and secondary consciousness.

Who are these old women who now and again appear in koans? They are who we really are, that wild old grandmother's heart of wisdom that does not engage in idiot compassion but cuts to the quick of the moment. She offers rice cakes and the refreshment of awakening tea. This staff of life, rice: common food for all. Tea: common drink for all. And Deshan got the special transmission outside the sutras, the supreme meal!

"Zen is poetry," said the scholar R. H. Blyth. What did he mean by "poetry"? Certainly he did not use the word in the sense of what we commonly call "verse." Rather, he meant that the essence of Zen, like the world of poetry, comes from the spontaneous energy of meeting reality directly. It is the unfiltered immediacy manifested by an old lady, nameless and by the roadside, selling rice cakes to any passerby. This quality of immediacy embodied by the old woman is in our everyday practice and is also reflected in the so-called literary body that we call koans.

The mystery of koans and their poetic veracity comes about because they are nondiscursive, based in life, full of allusions, and nonlinear. They are *not* commentaries on the sutras. Rather they invite us not to use the thinking mind but to allow the thinking mind to drop away by being absorbed completely into the koan body so that a genuine experience of intimacy can present itself.

The old woman selling rice cakes is that intimacy itself. She barks at the heady scholar: "Where is the mind that you wish to refresh with rice cakes, oh scholar? If you can answer this, you may buy a rice cake from me. If not, you'll have to go elsewhere for refreshment."

Practicing with a koan is like strengthening a muscle that gathers us up and releases us into the present. Like the old woman, a koan reduces us to who we really are. One strike, like a diamond hitting glass, and we are free of secondary reflections.

The experience of absorption into this poem-like case is similar and dissimilar to what we experience in meditation practice, of being with the present moment as it is, being the sutras, not commenting on the sutras.

Usually this "as-it-isness" is free of a medium, like a rice cake, like walking meditation, like this present moment. However, in the case of koan practice, the koan is dropped into the midst of this "as-it-isness" and lets the truth of things as they are shine through the matrix of its body. Using a jewel-like koan, a bright fragment of a past reality, as an inspiration and a guide in the immediacy of our very practice can enable us to be engulfed by truth; we become a kind of hook-line-and-sinker that is swallowed by the whole fish of life. Deshan got hooked and served up by one powerful, old, and nameless woman. He was fortunate to have the hunger to require some refreshments!

What can a scholar of sacred texts offer to the world that a wise baker can't? How would you answer the old woman's question? Where is your mind? Is it worth a rice cake?

74. Ling's Question

CHINA, PROBABLY NINTH CENTURY ·······································

ING XINGPO visited Master Fubei Heshang to pay her respects. They sat together and drank tea, and she asked him, "If a true word can't be spoken no matter how hard you try, how will you teach?"

Fubei said, "Fubei has nothing to say."

Ling was not satisfied. She placed her hands inside the opposite sleeves of her robe and cried out: "There is grievous suffering even within a blue sky!"

Again Fubei had nothing to say.

Ling said, "To be a human being is to live in calamity."

Jo POTTER'S REFLECTION

Reading this koan the first time made me laugh, because it reminded me of a possible scenario between a couple. Something like:

> Wife: "People can't read your mind, you know. So can you speak up?"
> Husband: "Got nothing to say!"
> Wife: "The kids need to hear something from you about going to summer camp!"
> Husband says nothing.
> Wife: "Talking to you is like talking to a brick."

This is one of those precious little Zen stories that often give me the feeling that I am squeezing drops of juice out of a dry prune!

Those tiny drops can be filled with intense wisdom, and it is worth the requisite koan interviews to harvest those drops. Let me share the drops I managed to squeeze out of Ling's interaction with Fubei.

In this koan we meet a great master, Ling Xingpo, a woman. Ling begins to prod Fubei by asking him about speaking true words. Ling is a keen-eyed teacher and I'm sure she knows that spoken words fall short of the truth. Consider what happens when eating very spicy Thai food: the truth of burning-hot chilis on the tongue needs absolutely no words of explanation in order for the brain to register alarm and pain. Words come much later than the truth of every particular situation. Ling is not particularly interested in the "truth," which she knows cannot be spoken, but she is definitely very interested in the *function* of the truth and wisdom. What do I mean by "function"? For example, it is not enough to register the truth that my neighbor is very sad after losing her husband. My function requires the additional step of visiting with her, comforting her, and listening to her talk about the loss.

Of course Fubei knows that if he answers Ling, his words will not be the truth. So in a technical sense his answer—"Fubei has nothing to say"—is correct. But for Ling, it is a useless way of being correct. Ling is pragmatic and she wants to know how Fubei will teach the great wisdom he has to others. What use is wisdom, if it cannot be shared? We have all experienced wise spiritual teachers who have the gift of clarifying life situations in such a way that our minds are changed and opened and we are inspired to reach for the stars. Ling's wise pragmatism points to using skillful means to know when to use words and when to use action. She prods at Fubei who seems to have stopped at one generic answer: "Nothing to say."

I love horses but will never be able to explain what it feels like to have a horse nibble on an apple in my hand—the velvet soft nuzzling of a huge nose, the shine in the horse's eye, the squirt of the apple juice, the no-word communication between me and the horse. But even though this experience is wordless, my function as a caring human being is to encourage others to approach a horse, open their palm, and offer an apple.

Ling persists with her prodding of Fubei. She perceives the suffering of the sentient beings even when the sky is blue. Ling keeps her heart open and knows that children are starving, loved ones are dying, war is being waged, and yet at the same time spring and summer bring masses of flowers and fruits, and parents are happily raising their children. I find myself liking Ling for exactly this persistence, this drive toward a practical application of wisdom and truth, and for her willingness to keep at Fubei, encouraging him to try to speak. We steadily apply ourselves to our practice in order to know, just as Ling demands to know from Fubei, how we are going to manage in this overwhelming world.

At the end Ling says, "To be a human being is to live in calamity." I get the sense that she is not daunted by this perception, but rather she has prepared herself to reach out and act in all the ways necessary to stay awake in the moment-to-moment situation with a compassionate heart and the determination to do her best. For me the bone of this koan is Ling's courageous wisdom and persistence. In our world today, we can acknowledge her example and develop courage to take another step and honor the precious light of each individual who touches our lives.

What difference would it make if you never read the newspaper or followed the news? In the midst of a moment of great joy, what do we do with the pain in the house next door?

75. Kakuzan Shido's Dagger

HE NUN Kakuzan Shido trained at the notoriously tough Rinzai monastery Engakuji. Her teacher, Tokei (whose name meant "Peach Tree Valley"), gave her *inka*, transmission and authority to be an independent teacher.

In the transmission ceremony, Shido took the seat in front of the altar and the monks asked her questions to test her skill. When it was the head monk's turn, he challenged her: "In our lineage, anyone who receives inka must give a discourse on the sutras. Are you really capable of doing this?"

Shido pulled out the ten-inch dagger carried by all women of the warrior class and held it in front of his face. "Every Zen teacher in the lineage of our master should teach the sutras," she said. "But I am a woman of the warrior line and I speak the Dharma face to face, with my dagger drawn. What need do I have for books?" He persisted with another question. "What was your original understanding before your parents were born?"

She answered by sitting in silence with her eyes closed. Then she said, "Do you understand?"

The head monk answered with a verse:

Here in Peach Tree Valley,
a wine gourd has been drained to the last drop.
Drunken eyes see ten miles of flowers.

Shido replied, "Was I not directed to the Way even before the births of my mother and father?"

Laura del Valle's Reflection

Kakuzan lived in a world of violence filled with uncertainty. Born into a class of woman warriors, she learned to cut off the fear of self-concern in order to defend others. At her transmission ceremony she cut through the patriarchal assumptions of Japanese Zen, showing that her practice was not an escape but a way to come face to face with the truth of her times.

She was asked if she was capable of expounding the Dharma. Although she respected those teachers who gave discourses, she had lived too long on the edge of the dagger to look beyond the truth that was right in front of her. The dagger is so unpretentious it heals.

I got my formal warrior's training in the late 1960s with the first Japanese Rinzai Zen teacher to come to Mexico City. Ejo Takata's eyes twinkled with humor, but his zendo was run like a boot camp. I learned to face my own terrors over and over as the *jiki jitsu*, or guardian of the zendo, usually a Mexican man acting like a samurai, stalked the zendo like a tiger, ready to pounce on whoever dared to shift even slightly. We had mandatory all-night sittings, so keeping still was a challenge. The sharpness of this strict practice cut through everything I was protecting about myself and pushed me to my limits, to the point where I thought I would explode, until I found the limitless and became more sure of myself: my own dagger was drawn.

Maestro Takata didn't teach much doctrine or establish elaborate rituals. In essence he gave us one koan: how can we help with the poverty and suffering around us? This question was to shape my life.

Like Kakuzan, I was born into a line of woman warriors. My grandmother and mother were immigrant women in the US, who as single mothers became fearless for the sake of their children. Although I was raised in Mexico City and Chicago, I ended up living and working as a doctor in rural Mexico, where many single mothers struggle for the survival of their children.

Isabel came to my clinic for help. She was a thin woman in her late twenties who held one hand over her mouth when she spoke to cover her few decaying teeth. She said softly, "Adam has taken the three children to live with his new prostitute girlfriend. I want them back." Adam had once hung her upside down from a tree. She didn't ask me directly for fear of losing hope. A long silence followed. We both knew that going to the law was useless. Adam, the father of her children, was a hard-core drug dealer who was off-limits to the state prosecutor and local police.

My mind was racing. I told myself, "You're a doctor, not a cop, you have no magic powers, you're not a tough guy with a gun, so just what do you think you can do?" Isabel was looking at the ground despondently. I said, "Get in the car and let's go get them." Adam wasn't home and the girlfriend turned over the kids without resistance.

An hour later Adam was at the clinic looking for me. Isabel and the kids hid. I came out to meet him. Once the knife is drawn, there's no turning back; the knife demands that you pay total attention to whatever unfolds. We stared at each other for a long time, both of us breathing heavily, before he spoke. "I should kill you, but you're a decent woman, you've fed my children, and I don't kill decent people." He left. Shortly afterward he did kill someone, and he was finally sent to jail, because the victim's parents had enough money and connections to go beyond the local authorities.

Working as a rural doctor for more than thirty years in a country with extreme poverty, lack of social services, and blatant government corruption, I have been called into action by my neighbors countless times. I've responded to medical emergencies, domestic violence, and human rights abuses, and I've organized town protests at public meetings. I lack the specialized knowledge to deal with most of the situations that confront me, but experts are scarce in this neck of the woods. I could have become paralyzed, or expounded Buddhist doctrine and done nothing, or turned away, assuring myself that someone else could deal with "it" better than I. Instead, I simply do the best I can on the spot. This is my way of living with the dagger drawn.

A nun draws a dagger—wait a minute, why would a nun, even a nun of the warrior class, have a weapon under her robes? Or was she carrying the bodhisattva Manjushri's sword of wisdom?
Can a person have the desire for awakening without knowing it?
What is the wine gourd in your own life?

76. The Old Woman and Naropa

 NE DAY, the great Indian scholar Naropa was quietly study-ing in his room. Suddenly, a shadow fell on the floor, and out of it an old, old woman emerged in front of him. She asked, "What are you reading?"

Naropa replied, "I'm studying the teachings of the Buddha."

The old woman asked, "Do you understand them?"

Without hesitation Naropa replied, "I understand every single word."

"How fortunate for this earth that such a scholar exists!" she exclaimed joyfully. Then she asked, "You understand the literal mean-ing of the teachings, but do you understand their inner meaning?"

Naropa replied, "Yes."

The expression of the old woman transformed from joy to sadness. With trembling heart, she cried, "To think that such a great scholar as you knows how to tell lies!"

The embarrassed Naropa inquired, "Is there anyone who truly understands the inner meaning of the Dharma?"

The old woman answered, "Yes, my brother, Tilopa."

Tears came to Naropa's eyes. He asked, "Where can I find this master?"

The old woman replied, "He is not in any particular direction; he could be anywhere. If your mind is filled with devotion and you yearn to meet him, that is the right direction." Then the old woman, who was actually Vajrayogini, an embodiment of enlightened energy in female form, disappeared like a rainbow fading in the sky.

Because of his deluded mind, Naropa had not been able to see her true form.

KARMA LEKSHE TSOMO'S REFLECTION

The legendary encounter of Naropa and the old woman is grist for many spiritual lessons. Born into an Indian Brahman family in the tenth century, Naropa became widely renowned as a great scholar who was peerless in philosophical debate. As a result of his superior knowledge and widespread acclaim, he became a bit cocky. With a nudge from the old woman in the story, he recognized his limitations. Seeking out the great yogi Tilopa, he went on to become a great meditator and perfected the Six Yogas of Naropa, advanced tantric practices still preserved today. He is counted as one of the eighty-four *mahasiddhas*, practitioners of great realization and power.

When the old woman asked whether Naropa understood the inner meaning of the Buddha's teachings, she alluded to the vast difference between book knowledge and inner awareness. Knowledge, especially knowledge of the Buddhadharma, is essential and a magnificent accomplishment. But scholarship without inner awareness is insufficient. Profound awakening requires a deep realization of the teachings that utterly transforms the mind.

As a result of his encounter with the old woman, Naropa set out on an arduous journey to find the fabled yogi Tilopa, her brother. His journey was literally a trek to the snowy Himalayas and also, metaphorically, to a place of inner realization. The journey was full of lessons, which only intensified once he finally found his teacher.

When Naropa began his search, he expected to find a glorious master surrounded by acolytes and admirers. Ultimately, instead, he found a naked *sadhu*, or holy man, eating live fish fresh from the river. As a rather stuffy Brahman and committed vegetarian, he was shocked by this unorthodox behavior. He immediately challenged Tilopa to explain himself, whereupon the naked sadhu released the still living fish from his mouth back into the river, exploding all Naropa's preconceived notions about spiritual mastery and his own intellectual superiority. Each step of the journey was a lesson and a fresh awareness in itself, validating the effectiveness of the teachings.

Vajrayogini, manifesting in the guise of an old women, appears at a critical junction to illumine Naropa on his inner journey. In an age when women's spiritual potential was rarely acknowledged, she turns the tables with her intuitive insight. Whether she appeared as a real, historical person or a miraculous archetype may be immaterial, since she triggered Naropa's epiphany. But her appearance in the body of a haggard women significantly broke through his brahmanical preconceptions about age, beauty, gender, and dirt. We do know that, as a consequence of her wisdom, manifest in female form, the lineage of Tilopa continued through Naropa to the present day. And although the old woman is unnamed and missing from the traditional lineages, she deserves to be included, not only as the full expression of feminine wisdom, but as a manifestation of Vajrayogini, the enlightened feminine in human form. Her appearance to Naropa, who was indeed an historical person, takes place at a time when he had reached the apogee of his scholarly career and her appearance was the catalyst that propelled him beyond his complacency.

The archetype of the woman who acts as a spiritual catalyst is a common trope in yogic literature. Often old, disheveled, seductive, or outrageous, she appears at a particular moment to awaken spiritual awareness, often in a man who is upper caste, highly accomplished, pedantic, or uptight. No doubt Naropa was well versed in the tantras (mystical rituals and practices) and had been practicing them in simulation mode for some time, but it took the goading of the old woman to awaken a higher level of consciousness and open him to new insights; in this case, she exposed his pride and the limitations of his perception.

Naropa's encounter with the old woman sparks a moment of direct intuitive experience in a way that is both ordinary and transcendent, altering his view of reality and creating space for further realization. It is not that his erudition is irrelevant—in fact, it is the fulfillment of his life's path up to that moment—but now a totally different level of reality is revealed. Embodying that revelation is all that remains to be done. And, for that, the old woman directs him to Tilopa, someone who "truly understands the inner meaning of the Dharma." Teachers such as these may appear at any time, in any form, to awaken our own Dharma wisdom.

How can you see another in his or her true form? How do you recognize Elijah when he comes to the seder table? What signs would you look for?

77. Lingzhao's Shining Grasses

CHINA, EIGHTH CENTURY ···

AYMAN PANG was sitting in his thatched cottage one day, studying the sutras. "Difficult, difficult, difficult," he suddenly exclaimed, "like trying to store ten bushels of sesame seed in the top of a tree."

"Easy, easy, easy," his wife, Laywoman Pang, answered. "It's like touching your feet to the floor when you get out of bed."

"Neither difficult nor easy," said their daughter Lingzhao. "It's like the teachings of the ancestors shining on the hundred grass tips."

JISHO WARNER'S REFLECTION

The members of the Pang family are the most famously enlightened lay practitioners in all of Chan. Layman Pang studied with Shitou and Mazu, the great masters of his time. A few stories present the wisdom of others in the family, especially Lingzhao, whose comments always go to the heart of the matter.

The family is cozily gathered at home. The Layman suddenly cries out. At this very moment, he is piercingly aware of life's tangles. He's been studying the sutras, a favorite occupation, but his cry is not about the subtlety of the sutras, it's about the difficulty of living. Life in a body is endlessly complex, seething with thorns and tangles, erupting with love and tenderness. Studying the sutras won't save you, zazen won't save you, being as enlightened as Layman Pang won't save you from difficulty.

The Layman explains what he means: "It's like trying to store ten bushels of sesame seed in the top of a tree." How frustrating to push heavy bushels up a tree, and all that sesame seed is just going to spill out and slither down the branches when the wind blows. It takes such effort to hold things in unstable combinations.

One day during a retreat I moaned to myself, "It's so hard," and I realized for the first time that I was simply describing my limited view. Of course that's how I feel when I'm boxed in by my delusions. "Difficult" is sometimes the feeling of the world pressing harshly on us, and sometimes the feeling of suffering arising in our hearts. "Difficult" is not inherent in the Dharma world, yet it is embedded in how we perceive and live. The world of myriad soft bodies coming and going is passionately beautiful, an endless marvel. And it's a world of stumbling and groping, dying as well as growing.

And here is Laywoman Pang, at her ease. What could be more straightforward than your feet reaching the floor when you stand up? Laywoman Pang speaks to us from the grounded viewpoint of unity, where no thing is divided from the rest of reality, where her body is not separate from the ground. When each thing is allowed to be as it is, and effort does not twist and force things out of shape, all is relaxed and open. Sometimes life unfurls softly for me, everything fitting like a box and its lid. If I try to hold on to that state, I find myself suddenly back in confusion, having lingered while life has moved on. And then I take my place in the flow again, in the endless moving stream that I never really leave.

It is crucial to know our undivided nature. It is a true side of life, the side where things are related to in terms of their sameness. The differences among people, trees, and stones are not accounted for here. So often, in the press of our hectic phenomenal life, Laywoman Pang's "easy, easy" looks like the goal, but despite our yearnings for life to be smooth, awakening is not an exit ramp from difficulty.

When Lingzhao says it's not the one or the other, she's not denying anything. The daughter is by birthright a synthesis of her father and mother. Reality is neither difficult nor easy: those are both opinions. Of course there is difficulty—that's our experience of feeling thwarted, but it's not what life is in itself. We forget this to our peril whenever we fall into the view that reality is only how it looks to us now. It is also not the case that life should be easy. Living beings encounter great hardship as well as great joy; we fulfill our humanity through both streams.

So how is it? "It's like the teachings of the ancestors shining on the hundred grass tips." Lingzhao offers us the living Dharma. She wove baskets to support her family, and here she weaves for us a basket of all the myriad phenomena, often spoken of in Zen as "the hundred grasses." In this interwoven universe, the many contain the one, at the same time that one contains all. "The teachings of the ancestors" are the wisdom of the Buddhadharma, which naturally shines forth from the tips of every swaying blade of grass. How could it be otherwise, when the myriad beings are themselves the one Dharma universe manifesting itself.

Wind-whipped seas and cerulean skies—
matching halves unite in a flash
in Lingzhao's grassy basket.

Is there a benefit to studying a spiritual text without understanding it?
Right now, for you, is the Dharma difficult, easy,
or something else entirely?

78. Qiyuan and the Lotus Sutra

CHINA, SEVENTEENTH CENTURY ···

SCHOLARLY LAYMAN AND a monk came to visit Master Qiyuan Xinggang and asked her to write an inscription in a copy of the Lotus Sutra that the layman had written out in ink mixed with his own blood. She refused.

When they insisted, she asked, "Where does the blood come from? Who is the one who copied out this sutra? If you can answer, then you will be able to break open the burning house and allow the true method to reveal itself. If the layman wants to truly understand this, the best thing would be to throw this copy of the sutra into the fire, so that not a single character remains. Then you will be happy."

STEPHANIE KAZA'S REFLECTION

The student comes to the teacher, homework in hand, the term paper dutifully crafted. "Please, give me an A! I worked so hard on this! It took me all night to finish this project." The teacher raises an eyebrow. "What is more important—your effort or the grade from the teacher?"

Qiyuan refuses to play this game with the layman who is asking for her endorsement. She is not impressed by his act of writing the sutra with his own blood, an intended act of piety. The student's effort is not clear. Can he answer her questions? Has he looked deeply into the source of his own blood? The water flowing from mountains, the soil becoming flesh and food, the sweat of his ancestors—does he really know who he is? Perhaps he thinks this act has purified his accumulated forgetfulness through pious devotion.

But the teacher sees only that the student has filled the empty space of the sutra's teaching with his own blood, his own ego, his own inflated self. To endorse such a view would only validate his self-projections of worth, the burning house of delusion. As a true teacher, Qiyuan seizes this moment to offer the true lifegiving option of liberation. "Why don't you just throw your homework into the fire? Get rid of your self-inflated views. Let every shred of ego burn in the flames of liberation. Then you will be happy."

The graduate student sits in my office, a first draft of her dissertation in hand. She struggles with self-doubt, with the exhaustion of her effort, with the fear that it won't be good enough, that she will fail. If she cannot pass this test, she cannot go on in academia. But the test is not about the writing, it is about her own courage, her willingness to break through the ego of self-doubt and persevere with the pure activity itself.

How can I compassionately help her confront these agonies of ego that permeate the high-stress competitive world of her chosen future? This moment is a chance for her to break through and see into the conditioning of judgment, see how she has been formed by being graded year after year, how she wants the good grades, how she doesn't want the bad grades, how she wants the teacher's (parent's) approval. I point out how thoroughly this culture of evaluation frames every aspect of higher education. Don't be fooled by this conditioned need for approval! Be bold! See who you really are!

I do not want to be swayed by the student's compliant devotion to her professor. Unexamined devotion offers a receptive field for intimidation. A teacher must be alert to the ever-present temptation to abuse the student's devotion to meet her own ego needs. Qiyuan stays far from this dangerous territory. Underneath her appearance of stern disdain is complete dedication to her task as a teacher.

Qiyuan pushes the student, "Go deeper, penetrate the falseness of this copied sutra, test your attachment—can you throw the sacred sutra into the fire?" The teacher holds firm to the true method, using this occasion to give the layman true teaching. Exactly because he has poured his own sweat and blood into the sutra, he is ripe for awakening. The layman has made the journey to see the teacher; he stands before her, wanting her response. How ready is he, she wants to know? Can she turn the momentum of his great effort and devotion toward his own liberation from false views? Qiyuan seizes the moment, shocking the layman with her fierce compassion.

You are the student; Qiyuan is the teacher. What have you made with the blood of your ego? What sacred text would you give your own life blood for? Walk right into the burning fire of those questions and find the true method. Don't expect the teacher's (or your partner's or children's) approval for your efforts. This is your own liberation you seek. You must match fire with fire; use the fierceness of your own willingness to go beyond shallow impressions of truth. Burn then, with the sutra—blood, paper, and ego all up in flames—until not a single character remains. This is the true path to happiness, to liberation from the suffering of ego.

We are always looking outside of our own life for salvation, though the Dharma encourages us to look within. So where does salvation come from? How important is self-discipline on the spiritual path? What about acts of great self-sacrifice and devotion?

79. Dieu Nhan's Without Words

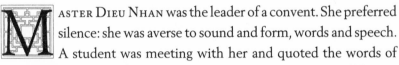

ASTER DIEU NHAN was the leader of a convent. She preferred silence: she was averse to sound and form, words and speech. A student was meeting with her and quoted the words of Vimalakirti from the Vimalakirti Sutra: "I am sick because all beings are sick." Then the student asked, "Why do you have an aversion to sound and form?"

Dieu Nhan quoted the Diamond Sutra, saying, "If someone sees me through form or looks for me through sound, that person is following a wrong path and cannot see the Tathagata."

The student asked, "Why don't you speak?"

Dieu Nhan said, "The Path is fundamentally without words."

EILEEN KIERA'S REFLECTION

Vimalakirti pointed to something that's true about human beings when he said, "I am sick because all beings are sick." We are not separate from each other. When people suffer, we suffer as a result.

One time a friend, who had adopted two young girls from Korea, was walking down the street with them. A neighbor who was a Vietnam veteran started shouting at my friend and his daughters, saying awful things. My friend quickly left with his kids. Later, another neighbor said, "That neighbor has posttraumatic stress disorder from the Vietnam War. After seeing your kids, he must have had a flashback."

When someone has suffered, that suffering manifests in the world. We cannot protect ourselves from the suffering in the world. We can distract ourselves, we can deny the suffering, or we can push it away, but then we're no longer in contact with what is here. We are cut off from ourselves and each other. We miss our lives, which are occurring right now.

There is something wonderful about the truth of not being separate. When we touch the first bloom of spring, something blooms inside of us. In March, when I arrive home quite late from practicing with the sangha, I'm always thrilled when I step out of the car to hear frogs singing for the first time in spring. It fills my whole being with joy.

When we realize that everything is interdependent and nothing is separate, then we see that even one kind word reverberates through the whole universe.

The student wants to know: If nothing is separate, why is Dieu Nhan averse to sound and form? But she does not feel aversion to sound and form: she is neither attached to sound and form nor caught by sound and form. The Vimalakirti Sutra warns against being caught in dualistic and discriminating thought. The sickness of the world presides where there is "you and me," "us and them," "right and wrong." Our sense of separation is the root of war and the destruction of the environment.

Dieu Nhan quotes the Diamond Sutra, saying, "If someone sees me through form or looks for me through sound, that person is following a wrong path and cannot see the Tathagatha."

Our practice lives when we're not caught in dualistic thinking. If we don't try to make things be the way we want them, or push away what we don't want, we can respond to each moment anew and each situation as it presents itself.

Yesterday, a friend and I walked down to Lake Jorgensen. We sat looking across the lake and talking. The sunlight shining on the water made the surface a silver reflection of everything surrounding the lake—the trees, the mountains, the clouds in the sky. The wind picked up, rippling the surface. It looked like a thumbprint. I turned to her and said, "It's like the thumbprint of God, everything reflected in the One."

Each and every one of us has been marked with the thumbprint of the divine, of the sacred. That print is eternal. It's always part of who we are. It's always part of the trees, the mountains, and the clouds. It is the true reality of existence and nonexistence, which Dieu Nhan is presenting when she quotes the Diamond Sutra. That thumbprint of the sacred, that illumination, is what we fundamentally are. It is beyond the dichotomy of thought and no-thought, sound and silence, form and no-form.

Yet the student doesn't understand and so says to Dieu Nhan, "Why don't you speak?" Dieu Nhan knows that the path is fundamentally without words. In springtime, the song of the frogs is just *"grok, grok."* There are no words or thoughts. There is no narrative to separate us from what is here. Out of that simple awareness arises the most selfless compassion. Truly there is no self and no other. Yet like gold hidden in countless grains of sand, our realization is found in the very midst of words. We use words to point to realization and we find realization mixed with the sand of countless words. Words aren't to be avoided. Our seemingly separate existence is the path in this life. Seeing through to nonseparation is the gold.

Our realization of the blooming witch hazel is to become one with that flower. No thought at all. Our realization of another person's life is to recognize our own face in their face. That experience of oneness is love. It is the thumbprint of the divine.

In order to find your own buddha nature, is it necessary to stop talking?
If so, why would anyone have an interview with a teacher,
and why would a teacher give a Dharma talk?

80. Shiji Doesn't Take Off Her Hat

CHINA, NINTH CENTURY ···

T HE MONK Jinhua Juzhi lived in a remote hermitage and begged for his food among the villagers. One rainy night a nun named Shiji came to his hut. She walked right in without knocking, and she did not take off her sedge rain hat. She circled around his meditation seat three times, holding up her traveling staff.

"Give me one word," she said, "and I'll take off my hat."

Juzhi said nothing.

She circled around him three more times and asked the same question, but he had nothing to say. And again, she circled around him, asked her question, and he said nothing.

As she went to the door, he said, "Wait! It's late. Why don't you stay here for the night?"

Shiji said, "If you say the appropriate word, I'll stay."

Again, Juzhi was speechless. The nun walked out.

Juzhi sighed and said, "Although I inhabit the body of a man, I lack a man's spirit." He resolved to leave his hermitage in search of understanding.

JUDITH ROITMAN'S REFLECTION

Juzhi became a great sutra master in his early twenties. When still young he withdrew from teaching—possibly due to the persecution and suppression of Buddhism in the late Tang dynasty—and lived alone in a hermitage. According to legend, his practice included devotional chanting of the mantra of Zhun Ti Bodhisattva, the mother of (it is said) seventy billion buddhas.

So this nun appears. Her name (and it's unusual that we're told her name) is Shiji, which means "true world." In the version of the story I know she is very tall. She walks in on Juzhi while he is sitting down. She has a long staff, like a walking stick, probably as tall as she is, with rings at the top that jingle when she strikes it on the floor. Shiji is an imposing figure, towering over Juzhi with her staff, and very rude. She doesn't bow. She doesn't even take off her hat. She circles around him three times without speaking. He is a great sutra master! Who does she think she is?

And then she challenges him: "Give me one word!" Three times she challenges him and he still can't speak. All he can do is croak out an invitation, and instead of being grateful this nun challenges him again. And walks out.

Juzhi realizes that in fact he understands nothing.

This is a fairly standard trope in Zen stories: a woman challenges a sutra master, and as a result of this encounter, he realizes that the sutras got him nowhere and he resolves to find a true Zen teacher. There are two aspects to this trope: practicing Zen is better than learning sutras and being shown up by a woman is shameful. Which is why, at least in this version, Juzhi says, ironically for a man devoted to the mother of seventy billion buddhas, that he "lack(s) a man's spirit." I doubt this irony was noticed at the time.

Gender politics aside, this koan resonates. We've all been stuck like Juzhi. Speechless. Unable to act. We've all been sitting in our metaphoric huts when suddenly—boom!—reality (another translation of "Shiji") appears.

What is being asked of Juzhi? What kind of word? Shiji isn't telling. This is terrifying! We want a hint; we always want a hint. We want to know what's expected of us so we can deliver it. But Shiji gives no hint. "Give me one word"—how can you respond to this? It's like getting a Facebook invitation that says "show up!" with no place and no time given.

So Juzhi freezes. He has no idea what to do. This is a common reaction when we are presented with something outside our expectations. And then he does something interesting: he realizes that he must change his life.

Forty-five years ago, back in college, a friend appeared in my doorway as unexpectedly as Shiji. But she wasn't strong and commanding; she was desperate, about to run away from overbearing parents. I wasn't stuck in samadhi like Juzhi; I was stoned on pain meds that barely touched my severe period cramps. Between pain and drugs I could barely comprehend what she was saying. Like Juzhi I froze. Like Shiji she disappeared. Unlike Shiji, she disappeared into a nervous breakdown. And, like Juzhi, I realized I must change my life.

And Shiji, what kind of woman is she? She appears as a commanding figure, completely in charge, completely free. She makes it seem so easy! But then I think of her times—ninth-century China, the convulsive and protracted end of the Tang dynasty—rebellions, warlords running amok, entire cities destroyed, and, as always in such times, women especially vulnerable. "Give me one word" takes on greater resonance than it seems to have at first glance. The challenge is deep. What is the one word that can end such suffering?

On my desk I have a portrait of the great Korean Zen master Man Gong, my teacher's teacher's teacher. Just now, between the last paragraph and this one, I found myself looking deeply into his eyes. It's easy to become complacent in our lives and comfortable in our practice. Man Gong's eyes tell me: Don't.

What is the most important word? How do you find it?
How do you greet a guest so that he or she knows you mean it?

81. Miaodao's Falling into the Hole

CHINA, ELEVENTH–TWELFTH CENTURIES ·······································

MONK ASKED Miaodao, "When words can neither describe reality nor reach the understanding of the hearer, what do you do then?"

Miaodao said, "Before you have defecated, you have already fallen into the hole." She went on, "Don't ask too many questions. Even if you are very fluent in debate, and even if you are clever enough to overturn mountains, these skills will do you no good at all in the realm of the Dharma. Originally, before the Buddha appeared, there was nothing whatever to be done."

GYOKUJUN LAYLA SMITH BOCKHORST'S REFLECTION

I read somewhere a description of a koan as "a knot in the current of our lives." For many years, probably the biggest knot in my life was a feeling that "I can't talk." I believed that in order to be a Dharma teacher I had to have great facility with words. In retrospect I think the main reason I left monastic practice was because I was expected to take on more teaching responsibilities, but I found speaking difficult. This koan is encouraging for those of us for whom speaking does not come easily, because it carries us beyond judgments about our speech.

Koans take us beyond our ideas of how things are. Although koans are words, they are trying to express a reality wider than words. With the amazing tool of human language, through stories and metaphor, koans help us to experience a deeper reality, larger than the bounds of language itself. Koans, like poetry, can resonate in many ways: each person responds uniquely to every koan. This is why it makes no sense to say there is any particular "answer" to a koan. The depth and richness of a koan is dependent only on the depth and richness of our response. Dogen Zenji says in the Genjokoan, "The moon is reflected in a puddle only an inch wide. The depth of the drop is the height of the moon." Yet "the depth of the drop is the height of the moon" doesn't mean that some understandings are deep and some understandings are shallow; it means there is no end to the depths of us. There are inconceivable, unknowable depths in every one of us.

So the monk asks about speech, and Miaodao's answer goes right past the monk's one-sided question. "Before you have defecated, you have already fallen into the hole." First we think, "Oh, I don't want to fall into the hole—that sounds bad." But "falling into the hole" is beyond positive and negative—it is the totality of reality, just as it is. Before a word comes out of your mouth, whether you speak or don't speak, whether you reach the understanding of the hearer or not, both you and the hearer are already in the hole together, fully manifesting the Dharma just as you are. You may have an idea that cleverness and skill with words are necessary to convey the Dharma, or that the hearer has to understand your words. But the hearer is already in the hole with you, so strictly speaking there is nothing to be done. You are never separate from others, Miaodao tells the monk, so why do you need to reach the understanding of the hearer?

I don't know how the koan of speech solved itself in my life, but it mostly has. It hasn't been a volitional process, and it hasn't been about acquiring any skill or fluency. It has been more a gradual accretion of the understanding that it doesn't matter. Ultimately, others do not need my help. I do not need to speak. There truly is nothing to be done.

But even if there is nothing to be done, we are always doing, we are always speaking. Even though others do not need our help, we must also recognize that it is our truest nature to want to be helpful. So it is an essential practice to continue to ask the question, "Then what do I do?" In "Ballad in Plain D," Bob Dylan asks, "Are birds free from the chains of the skyway?" We are not free from the chains of words, and we never will be free from the chains of words. But no matter; words are already in the hole with us. So just speak.

It helps to know that fluent speech and clever speech have nothing to do with truly expressing the Dharma. Yet with the question "Then what do I do?" I join the monk in his or her heartfelt path of practice. Ready to be scolded by my teacher for asking too many questions. Being willing to be in deep doo-doo because of my inevitably inadequate words, yet continuing nevertheless. Being willing to be caught by the chains of words, and being willing to speak when necessary, recognizing my desire to aid other beings.

So I just speak, encouraged by knowing that there is nothing particular to be said, and no special way to say it.

Are we ever not in the hole? How many questions are too many?

82. Miaoxin's Banner

SEVENTEEN MONKS, traveling in search of enlightenment, came to visit the famous teacher Master Yangshan Huiji. Before climbing the mountain to see him, they stayed the night in the temple guesthouse, and that evening they discussed the Sixth Patriarch's koan: "What moves is not the wind nor the banner, but your mind."

The nun Miaoxin was director of the guesthouse, a responsibility that had been given to her by Yangshan. She overheard the monks' conversation and said to her attendants, "What a shame that these seventeen blind donkeys have worn out so many pairs of straw sandals on their pilgrimages without even getting close to the Dharma."

One of the nuns told the monks what Miaoxin had said. The monks were humbled. They were sincere in their search for enlightenment, and so they did not dismiss Miaoxin's criticism as the impertinence of a woman. Instead, they bowed respectfully and approached her.

Miaoxin said, "What moves is not the wind, nor the banner, nor your mind."

All seventeen monks immediately awakened. They became Miaoxin's disciples and returned home without ever climbing the mountain to meet Yangshan.

MYOAN GRACE SCHIRESON'S REFLECTION

The fierce Chinese nun Miaoxin appears in Eihei Dogen's lecture "Raihai Tokuzui," or "Attaining the Marrow," which includes instructions about being willing to receive teachings without attachment to a teacher's formal title or rank. "Raihai Tokuzui" so emphatically supported women as equal partners in Dogen's Zen that twentieth-century Soto Zen nuns referenced it to reclaim their place as full Dharma successors in Dogen's lineage. "Raihai Tokuzui" is a treasure among Dogen's lectures, and Miaoxin sparkles boldly within it.

The story of wind, banner, and mind comes from early Zen monks arguing whether the wind moved a banner or the banner moved in the wind. The Sixth Patriarch elegantly intervened: "The wind does not move; the banner does not move; your mind moves." This story on the lips of the seventeen monks bored Miaoxin. She was unimpressed by their rehash of someone else's insight, just as we might be bored by Monday morning quarterbacking from spectators with no skin in the game. Why were these monks rehashing a centuries-old game? The real game is alive; it is not a discussion from the sidelines. Miaoxin had her own moves. She didn't need to rehash the Sixth Ancestor's, and she had the courage to enter the field.

Miaoxin was unafraid to surpass the teachings of the great Sixth Patriarch of Zen. Perhaps it was *because* she was a woman, not despite that fact, that the seventeen monks were intrigued by her teaching. They heard a bold voice from Yangshan's unusually highly placed woman leader. The very fact of her gender signaled her genuine transformation—enlightenment breaking through the barriers of culture, time, and place.

"What a bunch of losers," she exclaimed to her assistant. "They're wasting their energy visiting a great teacher, reviewing old plays instead of fully engaging on the Zen field." The assistant relayed Miaoxin's disapproval to the pilgrims, who became curious enough about her Zen view to question her. They ceased being spectators and stepped into Miaoxin's dangerous Dharma combat zone, willing to actually engage. Their surprise at such Zen power in a female form, combined with their lack of defensive maneuvering, must have played a part in their subsequent awakening with Miaoxin.

Miaoxin's disapproval of pilgrimage as a spectator sport reminds us of Zen's core teaching: get off the sidelines and jump in! She reminds me of my own experience as a sixteen-year-old. I arrived at the beach one morning to find six adults—blind donkeys, all—yelling out instructions, from the safety of the shore, to their own eight-year-old boy who was swimming and had been frozen with fright by the sudden ferocity of the ocean waves. I loved the ocean; I trusted its unpredictable rhythm with my own body. I did not trust the hand-wringing family, whose spoken advice separated them from actual contact. I suspected the same was true for our bobbing boy—adrift and alone, parental words floating and sinking on the ocean's surface. No comfort there. Fed up with the recycled wisdom of adults, I jumped into the wavy water and swam to him. My presence was all he needed to remember: he too could swim. The ocean's movement carried us back to land.

Dismissing the monks' foolishness, Miaoxin expressed her willingness to enter the ocean of this moment with its thrilling waves and its unknown outcome. In the wild water with them, she bellowed: "Come forth. The wind does not move; the banner does not move; the mind does not move!" The challenge hung in mid-movement: What moves? When we let go of our great knowing, our secure understanding of how Zen works, how life works, what moves? Are we brave enough to enter fully without knowing what will happen?

Miaoxin's skill led the seventeen monks to full presence and unknowing—preconditions to Zen enlightenment. Today, as Western Zen women, we are all Miaoxin. We have entered an originally male wisdom tradition. Knocked about by waves of uncertainty, we must find a way to express our wisdom bravely and boldly in our own words. The truth for Miaoxin is our truth: rehashing words from the male or female Zen ancestors won't do. We too can swim, we too can speak, we too can come forth. We need to fully inhabit our own teaching moment and shine our own surprising light.

So, I, Myoan Grace, say to Miaoxin, her successors, and all: "It isn't that the wind doesn't move; it isn't that the banner doesn't move; it isn't that the mind doesn't move. What moves me?"

How do you meet the ancient teachings in a way that keeps
them alive? What is required to tend a guesthouse?
And is it so bad to be a blind donkey?

I Saw You Fall Down So I'm Helping

The Path of Practice

83. Lingzhao's Helping

NE DAY, Layman Pang and his daughter, Lingzhao, were out selling bamboo baskets. Coming down off a bridge, the Layman stumbled and fell. When Lingzhao saw this, she ran to her father's side and threw herself to the ground.

"What are you doing?" cried the Layman.

"I saw you fall so I'm helping," replied Lingzhao.

"Luckily no one was looking," remarked the Layman.

JOAN SUTHERLAND'S REFLECTION

The Pang family has been the embodiment of enlightened house-holder life in China since the eighth century: living modestly, deeply committed to the Way and each other, full of humor and insight, unabashedly eccentric. During their lifetimes, a revolution in Chan was underway, and awakening was now understood as something that happens in relationship, in encounters and conversations. The earliest koans are records of such encounters, and the ones involving the Pangs show that deep realization is just as possible in domesticity as in monastic life, for women as for men.

Layman Pang renounced his wealth to live simply, befriending some of the greatest Chan teachers of his day. Mrs. Pang seems to have been simultaneously no-nonsense and profoundly connected to the mysterious. About their son we know little except that he worked in the fields, growing the family's food. For many, the most luminous member of the family is the daughter, Lingzhao, whose name means "spirit shining."

Lingzhao and her father were inseparable, supporting the family by making and selling bamboo utensils; later she accompanied him on his pilgrimages. Once when the Layman tripped, Lingzhao threw herself to the ground next to him. She explained herself with the immortal words, "I saw you fall so I'm helping."

Lingzhao's action obliterates the idea that there is a helper and a helped. Compassion isn't a commodity we deliver but a commitment, according to Chan, to help liberate the intimacy already inherent in any situation. "What is most intimate?" the koans suggest that we ask. Usually the most intimate response to another's difficulty begins with the willingness not to flee. Fleeing can take the form of abandoning the situation, and it can also mean escaping into "helping," into a whole constellation of ideas about what ought to happen. Intimacy is being willing to stay and accompany and listen, to be vulnerable and surprised and flexible. It's a willingness to fall with someone else, and see what becomes possible when we do.

Layman Pang's final remark does not mean that he's worried about some third person judging the event; the one who fortunately isn't looking is ourselves—that is, our inner tendency to monitor and pass judgment, distancing us from our interactions even as they're happening. How free it is when we aren't keeping score, how potentially generous a life lived with no one looking!

At another level, Lingzhao's gesture suggests that we are all falling together, lifetime after lifetime, through the universe. Right now we are falling through this world, which holds out an invitation to us: come see what life is like here. We find that it's made of flame and water, wind and earth, sorrow and beauty, love and fear, light and dark, and everything in between. As we fall, if we pick and choose, instead of accepting all of life as it offers itself, we're in some way refusing the invitation. If we say to life in this world, "I'll take your sunsets but leave your diseases," we're being stingy in a way that hurts ourselves most of all. In "Lingzhao's Shining Grasses" (page 271 of this book),

Lingzhao says that as we walk (or fall) the Way, the heart-mind of the ancestors—which is another way of saying the deepest reality—is in *every* blade of grass, and they all hold us up.

When Lingzhao throws herself down, her kindness is clear and unhesitating, completely without self-concern. It's also funny. Those are the qualities of her enlightenment. This is what it looks like when all the energy bound up in the small story we're constantly telling ourselves, in all our reactions and opinions and judgments, has been liberated into awakening. It's a free place, and Lingzhao lived there to the end. She, like others in the old stories, chose the time of her death: in the koan "Lingzhao Goes First" (page 185 of this book), she sat down, folded her hands, and disappeared. The Japanese poet Ryoan Keigo wrote that her basket had completely poured out its contents, and she shot out of life like an arrow.

Koans employ the language of art and myth to express the things that matter most in life. If you want to understand compassion, for instance, they offer no definitions. But they invite us to experience for ourselves what compassion feels like through completely absorbing and being absorbed by the koan. Over time the koans start falling down next to each other, illuminating each other, like Lingzhao, to help.

When someone you love is hurt, you want to help him or her. How do you find the appropriate response? How can anyone be helped? And is it possible to join another in suffering?

84. Faxiang's Recognition

CHINA, FIFTH CENTURY ···

HE NUN Faxiang often shared her clothing and food, giving the best to the nun Huisu. The other nuns admonished Faxiang, saying, "The nun Huisu is uncultivated and inarticulate. When she wanted to study meditation, no one would give her instruction because she is the worst of idiots. Why don't you sow the seeds of generosity in a more spiritually worthy field?"

Faxiang responded, "One would have to be a saint to know the spiritual accomplishments of the recipient of donations. I'm a very ordinary person, so I would rather do it this way."

Later, Huisu sponsored a seven-day meditation retreat with the community. On the third night, when the others arose from meditation, she did not get up, remaining in a deep meditation state until the end of the retreat. It was only then that the other nuns saw Huisu's extraordinary abilities, and for the first time they understood Faxiang's insight.

MISHA SHUNGEN MERRILL'S REFLECTION

Faxiang's story is everyone's story: How do we sincerely practice the *paramita*, or perfection, of generosity without falling into dualistic thinking? Our usual understanding of generosity is that there is one who gives things—materials, time, energy—and one who receives them. In the creation of "giver" and "receiver," however, we are already lost in delusion, misunderstanding the fundamental nature of generosity—ending separation between self and other.

At the beginning of the story, Faxiang is introduced as a generous practitioner, one who is willing to give her best offerings to the nun Huisu, whom the other nuns despise. They are perplexed by Faxiang's attitude and seem to think that generosity is meant only for the worthy.

Faxiang's response shows us the true quality of her practice. She believes that only a saint—someone she is not—could discern the depth of another's spiritual life. She understands that because ordinary people can never know another completely, they cannot judge another's worthiness.

Faxiang chooses to sow her "seeds of generosity" in what others consider an unworthy field. Because she is not attached to any outcome or preconceived ideas of Huisu's worth, Faxiang devotes herself to the simple act of pure giving. All too often I am like the other nuns, wanting to sow my seeds in the most fertile soil, where they will have the best chance of flourishing, where the risk factor is low and the possibility of appearing successful is high indeed! But if, like Faxiang, I am willing to sow my seeds anywhere without worrying about the outcome, I might be gratified by unexpected beneficial results. Faxiang's true generosity is not in the giving of things but in her willingness to look deeply and see Huisu for who she *really* is. She may be uncultivated, inarticulate, or even "the worst of idiots," but Faxiang knows that she is fundamentally a buddha, inherently perfect.

How often do we feel mistakenly judged, the victim of others' prejudices or baseless assumptions? How many Huisus have we ignored in the elevator or passed by on a street because of some misguided miserliness?

Many years ago I attended the Zen ordination of a friend, and during the reception afterward, I noticed a commotion around a sangha member who was lying ill on a sofa. Although we had only met that afternoon, I stepped forward to offer assistance, and to this day I don't know exactly what happened between us. As our eyes met, our hearts completely opened to each other. I saw her again a year later, and when I heard that her partner was ordaining, I asked if she too planned to ordain. She admitted that she would like nothing better but that her teacher had made it clear that she was not "monk material"—apparently for some of the same reasons that the nuns judged Huisu. This woman was not well-educated, and she had severe physical disabilities and a tendency to play the class clown, effectively hiding her inner depths. Unless you looked closely it was hard to see her passion for the Dharma. I decided to take a chance and told her that if she was serious and worked closely with me, I would ordain her.

More than ten years have passed since her ordination, during which time she has helped to form and co-lead another sangha and given hours of support as a volunteer hospice worker. Hundreds of people have benefited from her generosity, all stemming from that moment when we truly saw each other, buddha to buddha.

Henry David Thoreau wrote in *Walden*: "Nature and human life are as various as our several constitutions. Who shall say what prospect life offers to another? Could a greater miracle take place than for us to look through each other's eyes for an instant?" A miracle indeed! In looking through another's eyes, or standing in another's shoes—even for a moment—our entire view of self and other could drop away.

Faxiang truly *saw* Huisu when all others were blind to her. In doing so, she made it possible for Huisu to express her own generous buddha nature—something the other nuns could only see much later when Huisu showed her extraordinary abilities during a retreat. Faxiang shows us that it is possible to let go of our ideas of giver and receiver, of worthy and unworthy, of self and other. She knows that ultimately there is no giver, no receiver, just the gift—and that is the greatest gift of all.

Are there ways to judge the merit or power of another's spiritual practice? In emergency medical situations, doctors have to apply the principle of triage in deciding whom to help. How would you apply triage to the spiritual realm?

85. Sujata's Offering

SUJATA was the beautiful daughter of a landowner, and she prayed to the spirit of a banyan tree for a good husband and son. Her wish was granted, and every year, in gratitude, she made an offering of sweet, thick milk-rice at the foot of the tree.

Meanwhile, after six years of severe austerities, Siddhartha was close to death from starvation. One day he sat down in meditation beneath Sujata's banyan tree. That same day Sujata dreamed that she should make her annual offering. She sent her servant to prepare the place for the offering, and the servant ran back, crying, "A god is sitting under the tree!"

So Sujata made up the milk-rice in a golden bowl and carried it to the tree with her own hands. She offered it to Siddhartha, saying, "Just as my wish has been fulfilled, so may yours be granted."

He ate the milk-rice with gratitude, and it was the finest food he had eaten in many months. Then he cast the golden bowl into the river, saying, "If I am to fully awaken, may this bowl float upstream." The bowl floated upstream. Later that day, renewed by Sujata's offering, he sat down, determined to awaken, and his wish was granted.

Sujata and her son later became disciples of the Buddha and members of the sangha.

VIMALASARA'S, AKA VALERIE MASON-JOHN'S, REFLECTION

On a mythic level this story is so potent. It gives me goose bumps every time I think about the Buddha being offered milk-rice by a woman just before his enlightenment. Whether it was reality or myth, it reminds me of the Metta Sutta, the Buddha's words on kindness.

> Even as a mother protects with her life,
> her child, her only child,
> so with a boundless heart
> should one cherish all living beings.

The Buddha recognized the significance of women, and in this story one cannot help but think of the milk-rice as a metaphor for the breast milk that a mother gives to her newborn. Many centuries ago Siddhartha drank milk-rice from a woman and was reborn as a buddha; without breast milk or a suitable alternative a newborn—or indeed a reborn—would not survive.

Sujata demonstrates sympathetic joy, rooted in generosity. Upon seeing the Buddha she wishes for his good fortune just as she recognizes her own good fortune and the fulfillment of her dearest wishes. It's not surprising that she later became one of the Buddha's disciples, since generosity opens the doorway to practice and awakening.

I was raised in an orphanage run by Christians. The act of giving and receiving was at the heart of this charity. People donated so much to us orphans, and we in turn were taught to give. I learned that true generosity wasn't about just giving; it was also the act of receiving.

I remember being on a retreat, years later, and looking around and seeing no visible reflection of myself. Every other woman who was on the retreat was white. I said to myself, "Why I am here?" At that point I momentary let go of my attachment to my black self. In that moment I could see clearly that I was there because I was surrounded by people who had faith and who practiced generosity. This reflection resonated to the core of me. I was brought up by people who had let go of their worldly belongings to tend to the work of the Lord. Of course some had merely blind faith, but as a child I knew which adults had placed their hearts upon true spiritual values, such as generosity.

> If people knew, as I know, the results of giving and sharing, they would not eat a meal without sharing it, nor would they allow the taint of stinginess or meanness to overtake their minds.
>
> —The Buddha, Ittivutakkha 26

Sujata managed to remember every year to give thanks for the fulfillment of her prayers. She reminds me that I need to deepen my practice of gratitude and generosity. I need to give thanks for the many prayers that have been answered throughout my forty-nine years.

Sujata's story and actions are so simple and powerful, I wonder why so many women doubt themselves on the path. I was fortunate enough to be shaped by a feminist culture from the age of twenty. Although feminism was not enough to bring me to spiritual awakening, it certainly pointed me in the direction of Buddhism. Feminism taught me to love myself as a woman. It taught me that everything a man could do, I could do, and that I was not inferior or subordinate to men.

Eight years later I found Buddhism. I was surprised at how many women in my spiritual community lacked self-confidence. But here we have Sujata, thousands of years ago, who would have been under pressure to stay at home and nurture her family. But still she had the confidence to bless the Buddha and later join the sangha.

Women living in the West need to have this confidence in their own practice. We need to remember that the Buddha said, "All beings, male and female, have the potential for Buddha-hood." It's these words that inspire me to continue placing the teachings of the Buddha at the center of my life. I can see so clearly how I have moved closer to awakening. And I believe that if I continue to practice it is possible to gain insight in this lifetime.

Siddhartha's ideas about asceticism nearly killed him. Have you
held opinions about spiritual practice that got you into trouble?
Sujata did not know who Siddhartha was. If we express
gratitude toward the wrong person, does it matter?
What's the difference between a gift and an offering?

86. Laywoman Pang's Merit

 NE DAY Laywoman Pang went into the Deer Gate Temple and made an offering of food. The temple priest asked her on whose behalf she made the offering, so that he could dedicate its merit.

She took her comb and stuck it in the back of her hair. "Dedication of merit is complete," she said, and walked out.

AMY HOLLOWELL'S REFLECTION

This is one of the few traditional Zen stories in which the central character is not only a layperson but also a woman, a wife, and a mother. For these reasons alone, Laywoman Pang (or Mrs. Pang, as she is called in another translation) serves as an inspiration for many of us contemporary Zen women in the West. Add to that the fact that she has hair so long that it requires the use of a comb to hold it up (common for Chinese women in her day) and she might rise to quasi-heroine status for many female lay practitioners today, who may be confronted with a traditional, monastic-inspired Zen model in which an androgynous appearance is encouraged. I can almost hear the meditation hall ringing with a sisterly chorus of "You go girl!"

But of course there is more to this tale than gender issues, grooming techniques, and social and marital status. What matters here is that through these "ordinary" aspects of life, Laywoman Pang freely manifests a profound realization of the true nature of being. In the early days of my Zen practice, just as my partner and I were hoping to move into the small lay community that our Zen teacher was founding, I became pregnant with my second child. My joy was tempered by a fear that, with not one but now two children, our plan was most certainly doomed. But when I expressed this fear to my teacher, she didn't miss a beat: "Of course you can still come!" she exclaimed. "It will help us all to be creative." I wept sweet tears of gratitude. The essential point, I came to realize, was not lay or monk, man or woman, parent or not parent, but rather how we each respond here and now to our own particular situation.

This is exactly what makes the stories of Laywoman Pang and her husband, Layman Pang, a basket-seller in eighth-century China, so compelling in the West today. The Pangs and their two children devoted themselves to awakening and living an enlightened life not by setting themselves apart from others—taking monastic, priestly, or other special vows—but by fully engaging with the everyday stuff of their most "ordinary" lives. Their "chopping wood, carrying water" is our "changing diapers, paying bills."

So here comes Laywoman Pang, stopping by a temple to offer food. The priest inquires about the donation so that he can make the traditional dedication of merit, which involves posting a record of the gift with the donor's name, the date, and the name of the person for whom the gift was made. Merit? Dedication? Laywoman Pang, it seems, doesn't share the priest's views on the matter. Her entire life is an offering, and she therefore replies spontaneously, sharing with the priest her no-view: she doesn't discriminate when responding to the needs of all beings. Her gift to the temple is truly nothing special and she seeks not even a wink of recognition in return. Her action reflects the experience that she is not separate from others and that, as Gertrude Stein might have said, a comb is a comb is a comb, as perfectly sacred as every single being and thing.

Steeped in the boundless, creative heart of being, Laywoman Pang has no time for formalities, no space for fixed ideas about herself or others. You have hair? Here's a comb. You have two children? Love and care for them. It's raining? Here's an umbrella. She is adept at the wild home economics to which I aspire, simply functioning freely and compassionately with whatever is at hand, at home wherever she is.

In another story, rather than putting her hair up, Laywoman Pang lets it down. She comes into a temple during mealtime and the gate-keeper tells her to go back outside. In response, she removes the comb from her hair and sweeps up her footprints with her long hair—being completely herself, she leaves no traces of "her self." Departing, she says, "I've gone back."

Like Laywoman Pang, in those moments when I am able to let my hair down, when I hold nothing back, offering myself fully to washing the lunch dishes, working with disgruntled colleagues or meeting a homeless person in the street, I neither give nor receive, neither come nor go, I am neither early nor late, right or wrong, worthy of merit or not. Hair or no hair, not a single one is out of place.

Who benefits from your generosity? What are priests for?

87. Punna's Offering

P UNNA WAS a poor servant. One day she made a cake for herself of powdered rice-bits. Then she saw the Buddha on the road, bowed reverentially, and said, "Your Reverence, this cake is made mainly of broken rice-bits and has neither oil nor flour in it; it may not be sweet, but if you would be so kind as to accept it, you will enable me to obtain the sweets of nirvana."

The Buddha accepted the offering of the cake of broken rice-bits.

Punna said, "Your Reverence, just as this cake, when I offered it to you, became flavorful and worthy of you, so may I, who am a slave to others but have now come to you, be freed from the enslavement of desire."

"May it be so," responded the Buddha, and he went on to preach a sermon. At the end of the sermon, Punna obtained the divine cake of the stream enterer.

ADRIANNE ROSS'S REFLECTION

Reading this ancient story, I find the attitudes of both Punna and the Buddha deeply inspiring. Punna is open, direct, and unburdened by herself, despite being burdened by enslavement. I love her straightforward trust of her own value. In offering the simple cake, she is offering herself, exactly as she is, without apology, shame, or embarrassment. She seems to sense that if he can accept her rice cake, he is accepting the possibility for her to awaken, to taste the "sweets of nirvana." And the Buddha's acceptance of her offering acknowledges her inherent worth, regardless of her gender and class.

This empowers her to go further and take the next step, speaking aloud of her resolve to be free. Punna knows directly the painful bondage of slavery, but she does not ask to be free from enslavement to others. Instead she has the powerful intention to be free from the inner enslavement of desire.

As the Buddha responds, "may it be so," I think he is acknowledging the purity and determination of her wish to be free and also that it is absolutely possible for her—and thus for each one of us, right now—to enter the stream of awakening. The first stage of opening into the flow of awakening is termed "stream entry." One's Dharma eye opens to selfless true nature, rendering an unshakable conviction in the Dharma and the path to complete awakening. Once she has entered the stream, Punna is assured of following the flow to fulfill her heart's wish: complete freedom from desire, aversion, and ignorance.

I am so moved by Punna's ability to trust and her courage to not hold back: to trust that all she is, just as she is, is enough. I, and so many women I meet, struggle with trying to "get it right" and perfect ourselves. Practice can become a project rather than a simple offering. Punna is unburdened by painful comparisons; she has both humility and self-respect. So much of my life and practice has been about trying to be good enough—trapped in comparing, judging, and fixing. Each time I believe that I'm not enough—as a physician, teacher, mother, partner, or friend—I reinforce the sense that it's impossible to be free just as I am.

Whenever I identify with inadequacy I hold back. I can actually feel the contraction. I can feel my energy becoming blocked by "I can't" and "I'm not enough." I limit myself by my views, and my views of others limit them.

I am a physician. A man with multiple illnesses used to come to my clinic every week, and I would get caught in my desire to fix his many problems, and in my own inadequacy. One day as he was sitting in front of me, complaining bitterly, I felt myself contract into irritation and hopelessness—but then I really looked at him. I said "Life is so painful for you, isn't it? It must be really hard not to give up," and in the next moments of silence, our roles fell away. In the space where I was neither limiting myself with views of my inadequacy nor limiting him with my views of "difficult person," a warmth and creativity emerged from which we both saw possibilities for healing.

The Buddha and Punna exchanged gifts. She surrendered herself just as she was, with dignity, humility, and respect. The Buddha accepted her material offering completely and then conferred his confidence that the kind of freedom she really wanted would come about. Rarely do we give ourselves or each other the gift of being fully received and seen just as we are. Some years ago, in the midst of a very difficult time in my life and practice, a wise teacher gave me the blessing of fully receiving me and seeing me just as I was. Because I was so completely received, right in the midst of my own fear, hurt, and judgment, I felt the safety to let go, a miracle that allowed a deep understanding, compassion, and freedom to arise.

Punna's story inspires me as a practitioner and teacher to see the buddha nature in everyone I meet, no matter what their circumstances, and to be able to acknowledge that they too can awaken. May we all see and acknowledge the potential for awakening in each other and together make the commitment to help each other enter the stream, as the Buddha did for Punna that day, long ago.

What does it mean to give a gift that is made out of broken things you have patched together? Can the value of gifts be measured?

88. Khujjuttara Teaches the Dharma

KHUJJUTTARA was a slave woman in the palace of Queen Samavati. Every day the queen gave her eight coins to buy flowers to decorate the palace, but Khujjuttara would only use four of them for flowers and would keep the others for herself. One day, at the place where she bought the flowers, she happened to hear the Buddha give a discourse. His teachings penetrated her heart and she became a stream enterer, the first stage of awakening. Full of joy, she spent all the money she had saved and filled the palace with flowers. The queen asked Khujjuttara why there were so many flowers that day, and Khujjuttara told her of hearing the Buddha speak. Then she preached to Samavati and to all her woman attendants, and every single one was converted.

Queen Samavati, as the king's consort, could not leave the palace, so she asked Khujjuttara to go on her behalf to hear the teachings of the Buddha. Khujjuttara had an outstanding memory and she could repeat everything she heard. She went every day to the monastery and every day she would return to the palace and repeat the Buddha's discourses to the queen and her attendants.

Khujjuttara became renowned for her knowledge of the Buddhist canon and for her ability to preach the Dharma.

JEAN LA VALLEY'S REFLECTION

As I studied this story, I was touched by its practice-inspiring elements. I also worked with its "shadow" teachings—those elements of the story that initially irritated or confused me.

Queen Samavati and the slave Khujjuttara have different privileges and constraints. The queen has material well-being and position, but she cannot leave the palace. Khujjuttara is a slave, but she has the freedom to leave and to hear the Dharma. It is often hard to see the privileges and appreciate the constraints in our own lives. It can be even harder to understand when to live wisely within those constraints and when to attempt to move beyond them.

I am a woman who feels both blessed and buried by professional and familial caregiving duties. I have heard myself waxing rhapsodic about what a privilege it is to be closely connected to other people's lives and then, on another day, bemoaning the very same thing. In reading this story, I am reminded to move beyond my habitual rhapsody and my habitual bemoaning, to more deeply experience and learn from the role of caregiving within my community. I am also reminded to reexamine *how* I perceive the burdens and constraints of caregiving. In my situation I sometimes feel I have limited options, but this story suggests otherwise. A slave heard the Buddha teach and was enlightened. A queen heard a slave teach and was enlightened. Freedom can happen in any circumstance.

In this story, women sustain each other in a deep and dharmic way. There are no men here, as supports or foils or impediments. It seems likely that affairs of the world are being taken care of in other parts of the palace by the males of the governing class. The women create and experience a different world.

I recently co-led a weekend women's retreat with women from both the Zen and Vipassana traditions. We sat in silence, explored koans together, and shared our practice. Later, several of us met to review what had happened and how the retreat had affected us. One woman said, "During that whole weekend, I felt like twenty-seven other women 'had my back.' I felt like my practice was fearless. I had no idea that I had been practicing in fear until I felt the fear drop away, until I had the feeling of safety that came from being with women." This is a poignant reminder of the power of women practicing together and helping one another.

So there is inspiration and support in this koan. And then, for me, there is a shadow, an uneasiness, an irritation. I was bothered by ". . . and kept the others for herself." Rationally I understand that Khujjuttara wasn't awakened yet, nor had she heard the teachings; she was just like us. Until we are fully enlightened, we will have taints of one sort or another. And still, "knowing" all this, I was disturbed that Khujjuttara was stealing. So I paid attention and lived with this irritation.

Paying attention to reactions within myself that I don't understand and don't like is my favorite part of koan study. So I stayed with my reactivity. I saw how often I judge myself and others for unskillful behavior and how often that initial judgment has led to the thought, "I/they are *far* from enlightened." I saw how subtly that judgment takes me out of the present moment and closes me off to being open to freedom. Yes, we hear and practice both because of and in spite of taints. And being open in this very moment, we may find it possible to release our taints and become as full of joy as Khujjuttara.

The guideline I use when practicing with koans is this: "These stories are not about gaining anything. They are about illumination. They are not about rearranging the furniture in the room; they are about turning the light on in the room so you can see what's there." This story helps me to see what is in my own room—both light and shadow.

How can a limitation become exactly your liberation?
After the queen asked her to return to the Buddha,
did Khujjuttara go as a slave or a free person?

89. The Old Woman's Miraculous Powers

MAGU, NANQUAN, and another monk were on pilgrimage. Along the way they met a woman who had a teashop. The woman prepared a pot of tea and brought three cups. She said to them, "Oh monks, let those of you with miraculous powers drink tea."

The three looked at each other and the woman said, "Watch this decrepit old woman show her own miraculous powers." Then she picked up the cups, poured the tea, and went out.

MARY GRACE ORR'S REFLECTION

One can imagine the scene: three monks wait for the serving of their tea. They are tired, and thirsty, and also accustomed to receiving offerings. But then the woman who is serving them gives them a surprising challenge: "Let those of you with miraculous powers drink the tea." Silence follows. The monks look at each other. What do I do now? Will the other monks claim powers? One is not supposed to, as a monk. But we can imagine that they would want to claim the powers, and certainly they would want to drink the tea. I can even imagine the old woman chuckling a little at their dismay. And then she offers her teaching and shows her miraculous powers: she simply pours the tea.

Our minds are always leaning out into the future, into the hope of being something more, something special. Someday, we hope, we will not be ordinary. In the world of meditation retreats, students can get quite lost seeking remarkable mind states, or holding on to altered states when they do appear, or wanting to be enlightened, or to be special in some way. I remember with considerable embarrassment an early retreat interview of my own, when I described many strange images that were arising during meditation. I asked the teacher if I might be having past life memories—they were so exotic, so interesting! "No," she said, "I think you're just sleepy." Somehow I felt as though I had failed.

Mindfulness is a practice of being present with the truth of this moment. When we take the time to do this, we see that every moment is deeply miraculous. Recently I saw a video of the earth turning below the space station. Clouds, continents, and oceans in white, green, brown, and blue passed below; it is astounding to be here on this planet, surrounded by stars and galaxies, hanging in the vastness of space.

At some retreats I teach, I occasionally find clusters of meditation students gathered around a small hole in the ground, gazing raptly. I join them for a bit, to discover a small, whiskered nose and bright eyes that appear now and then at the hole, take one look, and vanish. The students, in the heart of their long, silent retreat, watch for long, long minutes. A gopher watching meditators, meditators watching a gopher: how much more miraculous do we want?

"Only a few people are awake and they live in a state of constant amazement," said Patricia in the movie *Joe Versus the Volcano*. The wise old woman of our story never saw that movie, but she seems to have known that within the very ordinary lies the miraculous. She understood that waking up to the present is actually the miracle. I notice that she is old, and I am reminded that the closer we get to our own dying, the more amazed we may be at being here at all.

You can pour tea! It is miraculous. The entire universe is present in this act. The sun, the rain, and the earth are in the tea leaves, in the fuel for the fire, in the muscles and neurons and blood cells involved in pouring. And on a grander scale, we know that all elements of our earth are derived from a supernova long, long ago.

There are many stories of people with miraculous powers who

can walk through walls, walk on water, and travel through time. But perhaps as we practice, we come to appreciate more and more the readily available miracles. And perhaps we even come to a point at which we can walk through the walls of our own minds. Maybe our hearts can become so vast that we can hold with kindness even those who are difficult for us. Maybe we can see clearly what is true in our lives and not have to hide from it. And this might be enough.

So that is the last thing: this old woman knew that her powers were enough, just as they were, in that very moment. No leaning out for the next thing, the better thing, the more powerful thing, the more interesting thing. She didn't even stick around to see or to hear the results of her teaching. She knew what was miraculous, and she did it. It was enough.

Just this. A cup of tea. Delicious! I hope the monks received this teaching—and that they remembered to say "thank you!"

How incredible that we are alive at all! How many times today have you considered this? What miracles have you performed today?

90. Bhikkhuni Kabilsingh Keeps the Precepts

THAILAND, TWENTIETH CENTURY ···

ENERABLE BHIKKHUNI Voramai Kabilsingh was the first Thai woman to receive full ordination as a bhikkhuni. As is required in bhikkhuni ordinations, she took three hundred and eleven precepts. A young man who was visiting her asked, "How can you keep all three hundred and eleven precepts?"

She answered, "I keep only one precept."

The young man, surprised, asked, "What is that?"

She replied, "I just watch my mind."

DHAMMANANDA'S REFLECTION

Thailand has been a unified country since the thirteenth century. Throughout its seven-hundred-year history, the community of monastics has only included male monks. This has been true despite the fact that the Buddha established the fourfold sangha: *bhikkhus* (monks), *bhikkhunis* (female monks), laymen, and laywomen, all of whom share the responsibility of upholding and practicing the Buddha's teachings.

But the full ordination of women never arrived in Thailand. According to the monastic rules, a woman who seeks ordination must be ordained by both bhikkhunis and bhikkhus, and because the requisite number of bhikkhunis from India never came to Thailand, Thailand did not have its own bhikkhuni sangha.

My mother, Venerable Bhikkhuni Voramai Kabilsingh, was the first Thai woman to receive full ordination and to take the three hundred

315

and eleven precepts of a bhikkhuni. She went to Taiwan in 1971 and received ordination from bhikkhus and bhikkhunis there. In Thailand, people believe that taking eight or ten precepts is better than taking five precepts, and, of course, observing two hundred and twenty-seven precepts, as a monk does, is even better. But people had never seen a bhikkhuni who observed three hundred and eleven precepts, so this initially caused much dismay and confusion.

In this story, Venerable Kabilsingh simply said that she takes only one precept: to watch her mind. The many precepts are ways of controlling the actions of body and speech, but physical and verbal actions are expressions of the mind. Once the mind is well controlled, all other expressions are purified. All the exercises of meditation are various ways to understand the nature of mind and to see things as they really are. This has always been the way of Buddhist practice. The well-known masters in the past practiced watching and training the mind; simply watching the mind allows one to see the nature of mind and leads to awakening, nirvana.

There is an old story about a monk who studied the texts and had great knowledge but did not practice. The monk became concerned that it was about time to start practicing, but he couldn't find anyone to guide him, as everyone thought he must already have so much wisdom. Eventually he was so desperate that he went into the forest and started crying. A nearby tree goddess came out and sat with him, also crying. He asked her why she was crying, and she said she was simply following what the monk did, since she assumed that it must lead to enlightenment. The monk was even further distressed.

Finally he came to a seven-year-old novice who was enlightened. The novice tested him by asking him to jump into the well nearby, as proof that he had really given up pride in his great accumulation of knowledge. He jumped into the well, and after he got out, the novice told him a story about how to catch a certain kind of lizard that makes three sounds—the sounds of greed, anger, and delusion—and lives in a place with six entrances. If a person closes five entrances and watches the sixth, he will be able to capture the lizard. The monk knew right away that he needed to close the five doors of the senses—eyes, ears, nose, tongue, and touch—and simply watch the sixth door, the mind.

Watching the mind, therefore, has always been the most important practice, as Venerable Bhikkhuni Kabilsingh explained. All the other precepts flow from this one.

But my mother also lived by the precepts. After she was ordained as a bhikkhuni, she had her own tiny room, and apart from her low bed there was hardly any space. Upon my return to Thailand from Canada, when I was twenty-eight, I slept next to her bed for the first two nights, happy to be close to her again. But on the third night, when I started to spread the bedding on the floor, she asked me to go back to my room. I was hurt. She explained that in the *vinaya*, the monastic code, a bhikkhuni cannot spend more than three nights with a laywoman. That is the rule, and that was what my mother was following.

When she was ninety-four she called me to announce that she wanted to leave her body. At that time I was only a *samaneri*, a novice bhikkhuni, so I told her, jokingly, that she could not leave while I was still a samaneri. She chose to pass away the next year, in 2003, just after my full ordination as a bhikkhuni.

How do you roll all good intentions into one? If there is only one precept, what is the point of all the others? If you were to watch your mind all the time, would you always behave well?

91. Uppalavana and the Precepts

INDIA, SIXTH CENTURY BCE
(REINTERPRETED BY EIHEI DOGEN,
JAPAN, THIRTEENTH CENTURY) ·······························

HE NUN Uppalavana was a disciple of the Buddha. She visited the home of some noble young women and encouraged them to become nuns. They responded, "We are young and beautiful and full of life. It would be hard for us to keep the precepts."

Uppalavana replied, "If you break the precepts, you break the precepts. First, leave the household and become nuns."

The women said to her, "But if we break the precepts, we will fall into hell. Why would you have us do that?"

Uppalavana said, "Go ahead and fall into hell."

The women all laughed and said, "Why would you suggest such a thing?"

She replied, "In a former life I was a prostitute and entertainer. One day I dressed myself in nun's robes in front of my customers, just as a joke, and because of this, in my next life I became a nun and took the precepts. But even though I was a nun, I was arrogant and broke the precepts, and as a consequence I fell into hell and its sufferings.

"Later, in this current life, I met Shakyamuni Buddha, ordained, developed great meditative powers, and became an arahant. In this way I learned that you can attain the fruit of the way even if you break a precept and fall into hell. The merit of receiving the precepts makes awakening possible, but if you never receive the precepts and do unwholesome things, you will never attain the Way."

THUBTEN CHODRON'S REFLECTION

As one of the great senior nuns at the time of the Buddha, Uppalavana was specifically praised by the Buddha as being the nun foremost in the six super-knowledges—psychic powers such as clairvoyance—possessed only by liberated beings. Uppalavana was no ordinary practitioner but someone whose life was dedicated to the Dharma and to benefiting others.

Her first exchange with the young women in the koan reminds me of conversations I've had with women (and men) who have expressed interest in becoming monastics but recoil when I encourage them, saying, "But I can't possibly keep the precepts! It's too hard!" Their negative self-image stops them from following the path to awakening.

While it may sound strange for Uppalavana to nonchalantly say, "If you break the precepts, you break the precepts," as if it were no big deal, she is in fact encouraging these women to go beyond their perfectionist tendencies and self-deprecation and give it a try. "Stop getting in your own way by telling yourself you're incapable of doing something that you admire. Have some confidence that you can realize your beautiful Buddha potential."

She knows they are capable of attaining awakening, and to prove this, she recounts her own experience in a previous life as a prostitute. In that life, as a joke, she put on monastic robes. Perhaps she seductively lowered the robes to reveal her breasts or raised them to reveal her legs, as if to say, "What fools these nuns are! Who in their right mind would want to be celibate and give up sensual pleasure?" But the symbol of the monastic robes touched something deeper in her, planting a seed so that in her future rebirth she could become a nun. Still, she was arrogant and defiant, broke the precepts, and fell into hell.

But hell is not an eternal state. When that karma was exhausted, Uppalavana was born once again as a human being; she underwent great suffering in her family life that is not recounted in this koan, and the whole time, despite her misery—much of which centered around sex, husbands, and children—the seed of liberation was being fertilized in her.

At last, Uppalavana became a monastic. Overcoming her fear and despondency, she practiced the path, and by taming her mind through keeping the precepts, she attained liberation. Had she never given this a try, she never would have become an awakened being.

When I speak to those with monastic aspirations who hesitate, I remind them that we take precepts because we are *not* capable of keeping them perfectly. If we were, we would not need to take them. If we never challenge ourselves—falling down in the process—we will not be able to transform our body, speech, and mind into those of a liberated being.

Uppalavana's story could equally apply to people who choose to remain householders and who keep the five lay precepts: to abandon killing, stealing, unwise or unkind sexual behavior, lying, and intoxicants. However, Uppalavana, like the Buddha himself, was a monastic. There is something precious about monastic life which is hard to describe in this day and age when people think that choosing to be celibate is strange. Having been a monastic for thirty-five years, I cherish the opportunity to hold precepts and live as a renunciate. Even though I have not kept my precepts perfectly, they support me on the path, subduing the mind and opening the heart.

Like the young women in the koan, I initially lacked confidence in my ability to keep the precepts. I tried following the example of the Tibetan nuns, being quiet, shy, and self-effacing, but it didn't work. I was a university-educated woman with a career, schooled in expressing my ideas. On the other hand, I was arrogant and full of attachment and anger; my physical, verbal, and mental actions definitely needed to be subdued. What held me steady in the Dharma despite the waves of my emotions and preconceptions was the knowledge that my mind is the creator of my happiness and suffering. There was nothing else to do but practice the Dharma—to transform my mind. Fortunately I had excellent spiritual mentors who guided me and whose instructions I had enough good sense to follow.

I am eternally grateful to the Buddha for initiating the monastic sangha and for the centuries of bhikshunis who have practiced diligently. Due to their kindness, the priceless option of becoming a monastic still exists today.

A courtesan puts on a Buddhist robe and is thereby reborn as a nun. How could a robe change a life? How can you vow to live by the precepts even though you know you'll break them?

92. Dipa Ma and the Thief

INDIA / UNITED STATES, TWENTIETH CENTURY ·····························

 STUDENT OF Dipa Ma had his radio stolen from his car, something that had happened to him several times before. When he told Dipa Ma, she burst out laughing.

"What's so funny?" the student asked.

Dipa Ma answered, "You must have been a thief in a former lifetime. How many more times do you think you will need to have your radio stolen? What did you do? What was your reaction when the car was broken into?"

The student replied, "I was really angry because it's happened so many times."

She looked at him in amazement. "You mean you didn't even think about the man who took your radio—how sad his life must be?"

She closed her eyes and started chanting quietly to herself, offering metta for the thief.

HEATHER MARTIN'S REFLECTION

This koan is about perception. I like how it reveals two very different ways of seeing the same event: from the usual self-concern or from the wise heart. The "what" of this story would appear to be about the radio, about being robbed, and the misfortune it entailed. Anyone can relate to such apparent "bad" luck, and to responding with anger, especially after repeated instances of the same event.

What I love is how Dipa Ma sees right through the apparently significant "what" into the underlying forces at play—the part we so readily miss, as we are blinded by things and fail to see the people. We are so accustomed to assuming that our happiness depends on getting and keeping our ducks (radios) in a row, and when they misbehave—get stolen, broken, or lost—we are upset.

Dipa Ma laughs: she's initially amused by the repeating pattern of loss this student is facing, and not perturbed in the least, seeing it as a beneficial teaching rather than a series of misfortunes. Then, when the student reports anger at the theft, Dipa Ma is amazed at his reaction. She's amazed at how the real story is missed, so obvious to her: the story that lies far beneath radios and robbers. This is a story of need, and she is moved by this to chant, gently, blessings for the thief.

I never met Dipa Ma, though what a beautiful being she must have been. She has been described as being fully present, with ease, stillness, and simplicity in whatever she did. When asked what was in her mind, she replied, "Just peace, concentration, and loving friendliness." Loving friendliness is a way of abiding, and Dipa Ma certainly seemed to abide in that state. How else could she have seen the sadness of the thief?

This koan reminds me of a story I often tell about my friend Carol's mother, a little, soft-spoken, Irish woman. One day she was visiting Carol in Canada and had to go to the bank. When she went up to the teller, the teller was very rude and unpleasant to her. Carol, who was waiting at the back, stepped up protectively, ready to interfere, just in time to hear her mother lean forward and say to her antagonist, "Have you ever thought of doing a different kind of work, dear?"

When I tell this story, my listeners and I all laugh, because it's so *not* the response we would make to a rude teller. But this kind old lady was far more interested in the teller's well-being than the rude words the teller spoke, and our laughter is at ourselves, and in delight at the possibility of a larger and lighter point of view.

Dipa Ma does the same thing—sees the real person and the real situation; sees right through the apparent event to the feelings causing it; and what's more, is compassionate with the perpetrator. In our koan, that perpetrator is very likely hungry, and most certainly living in some unenviable state, driven to theft out of pain.

A few years ago I encountered my own version of this koan. My teenage son had a party, and during the party someone went into my room and stole some of my favorite pieces of jewelry. I felt both the loss of the treasures and a creepy feeling of violation and broken trust.

For many months I suspected a nice young woman who worked at the local bakery and held her in the role of "suspect," regarding her with a secretly hostile attitude. When she handed me a cup of tea at the bakery, I could only see her through my "Are you a thief?" view. Her innocence was eventually revealed, and my view of and attitude toward her completely changed. We were both released from the prison of those roles.

It's how we see and don't see that creates our reality. It's true that we all swing between our small, self-centered point of view ("Thief, how could she?") and the bigger, broader, dharmic view of reality. The danger is in not realizing the difference and taking the little mind and its point of view as "reality."

It's not the act, nor the actor, but how we see them that makes our lives heaven or hell. Dipa Ma and Carol's mother created heaven wherever they went, because they could see beyond the prison bars, way beyond.

They say the road to hell is paved with good intentions. No one wants to create bad karma for themselves, even people who have never heard of karma. So how do you remember that someone who hurts you does so out of his or her own suffering? How is life different if it is lived with that view?

93. The Goddess and the Flowers

URING THE TIME of the Buddha, a great congregation of bodhisattvas, celestial beings, and monks were all gathered at Layman Vimalakirti's house, debating the teachings together. A goddess was there too, and one day she was so full of joy that she scattered celestial flowers over the whole congregation. The flowers that landed on the bodhisattvas fell to the floor, but those that landed on the monks stuck to them. The monks tried to shake the flowers from their robes, to no avail.

The goddess then asked the monk Shariputra, "Reverend Shariputra, why are you trying to brush away these flowers?"

Shariputra replied, "Because flowers are not proper for religious people."

Then the goddess spoke: "Why shouldn't flowers be proper for religious people? Flowers do not conceptualize or discriminate; you monks are conceptualizing and discriminating. Even though you have renounced your homes for the sake of the Dharma, if you make discriminations, you are not religious. If you make no discriminations, then you are truly religious.

"Evil spirits have power over the fearful but cannot disturb the fearless. So those afraid of forms, sounds, smells, tastes, and textures are under the power of the passions that arise from these things. The flowers stick to those who are afraid of them; they fall from the bodies of those who are free from the discriminations that lead to fear."

JAN WILLIS'S REFLECTION

This is a wonderful story on so many levels. It is basically a story about the error of focusing on religious "purity" and the observance of religious "rules" rather than on the core of religion and spirituality, which is the good heart. The story is also about fear, and it tells us that oftentimes it is fear that holds us back from acting freely and rightly in the world. Thus, if we want to act in accordance with the heart-core of practice, we need to loosen such discriminations and fears. Because Shariputra and the other monks have not done this, the flowers stick to them but not to the bodhisattvas, those who see the ultimate truth without discrimination and whose trademark is, therefore, the truly altruistic heart.

When the goddess asks Shariputra why he is brushing away the flowers she offered, he responds, "Because flowers are not proper for religious people." Here we see clearly that, for Shariputra at least, some things are "proper" and some things are not. There are rules! Moreover, he believes that following the rules ought to be paramount for "religious people." The goddess's response—that flowers do not discriminate and neither would the monks if they were truly religious—is a marvelous pronouncement. She points to the heart of the matter: namely, that "religious" folk need to put into practice the heart-teachings of their religious tradition and not just follow, by rote, its prescriptions.

Now, because I see myself as a Baptist-Buddhist, I also see a strong Christian parallel with this story in the parable of the Good Samaritan. You'll remember that in the parable, a man is robbed and beaten and left to die by the wayside on the road to Jericho. First a priest comes along and sees him. But the priest chooses not to help the man and instead crosses to the other side of the road. Next comes along a Levite, and he, too, passes over to other side. But then a Samaritan happens by, and seeing the man's poor condition—and without judging and discriminating about it—the Samaritan approaches the man, binds his wounds, places him on his own donkey, takes him to an inn, and gives the innkeeper money to continue the care of the man until his return. At the end of his narration of the parable, Jesus asks, "Now which of the three was truly the man's neighbor?" Or, put another way, which of the three was truly a "religious" man?

Perhaps the first two "religious" men, the priest and the Levite, were afraid that they would themselves be harmed if they stopped to help the wounded man. The robbers might still be around. Or perhaps they thought that stopping to help the wounded man might somehow be defiling to them because he might not be of their tribe or clan. Either way, it was the priest's and the Levite's fears that prevented them from acting religiously.

Interestingly, in Jesus's time, Jews regarded Samaritans with scorn. They considered them to be polluting and didn't want any physical contact with them. What a good thing that this particular Samaritan did not see the world this way! Rather than ask, "If I help this man, what might happen to *me*?" the good Samaritan asked, "If I don't help this man, what will happen to *him*?" In Martin Luther King's words, "the good Samaritan engaged in a dangerous altruism."

I was once soundly berated by a young African-American man, a newly "reborn" Christian, who told me that, by seeing goodness and virtue in the Buddha's teachings, I was not accepting Jesus Christ as my sole salvation and was therefore destined for eternal damnation. I told him that I didn't believe that Jesus himself would see it that way!

Discriminations and judgments usually serve only to alienate us, one from another, rather than bring us closer. According to Mahayana scriptures (where bodhisattvas figure so prominently), a tenth-stage bodhisattva—that is, a buddha—is referred to as a "cloud of dharma" because, like rain, he shares the teachings with all, equally and without discrimination. Whether we speak of Dharma rain or of the flowers of this story, the lesson is "Give up fear and don't discriminate and then you'll truly be practicing!" It seems very good advice.

You probably have ideas about socially appropriate behavior,
so if a beautiful young woman came into your church or your temple
wearing a bikini, what would you do? Could you respond without
self-righteousness? What is it that sticks to a person who
is afraid? Can anything truly stick?

94. Sona's Mother and the Thieves

INDIA, SIXTH CENTURY BCE ···

HERE WAS a wealthy lady at the time of the Buddha whose son Sona became a Buddhist monk known for his ability to expound the Dharma. Sona came to visit his hometown and so his mother built a pavilion where he could speak to the townspeople. She took her whole household with her to the gathering, leaving only a maid to look after the house.

During the talk, some thieves broke into the house; their leader went to the pavilion and sat near Sona's mother to keep an eye on her. The maid saw the thieves and ran to her mistress, but the lady only said, "Let the thieves take all my money, I don't care; don't disturb me while I'm listening to the Dharma."

When the maid went home she saw the thieves breaking into the room where the gold was kept. She ran back to her mistress. This time Sona's mother shouted, "Let the thieves take whatever they want! Don't you dare worry me again while I'm listening to the Dharma!"

The leader heard everything the lady said. He thought, "If we rob this noble person, we will surely pay a heavy price in some way." So he hurried to the lady's house and made his followers return everything. Then they went back to the pavilion. When Sona finished speaking, the leader told the noble lady what had happened, and they all asked for her forgiveness. Then Sona ordained them into the Buddhist order.

Sylvia Boorstein's Reflection

I have a framed cartoon by Nicole Hollander on my kitchen wall in which a frazzled middle-aged woman named Sylvia is typing a list called "Remarks You Most Hope to Be Able to Make Sometime." Two of the remarks on the list are "Yes, it *is* unusual to win the Nobel Prize and compete in the Olympics in the same year" and "I'll take the leather pants in a size 2, please." The final remark on the list, perhaps the one the cartoonist is suggesting ought to top the list, is "No, thanks. I have everything I need."

"I have everything I need" is, I think, the condition of a contented mind expressed in words. As Johnny Cash sang:

> The wealthiest person
> is a pauper at times
> compared to the man
> with a satisfied mind.

"Needing" is full of craving, which is a different state from simple "wanting." I do want. On a regular basis, I want to eat, and move around, and live among and communicate with others. I also want to work, to create, and even to play. These natural instincts seem to arise by themselves, and when they arise in nonproblematic circumstances in which they can be easily satisfied, then there can be comfort and a sense of ease.

And, because I know how problematic life circumstances are for many people in the world, I want there to be more equitable sharing of resources. I want wars to stop. I want people to care for each other so that the planet and life on it is sustained. This kind of want, although it inspires my passion for social activism, feels to me like a strong and motivating wish. It is a wish filled with determination but not with craving. It is a nonsuffering wish. It is full of clarity and free of suffering.

Sona, recognizing the truth that the highest happiness was a mind freed of craving, chose to live a renunciant life as a means of training his mind to be free.

Sona's mother, too, realizing that the Buddha's teachings provided the key to developing a mind free of suffering, refused to be distracted from those teachings even though it meant losing all of her material wealth. She understands that there is nothing, material or immaterial, more precious than a mind untroubled by neediness or craving.

The leader of the thieves, seeing that Sona's mother valued the Dharma much more than her worldly possessions, understood that all the riches in the world would not outweigh the "heavy price that he would pay" by not dedicating himself to enlightenment and the enduring happiness that was its fruit.

I trust that I—along with all human beings—have the capacity to train my mind to be free of craving. I trust that we can do it as lay people, too. I am committed to changing the habits of my mind from "This *must* be different now" to "I'll work as hard as I can for change because I wish things were different, because I wish for the whole world the end of pain and suffering." I think of this commitment as my invisible ordination.

What possession do you most value?
What could persuade you to give it away?

95. Songyong Doesn't Undress

ASTER HYANGGOK SUNIM, during a lecture on liberation, said to the nun Songyong Sunim, "I'll tell you what: if I undress, will you undress as well?"

Songyong replied, "If you undress that's fine; I'll undress as well. On second thought, I won't, because I fear sentient beings will fall into hell."

To this he said, "It's the same for me. Although I could undress in front of you, I fear for the negative karma of others, so I'll keep my clothes on."

They both laughed.

MARTINE BATCHELOR'S REFLECTION

I can imagine the scene: Hyanggok Sunim was a big man, twice the size of Songyong Sunim, and here he is challenging her in front of a group composed of the fourfold assembly (nuns, monks, laywomen, and laymen) that has gathered to hear a Dharma talk. He is saying to her that if he is capable of undressing without grasping and fear, can she, too, undress without grasping and fear? By that time both are old and wrinkly—what a sight it would have been if they had done it! They are both mischievous in this moment, but cool heads prevail and they both decide not to undress, out of compassion for sentient beings in the audience who might be shocked or might follow their example inappropriately.

Hyanggok Sunim was a great Korean Zen master of the twentieth century who was a strong supporter of Korean nuns; he felt that they were practicing as diligently and as seriously as the monks and possibly more so. The nun Songyong Sunim was the leader of the Zen hall at the nunnery of Naewonsa. This beautiful temple is nestled deep in the mountains near the southern tip of South Korea and specializes in Zen practice. Twice a year for three-month periods the nuns practice meditation for ten hours or more a day. They also do three-year retreats, and sometimes they do special retreats for a week or two where they sit in meditation every night, without lying down to sleep.

Hyanggok Sunim used to enjoy visiting these nuns, since they were so keen and so fun-loving at the same time. He greatly respected Songyong Sunim, and they would often have Zen exchanges. Songyong Sunim always gave as good as she got. Although Hyanggok Sunim was fierce, Songyong Sunim was never afraid of him, and he enjoyed sparring with her. She was very humble in daily life but in this exchange we see her coming into her own as a great Zen practitioner. She started out life poor and meek and encountered a lot of obstacles, but she found the courage to become a nun. By practicing hard, her inner strength and resilience were able to flower. She was renowned for her strong and deep meditative experiences.

When I was studying Zen in Korea, I went to Naewonsa and practiced with Songyong Sunim for a month. I was truly fond of her, while also respecting her immensely. She was so unassuming and so dedicated at the same time. For me she was the paragon of what a true nun could be: without any airs but with such a deep practice that one could not but be inspired by her. Before I left Korea in 1984, I saw her for the last time. She encouraged me to practice very hard while I was still young and energetic, and I took her advice to heart.

What is characteristic of these two great people and their interaction is the importance they give to the precepts. Some people think that having a Zen awakening means one can go beyond all boundaries and be totally unattached to any sense of morality. Hyanggok Sunim and Songyong Sunim were awakened Zen teachers; nevertheless, they chose to live by their ethical training, not just for themselves but also as an example to others.

In Korea there is a great emphasis on the practice of the "three trainings" of ethics, meditation, and wisdom. This story is embodying these three: because of wisdom Hyanggok Sunim and Songyong Sunim are not attached to or identified with their appearances; because of meditation they are stable and balanced and fearless; because of ethics they not only consider their own actions but the effects these actions could have on others.

I would like to leave you with a Zen poem of Songyong Sunim:

> Clear water flows over white rock,
> the autumn moon shines bright,
> so clear is the original face.
> Who dares say it is or it is not?

Real laughter rings across the universe. Does play have any place in the Dharma? What about affectionate flirtation?

96. Maurine Stuart's Whack

MYO-ON MAURINE STUART was leading a one-day retreat, and one of her students was soon to ordain as a priest. The student was walking behind Maurine during *kinhin*, or walking meditation, when she saw another woman start to wobble and fall. Without thinking, the student reached out her hand to assist the other woman. Maurine whacked the student's hand hard, twice. The other woman didn't fall.

The next morning, as the student was pouring tea for breakfast, Maurine turned to her, "Do you want to know why I hit you yesterday?"

"Yes," she said.

"You were being too helpful. You have to let people find their own balance. Don't be a crutch for them."

The student bowed deeply.

GYOKUKO CARLSON'S REFLECTION

Zen is not taught by words and ideas but primarily by relationship. It is dynamic, spontaneous, intuitive, and often baffling. Myo-on Maurine Stuart slaps a hand, hard and twice.

My relationship with my teacher, Jiyu-Kennett Roshi, was full of moments that brought me up short. When I first began working as her attendant, I was doing her laundry one day, and she complained that something had been done incorrectly. I thought she must be talking about somebody else, and only much later did I realize that her comment had been directed at me. Because I was so new in her service she was being circumspect in her correction. Later, when I had been in her service long enough for the trust to build, she would tell me what I had done wrong without holding back.

Just when I thought I knew what to do and how to do it, there would be a word, a look, or a gesture that gave me pause. At that moment I had several choices: to defer awkwardly while repressing anger and shame, to defer gracefully while letting go of my previous plans, to question my teacher and risk banishment, or to continue stubbornly with my previous course. I have come to feel that there is no perfectly right way to respond to correction, and equally there is no perfectly wrong way. But even doing a very bad job of responding can be the basis for deep learning and a profound turning. Conversely, responding well may be very satisfying but may also be tainted with smugness. Remembering that there is no single perfect way and no completely wrong way makes it easier for me to choose to act and respond.

The first time I read this little story, I went to my old pattern of wondering "Who is right?" Quickly, I saw that that is an unanswerable, irrelevant question. More useful is to reflect on these questions: How willing am I to have my hand slapped, to be interrupted in my present course, to interrupt someone else or to raise my hand? The relationships between students and teachers, and all practitioners with themselves, are where the Dharma comes alive.

The student whose hand was slapped was in training for leadership and a teaching position. If she gets stuck in imitating her teacher, she may, as a new teacher, slap and interrupt without discernment. If she gets stuck in the words "Everyone needs to find their own balance," she may leave everyone floundering without guidance or timely interruption. The art of teaching is to explore the heart and mind of the student with empathy but without entanglement, to be supportive but not permissive. The art of being a good student is to trust that what comes from the teacher could be important, but to remember that sometimes the teacher is just another human being having a bad day.

As I matured in my practice of Zen and came to know my teacher better, I saw that sometimes the corrections were coming from a place of deep compassion and skill, and sometimes they were not. None of us can manifest the perfection of an enlightened mind in every circumstance. We are not called upon to be other than human; we are called upon to be honest and true, to be as clear as possible each moment. To try to be perfect is overreaching and arrogant. To be human and humble is freeing.

When our teachers show their humanity, it is a gift. This is similar to the gift given us by old Gautama, who demonstrated his humanity by first becoming deathly ill in a very messy way, and then dying in public, fully demonstrating the frailty of the body. It is a gift given by our teachers when they belch or bark or snivel. This gift illustrates that we are all made of the same stuff, and therefore we all can receive Dharma and pass it on. All of us, with all our weaknesses, can enter into these dynamic, baffling relationships and come alive in them. We can know what it is to move freely, making mistakes and facing our humanity without fear.

A newborn baby is completely dependent on her parents. The parents' job is to help that child grow up and leave them behind. How do you know when to let your child or your student make her own mistakes? Can you let someone fall in front of you?

97. Fish-Basket Kuan Yin

CHINA, NINTH CENTURY ···

DURING THE TANG dynasty, a beautiful girl with a basket of fish appeared near the golden-sand beach of Shanxi, an area where people had no interest in Buddhism. Every day she came to the beach, always with two living fish in the basket. All the young men wanted to marry her. She said, "I will marry any man who can memorize the 'Universal Gateway' chapter of the Lotus Sutra in one night." The next morning, twenty men passed the test.

"I can't marry you all," she said. "Please memorize the Diamond Sutra." Ten of them could recite it in the morning. Then she asked them to memorize the entire Lotus Sutra. This time, only a man named Ma succeeded.

He made wedding preparations, but when she arrived at his house, the girl fell ill and died. She was buried, and several days later an old monk in a purple robe came and asked Ma to show him the tomb. The monk opened the tomb. Inside were bones linked together with a golden chain. The monk told the onlookers, "This girl was a manifestation of Kuan Yin, the bodhisattva of compassion, who came to teach you the sutras and the way of Buddha." Then he ascended into the sky, carrying the bones. Many people in that region converted to Buddhism.

Master Fengxue Yanzhao was asked by a monk, "What is the pure Body of Dharma?" He answered, "Ma's wife of golden-sands beach."

JISAN TOVA GREEN'S REFLECTION

I first heard of the fish-basket Kuan Yin on a pilgrimage to Kuan Yin sacred sites in China led by Eijun Linda Cutts and Rusa Chiu in 2005. Near the end of our journey we arrived by boat at the island of Putuo Shan in the China Sea, which has many Kuan Yin temples and other sacred sites. Overlooking the harbor of Putuo Shan looms a huge golden statue of Kuan Yin, a beacon to fishing boats at sea. Kuan Yin reputedly saved the lives of many fishermen endangered by storms, turbulent waters, and the island's rocky coast. In the Putuo Shan shops we saw images of Kuan Yin holding a fish basket and learned that she carries a copy of the Lotus Sutra carefully wrapped under the fish in her basket.

The beautiful young woman in the story above is a manifestation of Kuan Yin. She uses her beauty to awaken people to the Dharma. I chose this story to write about because at first I found it disturbing. I questioned whether it is an example of deceit or the misuse of sexuality, or an example of skillful means. This question inspired the following verse:

> What lures us to practice?
> Healing nectar,
> the words of a sutra,
> food for the spirit
> carried in the hands
> of someone
> we find beautiful.

When I first encountered Zen students at a Buddhist Peace Fellowship gathering, I was impressed by their warmth, openness, and uprightness. I wanted to be like them. I began sitting with them at Berkeley Zen Center and at Green Gulch Farm. This was before I knew about Kuan Yin, but she was manifesting through the lives of my Zen friends.

When Kuan Yin appeared in the guise of the beautiful young woman with fish in her basket, was she offering fish, her beauty, or something else? There is the adage "Give someone a fish, food for a day; teach someone to fish, food for a lifetime." Perhaps she was offering food for a lifetime. What better way to introduce Buddhist teachings than to encourage people to read, memorize, and recite them?

My teacher, Eijun Linda Cutts, encourages students to copy, memorize, and recite the texts we study with her. In memorizing "The Parable of the Herbs" in the Lotus Sutra I was drawn to its message of rain falling equally on all plants and trees, large and small alike, giving each what it needs. The Buddha's teachings are available to everyone, no matter their age, race, class, gender, or sexual orientation. This parable helps me appreciate the uniqueness of each member of our sangha, including those who are very different from me. It also helps me to be friendly when I open the front door, not knowing whether I will be greeting the UPS delivery person, a homeless man or woman asking for food, or a sangha member coming for a class.

When I memorize a phrase of a koan or a paragraph of a sutra it is always with me. I can call on it when I am meeting with a student in a practice discussion, giving a talk, teaching a class, or when I simply need inspiration.

As I have sat with the story of the fish-basket Kuan Yin, I have come to see the challenges she offers to her suitors as examples of skillful means. She found a way, through working with their desire for her, to introduce them to the Dharma: food for a lifetime. In that way she brought accessible and profound Buddhist teachings to a place where, prior to her coming, people had no interest in Buddhism. Although the beautiful maiden was (at least on the surface) a lowly fishmonger, she offered priceless gifts to those who courted her, even sacrificing her life to transmit the teachings.

I, and many of my Dharma sisters, never imagined as young women that we would grow up to be Dharma teachers. I often ask myself, with astonishment and appreciation, "What is a nice Jewish girl from a working-class family in the Bronx doing in priest robes?" I feel fortunate to have met my teacher, who inspired me to embrace this life of vow.

Zen practice is transmitted "warm hand to warm hand." Each of us may be a beacon for others we encounter, like the golden statue of Kuan Yin above the harbor of Putuo Shan or the maiden with her basket of fish.

Is it ever helpful to make a promise you might not keep? Is it ever appropriate to trick people for their own good? And what about those fish in Kuan Yin's basket?

98. The Old Woman and the Fire Poker

JAPAN, EIGHTEENTH CENTURY ···

ASTER HAKUIN EKAKU used to tell his students about an old woman who had a teashop nearby, praising her understanding of Zen. The students didn't believe that such a person could have much wisdom, and so they would go to the teashop to find out for themselves.

Whenever the woman saw them coming she could tell at once whether they had come for tea or to look into her grasp of Zen. In the former case, she served them graciously. In the latter, she beckoned them to come behind the screen to the back of the teashop. The instant they obeyed, she struck them with a fire poker.

Nine out of ten of them did not escape her beating.

JANE HIRSHFIELD'S REFLECTION

"There are mountains hidden in mountains, there is hiddenness hidden in hiddenness," wrote Eihei Dogen. Hiddenness steepens also this story of the unrecognized teacher outside the gate, who keeps her abbot's stick, a handy fire poker, tucked behind a rice paper screen.

Preconception hides the actual behind a screen. One preconception here is surely gender—these monks are skeptical of the practice of a woman. Status can blind as well. The monks are home-leavers, wandering clouds. The old woman lives in the world of commerce and thirst, of road dust and fatigue. How could her understanding compare to their vows, long effort, and strict meditation?

Another story punctures similar issues. Two monks find themselves on the bank of a fast-flowing river alongside an old woman who also needs to cross. One lifts her onto his shoulders. Many miles later, the other turns and asks how he could defile himself so, breaking the precepts by touching a woman. The first monk replies, "I put that grandmother down hours ago; why are you carrying her still?"

Who, then, lives in the relative and in preconception: the woman who simply serves tea and then wipes the counter with a clean rag, or the robed monks who question her practice's heart? This koan unravels both fabrics. Come into the shop with anything extra— competitiveness, self-importance, comparative ego—and the fire poker waits. For those who enter with wholehearted thirst, who taste with their own tongues, fragrant green leaves will appear.

This koan offers a path without extra. Its affection for us is a flavor poured without category, beyond definition. Lay practice is acknowledged in Zen, at least in theory. Vimalakirti, Layman Pang and his family, the oxherding pictures: each shows a thorough practice not separate from others. But this old woman goes even further; she just makes tea. Nameless, almost invisible, a person of no rank expressing wisdom as naturally as she might reach back in the night for a pillow—throughout Zen, we find realization described in such images, a mountain whose grasses any donkey can browse. "What is Buddha?" one student asks. "Have you eaten your breakfast?" the teacher replies. "Yes." "Then wash your bowl." The sixth Zen ancestor—whose practice had been in the kitchen, sorting rice—he too is in this old woman's family tree.

When I left my years of formal training in Zen—years I still feel as the gyroscope and diamond at my life's center—and began to make my way as a poet, I didn't hide my Zen background, but I didn't announce it. I didn't want my poems hung on a Buddhist coat peg or read with any preexisting expectation. As a young student, I'd learned of the four traditional paths of practice—priest, monk, layperson, teahouse lady. As I moved back toward poetry, the old woman's wholehearted yet invisible practice simply felt right: to live and write with an unlabeled and unlabeling awareness. Then, in 1999, Bill Moyers interviewed me for a poetry documentary on public television, and surprised me by asking, "I've heard that in your Zen you do something called 'teahouse practice.' What does that mean?" I could say only, "It means we've just burned down the teahouse." Then I told the story of the old woman's practice of boiling water and hidden, fragrant leaves, how people liked to stop at her teahouse without knowing why.

The woman of this story has a Western sister—a barmaid in the Sumerian epic *Gilgamesh*. The hero, wild with death-grief, searching for an herb that will make him immortal, asks for directions from the barmaid. She counsels him to accept death, return home, love his wife, raise his children, enjoy the warmth of sun and the coolness of rain. Gilgamesh ignores her, finds and then loses the herb, and goes home to build an immense wall around his city. This image, to me, is no symbol of civilization's beginning, nor even of a necessary individuation. Rather, Gilgamesh makes a choice toward ego and self-separation, born of death's denial and acceptance's failure. We call *Gilgamesh* the first epic. Might it not equally be our earliest tale of the tragic? The barmaid and the old lady of the teahouse meanwhile keep offering this moment's generous, fragrant cup, washing it clean again when it's been emptied.

Walk into the old woman's teashop today, you'd still get either tea or a thrashing. But her koan? This book? She'd burn them right up, stirring the ashes gladly with her plain iron poker.

If you try to prove that someone else is a fool, you're bound to be made a fool of. But how do you investigate the wisdom of another? Would you go to that old woman for tea or for her Zen beating? What did her tea taste like?

99. Let's Become Enlightened Together

···

HE AUSTRALIAN NUN Chi Kwang Sunim had the opportunity to meet a 102-year-old Korean nun, Kye Jeon Sunim,
who had meditated for years. When Chi Kwang came into
her presence, the old nun was sitting upright, with a rosary of black
beads and a rosary of white beads twirling together in her left hand,
silently repeating her mantra and gazing into space in front of her.
The old nun grabbed Chi Kwang's hand and pulled her close.

When Chi Kwang yelled in the hard-of-hearing nun's ear, "I'm a
foreigner!" the old nun held up the mingled black and white beads
and said, "Let's practice together."

When Chi Kwang asked the old nun about her past, she replied,
"What past?" Then the old nun smiled and said, "Let's become enlightened together."

ALEXANDRA PORTER'S REFLECTION

This koan is from the Korean tradition. When I was young, I traveled to
Korea, and there I met a lot of wonderful and powerful Korean nuns.
Some of them ran their own temples, taking care of anyone who came
to explore the Buddha's path. During my first visit, one of those nuns
inspired me to practice meditation, not by trying to teach me anything
or by asking questions, but just by being helpful and human. She
was just there, providing what I needed. Her example made a strong
impression on me and now I have been practicing within the Korean
tradition and running a temple myself for more than twenty years.

This koan has three important points:

The first one is about two people connecting, just sharing their life experience and their practice. Buddha said: "If beings knew, as I know, the results of giving and sharing, they would not eat without having given. Even if it were their last bite, their last mouthful, they would not eat without having shared." Of course, Buddha's teaching is not only about sharing food but about sharing whatever you can. And so the old nun shared her wisdom with Chi Kwang Sunim, reminding her: "Let's practice together."

There is a Buddhist story about a well in a meadow, beside a mountain path, where passersby stopped to drink fresh water. One day somebody covered this well, so it wasn't used any longer, and consequently it dried out and was forgotten. In just this way, if we cease sharing with one another, something in us dries up.

So sharing gives and brings life.

The second point I see in the koan is about using our skills when communicating with others. In Zen training, teachers use all kinds of ways to help students see their conditions, blocks, and attachments, and this is only possible when we—both teachers and students—are not occupied with our own agendas. Only then can we stay in touch with what is happening, moment by moment.

In the koan, the Korean nun is quite old but is still clear and vivid, using the situation to emphasize the importance of staying focused and keeping a present mind.

Finally, the third point I see in the koan is about relationships: how do we manifest in this world? For instance, are we self-centered or not? The two nuns are playing together, wrestling, the same way as we do in our relationships.

In my own marriage I used to fight with my husband about everything: how to raise children, what to cook for dinner, what to do in the evening. I was endlessly trying to force my point of view on him. Thanks to strong meditation practice, I finally learned how to put down smaller issues and engage with the bigger ones. It worked much better for all of us.

In the Korean tradition we learn that it takes three things to practice Zen—a great question, great courage, and great faith. In this koan the core question is this: What did the old nun attain that enabled her to just sit quietly, with an unmoving mind, simply repeating her mantra? This is a question for everybody. What do we want from our practice, from our life? What do we really want? What is our life? In the Korean style, it's absolutely necessary to go back to these essential questions over and over again. In this way we keep beginner's mind, or as we call it, "don't-know mind." If we have this don't-know mind, we are on a good path to liberation.

We keep forgetting the big questions, like "What is this? Who am I?" We are often totally absorbed in our worries, and the koan's job is to bring us back to this moment. Then we can let go of our conditioned way of looking at ourselves and others and respond to situations in a fresh way.

Both nuns were familiar with this practice, and so they kept trying. To continue being a nun, one needs to have great faith in one's own buddha nature and great courage to take care of this for all of one's life.

The questions in koans bring our meditation and mindfulness alive. This koan suggests two more questions to me:

White beads and black beads—are they the same or different?

What would you do if someone yelled in your ear?

What is the past, with its stories and apparently reality "back there somewhere"? For that matter, what is the present? How old do you have to be in order for the past to lose its interest? What does it mean to be a foreigner, anyway?

100. Darlene Cohen's Skillful Means

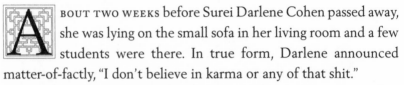 BOUT TWO WEEKS before Surei Darlene Cohen passed away, she was lying on the small sofa in her living room and a few students were there. In true form, Darlene announced matter-of-factly, "I don't believe in karma or any of that shit."

One of her students asked, "If you don't believe in any of that, what do you believe in, here on the threshold of life and death?"

Without a moment's hesitation and with much laughter and delight, Darlene said, "I believe in skillful means, which means I am willing to lie about anything."

LESLIE JAMES'S REFLECTION

This koan is about my dear friend Darlene Cohen, who died January 12, 2011. Exactly one year later, my granddaughter was born, and I thought, "Maybe it's Darlene coming back." But then, since I'm her grandmother and I have to watch her mother bring her up, I thought, "I hope she's not *too* much like Darlene, because she would be such a handful!"

I met Darlene in the mid-seventies when I first came to San Francisco Zen Center. She was a really beautiful woman, vibrant and alive and feisty. Then, in her early thirties, when her son was only three years old, she developed severe rheumatoid arthritis. Her hands and legs were deformed and crippled, though she was still beautiful and lively. Eventually, years later, she had cancer, and the medicine for the cancer would counteract the medicine for the arthritis; she had to keep choosing which one to take. Through it all she would say, "I'm going to live my life completely."

I think she was surprised, over time, to find herself becoming a teacher. She had a lot of trust in her wisdom, but to actually find herself being beneficial to people, in a practice way, surprised her. And as I watched her over the years, this came to be the most important thing to her: teaching people and helping people. She really studied how to make the Dharma available to people, because she knew it had helped her so much. She did it in her own way though, with her own skillful means. For instance, I remember that when she and an old friend taught workshops together, they would sometimes bring squirt guns, and then they would hide behind bushes beside the path and squirt people as they walked by!

Her commitment to do whatever it took to teach continued right through her last illness. She had various kinds of chemotherapy for the cancer, and they would work for a while, but finally the doctors said, "You have probably a couple of months to live." In the last weeks of her life, when she was really weak, she even finished a Dharma transmission ceremony for two of her students, which took a tremendous amount of time and energy. I saw her for the last time a few weeks before she died. She was totally alive until the last minute, but also recognized what was happening.

So in this koan, what does she mean when she says, "I don't believe in karma or any of that shit"? Karma is, of course, one of the main teachings of Buddhism. I think she was saying, "I don't believe in feeling like my karma is limiting me. And I don't want you to feel like, 'Oh, this is my karma, and now this is going to happen because I've done that.'" Darlene's sicknesses were real in her life. I'm sure she thought, at times, "This is terrible. I'm all crooked and crinkled." But she never let that limit her. She continued to wear black lacy clothes from antique stores, saying, with her whole body, "Don't let these beliefs stifle your life."

In this koan, someone then challenges her, saying, "Well, here you are, in this real situation. What do you believe in now, what do you rely on?" She says she values skillful means above everything, and she says she is willing to lie if necessary. Darlene did lie, when she was younger, to tease someone or get her way, but when she became a teacher and felt that responsibility, her reasons for lying shifted, and became about how to be most helpful. Even in her relationships with her students—if you want to call this lying—she would say, "Okay, my students can think I'm wonderful, even though I may need to go home and climb into bed and eat chocolate chip cookies under the covers and not come out for a few days. They don't need to know everything about me. They can still call me their teacher."

It's hard to believe that such a life force is gone, and yet, that is what happens to us: this very unique life force that we all carry goes away. So I think Darlene's teaching was this: "Use it. Use it fully, whatever you are. Don't try to be me, it would be impossible"—it *would* be impossible to be Darlene—"but be whoever you are, and use it to benefit others."

A Dharma teacher once told a woman with breast cancer, "That's your karma." Was that skillful means or something else entirely? How do you know if expressing your imperfect self will help others?

Acknowledgments

THIS BOOK CAME into being through the inspiration, collaboration, and help of many people. Indeed, like the koans themselves, it arose from relationship and generosity. First, we would like to thank our teacher, Zoketsu Norman Fischer, for the work he has been doing for many years to bring forward the history and importance of Zen's women ancestors, and for his personal support and encouragement to both of us, also over many years. We would also like to offer bows to the Zen teacher and translator Joan Sutherland, for her innovative, practice-centered approach to women's koans.

We are grateful to many translators, without whom we would not have had access to these stories and koans, and who also provided us with information on various fine points of Chinese Buddhist idioms and expressions. In particular we would like to thank Beata Grant, Wendi Adamek, Thomas Cleary, Bill Porter, Andy Ferguson, and Miriam Levering.

We would also like to pay our respects to a few of the scholars and writers who paved the way for us. Caroline Rhys Davids made the first English translation of stories about Buddhist women, with her 1909 translation of the *Therigatha*. Susan Murcott published *The First Buddhist Women*, also from the *Therigatha*, in 1991, ushering in an era of increasing interest in Buddhist women's history. In the twenty-first century, Sallie Tisdale, in *Women of the Way*, and Grace Schireson, in *Zen Women*, helped to familiarize Westerners, including us, with the biographies of many Buddhist women ancestors.

Barry Briggs of the Kwan Um school developed the first website of women's koans, *Zen Women*. His website was invaluable in the beginning of our koan collection process, and he was unfailingly generous to us throughout the development of this book. Thank you, Barry. And thanks to Kaz Tanahashi who steered us early on to sources for koans about women and to Nelson Foster who gave us excellent advice during the embryonic stage of the book.

Jean La Valley of the Bellingham Insight Meditation Society and Chris Fortin of Everyday Zen have both helped us to bring these koans and stories to groups of women in retreat. We also wish to thank our Dharma sisters who have participated in these retreats and in ongoing koan study groups. We commend them for their courage and willingness to leap out of their familiar ways of practicing the Dharma into the uncharted waters of koan study.

Taigen Dan Leighton and John Maraldo critiqued our introduction from the perspective of Buddhist scholars. Others who generously consulted with us about the manuscript at various points along the way are Barbara Briggs-Letson, Dave Evans, Monica Heredia, Michael Hofmann, Keatin Holly, Jean La Valley, Jane Lazar, Patrick McMahon, Charlie Pokorny, Kathleen Martin, Harriet McNeal, Wendy Egyoku Nakao, and Laurie Senauke.

We had several intensive writing retreats together while working on the book, and we would like to thank Sonoma Mountain Zen Center, Tracy Grubbs and Richard Taylor, and Shoalwater House for generously providing peaceful and pastoral retreat space for us.

A number of women shared stories about their own beloved teachers with us. We thank Amita Schmidt, Andrea Thach, Beata Chapman, Beth Goldring, Chi Kwang Sunim, Dhammananda, Peg Syverson, and Susan Jion Postal for their generosity.

If the stories and koans are the bones of the book, the reflections are its flesh. We thank our commentators for giving this book its body. They brought themselves to their respective koans with ardor and openness. Some lived with their koans for months as they reflected on them, and all endured our edits and revisions with patience and willingness. We thank them for their great hearts of practice.

We owe a particularly deep, astonished, and wholehearted thanks to Alison Reitz for copyediting the whole manuscript for us before we sent it to the publisher, as well as offering us her counsel every time we sought it. Her meticulous effort and wise responses were labors of love. Her generosity was stunning.

Josh Bartok, our editor at Wisdom Publications, was enthusiastic about our book from the start. We wouldn't have had the endurance to complete such an ambitious project without knowing that Wisdom wanted to publish it, and Josh and his colleague Laura Cunningham continued to be supportive and encouraging throughout. The beautiful cover design was created by Phil Pascuzzo. We also wish to acknowledge the artist Michael Hofmann, for his support and help in developing ideas for the cover.

Finally, we offer our deep bows to the many women, known and unknown, who have kept the lamp of the Dharma burning through the centuries.

Glossary and Background Information

Arahant (Pali, *arhat* in Sanskrit) is term used to refer to someone who has reached total awakening and gone beyond greed, hate, and delusion. An arahant enters *nibbana* (nirvana) upon his or her death. Most of the ordained disciples of the Buddha, male and female, were arahants.

Akshobhya Buddha, Sanskrit for "Immovable One," is one of the Five Wisdom Buddhas, and he represents consciousness as an aspect of reality. He is lord of the Eastern Pure Land Abhirati ("The Joyous"). Akshobhya is the embodiment of "mirror knowledge": the mirror is mind itself—clear like the sky, empty yet luminous.

Amida Buddha is the Japanese form of the Sanskrit name *Amitabha*, which means "the Buddha of infinite light." Many people in Japan are followers of the Pure Land doctrine, in which he is a central figure. According to Pure Land doctrine, the Buddha Amitabha created a paradise in the West for those who would take his name with faith. From this Pure Land it was easy to attain final nirvana.

Ananda (Indian, sixth century BCE) was the Buddha's cousin and his attendant. He did not become an arahant until after the Buddha's death.

Ann Aitken (American, 1911–94) cofounded Koko An Zendo in Hawaii in 1959 with her husband, Zen teacher Robert Aitken. They later cofounded the Maui Zendo and established the Diamond Sangha, one of the significant Zen lineages of the West. She studied with Soen Roshi, Yasutani Roshi, and Yamada Roshi, and, although never formally a teacher, she inspired and supported generations of Zen students, particularly women.

Anoja (Indian, sixth century BCE) was a noble-born queen and the wife of King Mahakappina. Together they ruled the kingdom of Kukkutavati at the time of the Buddha. She followed her husband to the Buddha and was ordained by Uppalavana.

Asan (Japanese, seventeenth–eighteenth centuries), or "Old San," was a laywoman from the town of Shinano. She was a student of the Soto master Tetsumon and considered greatly enlightened. She also met with Hakuin.

Bhadda Kapilani (Indian, sixth century BCE) was married to Mahakassapa, but they decided to renounce the world together. In one version of the story, they had married many times in previous lives. The women's sangha was not yet formed, but when it came into existence, Bhadda Kapilani ordained and became known as foremost among the nuns in the ability to recall and understand past lives, her own and others'.

Bhadda-Kundalakesa (Indian, sixth century BCE) was a wandering Jain ascetic famous for her debating skills. After being defeated by Shariputra in debate when she was an old woman, she met the Buddha, immediately grasped his teaching, became an arahant, and joined the Buddhist order as a nun.

Bhikkhuni Voromai Kabilsingh (Thai, 1908–2003) was the first Thai woman to receive full bhikkhuni ordination. After being a journalist, householder, and mother, she traveled to Taiwan in 1971 and was ordained there, since full ordination for women is not possible in Thailand. Her daughter, Bhikkhuni Chatsumarn Kabilsingh, is a nun as well, and a contributor to this book.

Bingdian An (Chinese, ninth century) was a Chan master and a contemporary of Linji. His sister-in-law was also a Chan adept.

Bodhidharma (Indian/Chinese, fifth–sixth centuries, died circa 532) was an Indian monk credited with bringing Chan to China. He is considered the twenty-eighth Zen ancestor.

Bodhisattva is a being on the path to buddhahood. The Buddha was once a bodhisattva. In the Mahayana tradition, bodhisattvas vow to be reborn until all beings are liberated.

Changjingjin (Chinese, eighth century) was the daughter of Administrator Murong of Qingzhou. She and her mother both ordained with Master Wuzhu. It is said that she and her mother became "leaders among nuns."

Chen (Chinese, Tang dynasty) was a laywoman from En Province who realized enlightenment with Master Jing of Changlao.

Chi Kwang Sunim (Australian). See her biography in contributor biographies.

Chiyono (Japanese, 1223–98) was the first Japanese woman whose enlightenment was recognized and who received transmission in a Zen lineage, from Chinese Master Wuxue Zuyuan. In one version of her story, she was said to be the daughter of a high-ranking family but was employed as a servant in a Zen convent in Hiromi in Mino province. She founded several convents in Kyoto, including Keiaiji, the leading women's monastery in Japan's medieval period. Chiyono was her secular name. Her Dharma name was Mugai Nyodai, or Mujaku Nyodai. There are many versions of her life story.

Chokan (Japanese name for Chinese folk figure) was the father of Senjo in a famous Chinese folktale. He is also known as Zhang Kien in Chinese versions of the tale.

Chuan-deng Jing-di (British, 1930–2011), also known by his English name, John Crook, was the founding teacher of the Western Chan Fellowship and received Dharma transmission from the great Chan Master Shen Yeng.

Dahui Zonggao (Chinese, 1089–1163) was a disciple of Yuanwu Keqin in the Linji lineage, known for teaching many laymen and laywomen. He had two female Dharma heirs: Miaozong and Miaodao. He is often referred to in texts as Ta-hui.

Daofu and Daoyu (Chinese, fifth–sixth centuries) were two of the four primary disciples of Bodhidharma mentioned in the *Jingde Records of the Transmission of the Lamp*. In some versions of Chan lineage, Daoyu was Bodhidharma's primary Dharma heir, rather than Huike.

Darlene Cohen (American, 1942–2011) became a student of Suzuki Roshi at San Francisco Zen Center in 1970. When she was a young mother and wife in her thirties, she contracted severe rheumatoid arthritis, and much of her life was devoted to working with people in chronic pain. She ordained in 1999 and founded the Russian River Zendo and several other sanghas. She published several books on working with pain and suffering. Her Dharma name was Surei Kempo.

Deshan Xuanjian (Chinese, 782–865) was originally a lecturer on the Diamond Sutra in Sichuan, but due to his encounter with an old woman, he became a disciple of Chan master Longtan Chongxin and later became his Dharma heir. He is sometimes referred to as Te-shan.

The Diamond Sutra (Vajracchedika Prajnaparamita Sutra in Sanskrit) is part of the collection of sutras known as the Prajnaparamita sutras, or Perfection of Wisdom sutras, written in Sanskrit in India and forming the foundation of Mahayana thought. The Diamond Sutra is an exploration of emptiness and is an important sutra for the Zen school.

Dieu Nhan (Vietnamese, 1042–1113), or "Wondrous Cause," was the eldest daughter of Lord Phung Yet, and she was brought up in the imperial palace. She was married to a provincial governor, but when he died she became a nun and practiced with Chan Dang, who appointed her head of the Huong Hai Convent.

Dipa Ma (Indian, 1911–89) was born in an Indian Buddhist family. She married at twelve and moved to Burma. When her husband and her youngest child died, she began practicing with the Burmese teacher Anagarika Munindra. At fifty-three, she awakened. She moved to Calcutta in 1968, where she taught. In 1980 and 1984 she came to America to teach at the Insight Meditation Society.

Dongshan Liangjie (Chinese, 807–869) was the founder of what became the Cao-dong school in China, which later became the Soto Zen school of Japan. He spent a large portion of his early life on pilgrimage. He received Dharma transmission from Yunyan Tangsheng. His name in Japanese is Tozan Ryokai, also translated in Chinese as T'ung-shan Liang-chieh.

Eihei Dogen (Japanese, 1200–53) was the founder of the Soto Zen school in Japan and a prolific writer and philosopher. His most famous work is the monumental *Shobogenzo (The Treasury of the True Dharma Eye)*. He traveled to China to receive teachings and received Dharma transmission there.

Engakuji is an important Rinzai temple and monastery in Kamakura, Japan. It was founded in 1282 by the Chinese master Wuxue Zuyuan and is considered the second of the "five mountains"—the five Rinzai monasteries of Kamakura.

Eshun (Japanese, circa 1364–1402) was the younger sister of the monk Ryoan Emyo. She studied both Rinzai and Soto Zen and founded the temple Saijoji. She was ordained by her brother in 1394. She was famous for her fearlessness, and when she was close to death she lit a bonfire and sat upright in it until she died.

Faxiang (Chinese, 375–453), or "Mark of the Law," was from northwest China. She married, but when the Qin dynasty was overthrown, all her relatives disappeared or died. She became a nun and lived at Great Mysterious Terrace Convent.

Fengxue Yanzhao (Chinese, 896–973) was a Chan master and Dharma heir of Nanyuan in the lineage of Linji.

Fubei Heshang (Chinese, eighth–ninth centuries) was a Chan master and Dharma heir of Mazu.

Ganji (Chinese, ninth century) was a workman; like Layman Pang, he and his entire family were considered Zen adepts. He did the practices of Samantabadra, and his awakening was recognized by Yantou.

Guanxi Xian (Chinese, died 895) was a disciple of Linji and Moshan Liaoran. He was a Dharma heir of Linji and later became a Chan master.

Guishan Lingyou (Chinese, 771–853) was a student of Baizhang and taught at Mount Guishan. He had a number of Dharma heirs, including Liu Tiemo ("Iron Grindstone Liu") and Yangshan Huiji. His lineage died out several generations later.

Hakuin Ekaku (Japanese, 1685–1768) was one of the most influential figures in Japanese Zen Buddhism. All Rinzai Zen masters today trace their lineage through him, and many modern practitioners of Rinzai Zen use practices directly derived from his teachings. He was also known for his calligraphy and Zen painting.

Hakuo Dotai (Japanese, died 1682) was a master in the Obaku school at the small temple Daikyu-an, and the teacher of Ryonen Genso.

Huike (Chinese, 487?–593) was one of the four primary disciples of Bodhidharma mentioned in the *Jingde Records of the Transmission of the Lamp*. In most versions of Chan lineage, he is the primary Dharma heir of Bodhidharma. He is also known as Dazu Huike and in Japanese as Taiso Eka.

Huisu (Chinese, fourth–fifth centuries) is known primarily for her role in the life of Faxiang. She lived with Faxiang in the same convent, the Great Mysterious Terrace Convent, and was seen as a poor, uneducable practitioner before surprising the nuns with her deep meditation practice.

Hyanggok Sunim (Korean, 1912–78) was one of the teachers of Songyong Sunim. He lived in a temple near Pusan.

Ika (Japanese, fourteenth century) was one of the attendants of Yodo, the fifth abbess of Tokeiji.

Ikkyu Sojun (Japanese, 1394–1481) was a Rinzai monk and poet known for his eccentricity, unabashed sexuality, and iconoclastic approach to Zen. He was quite possibly an illegitimate son of the emperor Go-Komatsu, and his poetry is renowned in Japan and the West.

Indra (Indian mythology) is the king of the devas, or gods. He is also associated with thunder and war.

Iron Grindstone Liu, or Liu Tiemo (Chinese, ninth century), was a nun and Dharma heir of Guishan Lingyou. She taught in a style described as "precipitously awesome and dangerous," and exhibited iron-like strength in Dharma combat. There are references to her being a "leader of a congregation" as well. She is the only woman with a name who appears in either the *Book of Serenity* (Case 60) or the *Blue Cliff Record* (Case 24).

Isso (Japanese, eighteenth century) was the patron and later husband of Ohashi, and a student of Hakuin.

Jain is a term for someone who practices Jainism, an Indian religion of nonharming that predates Buddhism.

Jianyan Yuan (Chinese, twelfth century) was a Chan master who had an exchange with Miaozong. Nothing more is known of him.

Jiaoan (Chinese, eleventh–twelfth centuries) was the niece of a high official of the Song dynasty. She decided early on not to marry or bear children and experienced awakening at the words of Yuanwu Keqin.

Jingxuan (Chinese, seventeenth–eighteenth centuries) was a nun-disciple and attendant of Ziyong Chengru in the Linji lineage. Jingxuan was with her teacher when she died, and she compiled some of the discourses in the record of Ziyong.

Jinhua Juzhi (Chinese, 810–80) was known as the "one finger" master, since he held up one finger in answer to any question. The nun Shiji spurred him on toward his enlightenment encounter with his teacher, Hangzhou Tianlong. He is better known by the Japanese form of his name, Gutei.

Jiyu-Kennett (English, 1924–96) was a prominent Western Soto Zen teacher. Born Peggy Teresa Nancy Kennett in England, she ordained as a bhikkhuni in China and practiced at Sojiji, and she was the first woman to be sanctioned by the Japanese Soto school to teach in the West. She founded Shasta Abbey and the Order of Buddhist Contemplatives. Her full Dharma name was Houn Jiyu-Kennett.

Joko Beck (American, 1917–2011) was a pianist and a mother of four who began Zen practice with Maezumi Roshi when she was in her 40s. She also studied with Yasutani Roshi and Soen Roshi. She received Dharma transmission from Maezumi Roshi and founded the San Diego Zen Center in 1983. She later founded the Ordinary Mind school. She was known for her iconoclastic teaching and penetrating insight. Her book, *Everyday Zen*, remains a major contribution to Western Zen practice.

Kakuzan Shido (Japanese, 1252–1305) was a member of a powerful samurai family and was married to the shogun Tokimune. She studied with the Chinese teacher Wuxue Zuyuan, who was also the teacher of Chiyono (Mugai Nyodai). Chiyono and Kakuzan were related. After the shogun's death and the bloody power struggle that followed between her own family and her husband's family, Kakuzan became a nun and was the founder and first abbess of the famous Rinzai temple Tokeiji, the sister convent to Engakuji.

Kannon—see entry for Kuan Yin.

Keizan Jokin (Japanese, 1268–1325) was a Soto Zen monk and teacher. He is considered one of the two founders of Soto Zen in Japan. He founded Sojiji, still one of the two primary Soto Zen training temples in Japan. His mother became an abbess of a Zen convent, and he had many women disciples.

Khujjuttara (Indian, sixth century BCE) was a slave woman in the palace of Queen Samavati of Kosambi, who became known for her tremendous knowledge of the Buddha's teachings.

Kisagotami (Indian, sixth century BCE) was the wife of a wealthy man. When her six-month-old child died, she went to the Buddha to be helped in her grief, and through his teachings she ordained as a nun and became an arahant.

Kongshi Daoren (Chinese, 1050–1124) was a Dharma heir of Cixin Waxin and a nun, teacher, and poet. She wrote the "Record on Clarifying the Mind," which circulated throughout China. When still young, she left her husband and asked her parents to allow her to ordain, but they refused. After her parents' death, she ran a bathhouse and wrote Dharma poetry on the walls. She was praised by masters like Yuanwu and Foyan, and she finally became a nun in old age. She was also known as Weiju, or by her lay name, Zhidong.

Kuan Yin (known as Kannon in Japan or Guanyin in China) is the female manifestation of Avalokiteshvara, the bodhisattva of compassion. She is an important figure in China, Japan, and Korea.

Kye Jeon Sunim (Korean, 1891–1995) was a Korean Zen nun who lived to be 104.

Langye Huijue (Chinese, 980–1050) was a disciple of Fenyang in the Linji lineage.

Layman Pang (Chinese, 740–808) was the most famous lay Chan Buddhist in Chinese history. He came from Hengyang (southern Yunan province). He studied and gained realization under the two great teachers of his time, Shitou and Mazu. His wife, son, and daughter (Lingzhao) were also Chan adepts.

Laywoman Pang (Chinese, d. 808) was part of the most famous lay Chan Buddhist family in Chinese history.

Ling Xingpo (Chinese, eighth–ninth centuries) is mentioned in the *Record of the Transmission of the Lamp* of 1004, in a biography of Mazu's heir, Fubei Heshang. Her encounter with Fubei forms the bulk of his story. She was also highly praised by Zhaozhou, who exchanged poems with her.

Lingzhao (Chinese, died 808) was the daughter of the famed Layman Pang and his wife, and was also noted as a Chan adept. She traveled with him in poverty, seeking teaching and doing cave meditation. She died just before her father. Her name means "Spirit Shining."

Linji Yixuan (Chinese, died 867) became a monk at an early age and later received Dharma transmission from Huangbo Xiyun. He was the founder of the Linji school, which later became the Rinzai sect in Japan. He was known for a vigorous, abrupt teaching style and often used shouts and blows.

The Lotus Sutra (Saddharma Pundarika Sutra in Sanskrit) is one of the most revered Mahayana sutras, particularly in China and Japan. It was written between 100 BCE and 200 CE. It is treated with great reverence, and in some schools of Buddhism, people chant or write out the whole sutra as a devotional practice.

Magu Baoche (Chinese, eighth–ninth centuries) was a Dharma heir of Mazu.

Mahakappina (Indian, sixth century BCE) was the husband of Anoja and the king of Kukkavati at the time of the Buddha. He left his kingdom to become a monk, offering all of his secular power to his queen, Anoja, who refused it and also ordained.

Mahakassapa (Indian, sixth century BCE) was married to Bhadda Kapilani, but they decided to renounce the world together. In one version of the story, they had married many times in previous lives. He became one of the principle disciples of the Buddha. Within the Zen tradition, it is said that the Buddha held up a flower in silence and Mahakassapa smiled in recognition, thereby becoming the first Zen ancestor.

Mahapajapati (Indian, sixth century BCE) was Shakyamuni's aunt and foster mother. She challenged the Buddha's exclusion of women from the monastic order and won women the right of ordination, thereby becoming the founder of the nuns' sangha. She was considered chief among Buddha's women disciples. When she died, miracles occurred, much like those at the Buddha's death.

Mahayana refers to a form of Buddhism that began near the beginning of the Common Era in India, in which the path of the bodhisattva is of primary importance. The Heart Sutra is a primary sutra for Mahayana practitioners, and the philosophy of both Zen and Tibetan Buddhism are strongly influenced by Mahayana sutras.

Manjushri is the bodhisattva of wisdom. He is strongly associated with the Perfection of Wisdom sutras and is particularly beloved in the Zen sects. In China, Mount Wutai is considered the home of Manjushri.

Manseong (Korean, 1897–1975) was born into a peasant family and was married and then widowed at an early age. She practiced with Mang Gong, the great revitalizer of Korean Zen. She was ordained in 1936 and received Dharma transmission from him in 1941. After his death she became a wandering monk for nine years. In 1955 she took over the leadership of Taeseong-am, a small nunnery, and taught there for the rest of her life.

Mara is a mythological demonic figure who represents unskillfulness, ignorance, and death. In the Pali canon he often attempts to seduce the Buddha and his disciples away from the spiritual path.

Mazu Daoyi (Chinese, 709–788) was the sole Dharma heir of Nanyue Huairang. He was one of the most prominent of the Tang Chan masters and shaped the directness of teaching styles through his use of the shout, stick, and glare. In contrast to his teacher, he had 139 Dharma heirs.

Metta is a Pali Buddhist term often translated as "loving-kindness." It is one of the Four Divine Abodes advocated by the Buddha, along with compassion, sympathetic joy, and equanimity. There are specific meditation practices aimed at developing boundless loving-kindness, as well as the *Metta Sutta*.

Miaodao (Chinese, eleventh–twelfth centuries) was a nun, Dharma heir of Dahui, and an important teacher with many recorded sermons and teaching dialogues with monks.

Miaoxin (Chinese, ninth century) was a nun disciple of Yangshan Huiji, and he spoke highly of her understanding. She was appointed director of the gatehouse at Yangshan's monastery. We know of her through Eihei Dogen's fascicle, "Raihai Tokuzui."

Miaozong (Chinese, 1095–1170) married a scholar-official but gradually devoted herself to spiritual pursuits. After studying with a number of teachers, she became a lay student of Dahui Zonggao, under whom she was enlightened. She was ordained in 1162 and became abbess of Cishou nunnery, where she had Dharma heirs. Her lay name was Wuzhuo.

Mokufu Sonin (Japanese, fourteenth century) was a benefactor and student of Keizan Jokin. She and her husband (Myojo, ordained a few years later) gave land to Keizan and invited him to found Yokoji. She ordained in 1319, received Dharma transmission from Keizan in 1323, and later became abbess of Entsu-in, an important convent. Keizan called her the reincarnation of his grandmother and said that he and she were inseparable.

Moshan Laoran (Chinese, ninth century) was well known in her time and referred to by many later writers. She is one of the women role models prominently cited for their wisdom by Dogen in his essay "Raihai Tokuzui." She was a nun, a disciple of Gaoan Dayu, and the first woman Dharma heir in the official Chan transmission line, with a chapter about her in the *Jingde Records*.

Mount Hua, or Hua Shan, is located in Shanxi Province, China, and is considered one of China's Five Great Mountains. This massive mountain was particularly important to Daoists and was associated with immortality.

Mount Wutai, or Wutaishan or Daishan, is located in Shanxi, China; the pilgrimage trail to Mount Wutai passes the monastery where Zhaozhou Conshen practiced. Mount Wutai has long been identified as the dwelling place of Manjushri, the bodhisattva of wisdom. It is regarded as the most sacred of the four Buddhist Mountains in China. Pilgrims, then and now, sometimes see visions of Manjushri there, encountering him in the form of a monk or pilgrim.

Myo-on Maurine Stuart (Canadian, 1922–90) was a musician and Rinzai teacher who was ordained by Eido Tai Shimano and received Dharma transmission from Soen Nakagawa. She was the spiritual director of the Cambridge Buddhist Association before her early death from liver cancer.

Nagas were mythical beings with human faces and serpent bodies who lived in palaces at the depths of lakes, rivers, and oceans. They were considered the guardians of the treasures of the ocean and of the regenerative power of life, and in the Mahayana tradition they are also the guardians of the Perfection of Wisdom sutras and therefore associated with wisdom.

Nanquan Puyuan (Chinese, 748–835) was a Dharma heir of Mazu Daoyi and had seventeen heirs, among them Zhaozhou Congshen. "Nanquan Kills the Cat" is the most well-known of the many koans about Nanquan. He is also known as Nan-chuan, or Nansen in Japanese.

Naropa (Indian, 956–1041) was a scholar-monk who eventually became the disciple of Tilopa and the teacher of Marpa. These three began the Kagyu Buddhist sect of Tibet.

Nirvana (*nibbana* in Pali) is a Sanskrit term for the mind of complete peace, liberation, and luminosity. The term is used in both Theravada and Mahayana Buddhism, with slightly different meanings.

Nyozen (Japanese, thirteenth–fourteenth centuries) was the wife of a retainer to a powerful family. Later she became a nun at the Rinzai women's temple of Tokeiji and trained under Gen-o, the founder of Kaizoji Temple. In 1313 she awakened.

Ochu (Japanese name for Chinese folk figure) was the cousin and later husband of Senjo in a traditional Chinese folk-tale. He was known as Wangzhao in some Chinese versions of the story.

Ohashi (Japanese, eighteenth century) was the daughter of a samurai who lost his position, and so she sold herself into a brothel to support her family. She had an enlightenment experience that was verified by Hakuin, married a patron (Isso), and later ordained. Her Dharma name was Erin.

Patacara (Indian, sixth century BCE) went mad from grief after her children, parents, and husband died in one day. Eventually she met the Buddha, who calmly told her to recover her presence of mind, and thus she was cured. She became a highly influential teacher who brought many women to the Dharma and had many disciples. Her name is pronounced "Patachara."

Precepts are guidelines for ethical conduct. Originally they referred to the many hundreds of rules and guidelines for monks and nuns. In the Theravadin tradition, many lay people take five precepts, and in Zen lineages in Japan, both lay and ordained people take sixteen precepts.

Punna (Indian, sixth century BCE) was a servant woman who made an offering of broken rice cakes to the Buddha and later became a stream-enterer.

Punnika (Indian, sixth century BCE) was a slave woman who carried water from the river and was a disciple of the Buddha.

Qiyuan Xinggang (Chinese, 1597–1654) was the only child of a retired scholar. She was engaged as a young woman, but her fiancé died. She wanted to enter the religious life but did not ordain until she was thirty-five, after serving her parents and in-laws. She received Dharma transmission from Shiche Tongshen in the Linji lineage. She later spent nine years in solitary retreat. In 1647 she became abbess of the Lion Subduing Chan Cloister, a convent in Jiaxing. Over one hundred nuns lived in her community.

Rahula (Indian, sixth century BCE) was the son of Shakyamuni Buddha. He joined the Buddhist sangha as a monk when he was still a young boy.

Ryonen Genso (Japanese, 1646–1711) was from an aristocratic family and served the empress as a young woman. She left her husband and children to become a nun and practiced at the Rinzai nunnery of Hokyoji. She then traveled to find a teacher from the Obaku school. After being refused by one Obaku teacher, she met with Hakuo Dotai, who also refused her. After scarring her face, she returned to Hakuo, who admitted her into his monastery and gave her Dharma transmission. She later founded and became an abbess of her own temple, Taiunji.

Saijoji Temple, in Japan, also known as Doryo-son, was founded in 1394 by the nun Eshun's brother, the monk Ryoan Emyo, who had trained at Engakuji and also with Soto Zen teachers. It is still in existence, and a sub-temple there is dedicated to Eshun.

Samadhi is a Sanskrit Buddhist term referring to a state of blissful concentration and meditative absorption.

Samantabhadra is an important bodhisattva figure in Mahayana Buddhism, associated with the union of meditation and enlightened activity. He is a figure in the Lotus Sutra and the Flower Ornament Sutra, and his ten great vows are delineated in the latter. The vows became a common practice in East Asia, particularly the tenth vow of dedicating all personal merit to the benefit of all beings. Samantabhadra is often depicted sitting on an elephant.

Samavati (Indian, sixth century BCE) was a queen in the court of King Udena of Kosambi and a follower of the Buddha's teachings as they were passed on to her by her slave woman, Khujjuttara.

Samsara is a Sanskrit term describing the world of birth and death and suffering, the continuous flow from one life to another, and the mind that is caught in these ideas.

Sarvastivada was an early Buddhist sect based in what is now northwestern India and Afghanistan. The Sarvastivada ideas about women and their capacity for enlightenment were generally less repressive than some other early Buddhist schools. This sect is no longer extant.

Satsujo (Japanese, eighteenth century) was a niece and student of Hakuin. She was a Zen adept from a very young age, and her enlightenment was verified by Hakuin. She remained a laywoman, though she was known for vanquishing others in Dharma combat, including—on occasion— Hakuin himself.

Seisho Maylie Scott (American, 1935–2001), or Kushin Seisho, was an activist for peace and social justice, a Soto Zen priest and teacher. She studied with and received Dharma transmission from Sojun Mel Weitsman of Berkeley Zen Center, in the Soto lineage of Shunryu Suzuki. She was also a student of the Rinzai teacher Maurine Stuart. She was the founder and teacher of Rin Shin-ji, a Zen temple in Arcata, California.

Senjo (Japanese name for Chinese folk figure) was a young woman who ran away with her lover in a traditional Chinese folktale. She is known as Ts'ing in some Chinese versions of her story.

Shanxi is a land-locked province in northern China.

Shariputra (Indian, sixth century BCE) was one of the primary monk-disciples of the Buddha, considered "foremost in wisdom," but in Mahayana sutras he is often the "fall guy," portrayed as holding to a too-rigid understanding of the Dharma.

Shiche Tongshen (Chinese, 1593–1638) was a student and Dharma heir of Miyun Yuanwu in the Linji lineage. He had three Dharma heirs, one of whom was the nun Qiyuan Xinggang.

Shiji (Chinese, ninth century) was a little-known nun, of obvious Chan attainment, who appears in the biography of Jinhua Juzhi.

Shotaku (Japanese, fourteenth century) was the wife of Sakurada Sadakuni, the chief retainer of the Kodo family. In 1331 he was slain, and she entered the Rinzai convent Tokeiji. She studied at Engakuji and later became the third abbess of Tokeiji. Her lay name was Sawa.

Soma (Indian, sixth century BCE) was a disciple of Shakyamuni Buddha. She was the daughter of a minister of King Bimbisara. She was first a lay disciple, then a nun, then an arahant.

Sona (Indian, sixth century BCE) was a monk disciple of the Buddha from a wealthy family.

Songyong Sunim (Korean, 1903–84) was ordained at nineteen. She was a student of Master Man'gong and became the leader of Maewonsa Nunnery in Korea.

Stream enterer, also called stream winner, is a person who has attained the first of the four stages on the path of the arahant. A stream enterer has eradicated greed, hate, and delusion and will move forward toward *nibbana* (nirvana, total cessation) within seven lifetimes.

Sudhana is the main character in the "Gandavyuha" chapter of the Avatamsaka Sutra (the Flower Ornament Sutra). He is a young man on a pilgrimage at the behest of the bodhisattva Manjushri. Sudhana converses with fifty-two enlightening beings in his quest for enlightenment.

Sujata (Indian, sixth century BCE) offered the Buddha the milk-rice that ended his time of austerity before he awakened beneath the bodhi tree. She was the wife of a landowner.

Tang dynasty (China, 618–907) was a Chinese imperial dynasty, often considered a golden age of Chinese culture and Zen.

Tara is a much-beloved female form of the bodhisattva Avalokitshvara in the Tibetan tradition. She is known as "the mother of liberation" and is associated with the qualities of activity and compassion. She is also sometimes considered a female buddha.

Tathagatha is one of the honorific names for the Buddha. It has been translated as "the one who has arrived at suchness" or "the one who has thus come."

Tetsumon (Japanese, seventeenth–eighteenth centuries) was a Soto Zen master, contemporary with Master Hakuin (1685–1768), and he probably taught in or near the town of Shinano.

Theravada (Buddhist term) is a school of Buddhism that developed in the first few hundred years after the Buddha's death and is still extant today in Southeast Asia and the West. The name means "The Teaching of the Elders," and the teachings are based on the sutras in the Pali Canon. Vipassana ("insight meditation" in English) is a Theravada meditation practice.

Tilopa (Indian, 988–1069) was born into the Brahman caste but under the influence of a dakini became an itinerant tantric practitioner. His most famous student was Naropa. He is considered the founder of the Kagyu sect of Tibet and he developed the method and study of Mahamudra.

Tokei (Japanese, 1240–1306) was the fourth abbot of the Rinzai monastery Engakuji and the teacher of Kakuzan Shido, the first abbess of Tokeiji.

Tokeiji is a Buddhist temple and former nunnery of the Rinzai lineage, in Kamakura, Japan, founded by the nun Kakuzan Shido in 1285. It was a refuge for women seeking divorce from abusive husbands and a sister temple to Engakuji. It was famous for "mirror zen" and for its Buddha's birthday celebrations. No man was allowed to enter it for nearly six hundred years. Many abbesses were the daughters of aristocrats or even emperors.

Uppalavana (Indian, sixth century BCE) was one of the Buddha's nun-disciples, believed to be foremost among the nuns for her supernormal powers, which include telepathy, clairaudience, and knowing past lives. She is also known as Uptalavarna in Sanskrit.

Vasumitra (Indian literary character) was an enlightened courtesan in the city of Ratnavyuha. She is a character in the "Gandavyuha" chapter of the Avatamsaka Sutra (the Flower Ornament Sutra) and one of the fifty-two teachers met by the pilgrim Sudhana.

Vimalakirti (Indian, probably mythological) is the main character in the Vimalakirti Sutra, an early Mahayana sutra. The Vimalakirti Sutra was likely composed in India in approximately 100 CE. Its central figure is Vimalakirti, who is presented as the ideal Mahayana lay practitioner and a contemporary of Shakyamuni Buddha. Vimalakirti manifested being ill in order to bring many wise beings into his house to debate and bring up the Dharma together.

Wanan (Chinese, twelfth century), also known as Daoyen, was a disciple of Dahui Zonggao and the head monk at his monastery.

Wuzhu (Chinese, 714–74) was a Chan master in Sichuan who claimed descent from Korean master Wuxiang (684–762) and taught at the Bao Tang monastery in Yizhou. The Bao Tang sect appears to have been short-lived, and Wuzhu's teachings are known mainly from a text called the *Lidai fabao ji* (*The Record of the Dharma-Jewel through the Generations*).

Wuzu Fayan (Chinese, 1024–1104) was born in Sichuan Province and taught at Mount Wuzu (also called "East Mountain") in Hubei Province. He was in Linji's lineage, and his most famous disciple was Yuanwu Kiqen. In Japanese his name is Goso Hoen.

Yamada Koun (Japanese, 1907–89) was a Japanese businessman who became a serious Zen student of Haku'un Yasutani and later received Dharma transmission from him. Yamada was the leader of the Sanbo Kyodan lineage, an independent lay sect derived from Soto Zen and founded in 1954. He gave Dharma transmission to many influential Western Zen teachers, including Robert Aitken and a number of European women.

Yangshan Huiji (Chinese, 807–83) was a student and Dharma heir of Guishan and the Dharma brother of Iron Grindstone Liu.

Yantou Quanhuo (Chinese, 828–87) studied Chan under Deshan and received Dharma transmission from him. He lived through a time of persecution of Buddhist monks and nuns and was a ferryman on a lake for a while. Later he was the master of his monastery. He died violently at the hands of bandits.

Yasodhara (Indian, sixth century BCE) was the wife of Shakyamuni Buddha. She later ordained and became a nun in the Buddha's sangha.

Yodo (Japanese, fourteenth century) was the daughter of Emperor Godaigo and an imperial princess. When her younger brother was killed, she took Buddhist vows. She became the fifth abbess of the Rinzai temple Tokeiji.

Yoshihime (Japanese, thirteenth–fourteenth centuries) was a nun and the student of Ninpo, an abbess at Tokeiji. She was the daughter of General Kanazawa Sada. She was "ugly and exceptionally strong." Her nickname was Devil-girl.

Yu Daopo (Chinese, twelfth century) was the only Dharma heir of Langye Yongqi and apparently remained a laywoman. She was awakened upon hearing the teaching of "the true person of no rank." After her powerful encounter with the master and abbot Yuanwu, he recognized her accomplishment and she was sought out by many monks.

Yuanji (Chinese, eighth century) was a nun who studied with Huineng, the Sixth Ancestor, along with her brother. She practiced meditation in a cave and wrote a book called "The Sound of Perfect Enlightenment," which was said to be comparable in insight to a book by Yongjia, a Dharma heir of Huineng.

Yuanjue (Chinese, eighth century) was a monk who studied with Huineng, the Sixth Ancestor, along with his sister, and later practiced as a teacher on Mount Wutai. In another, later version of the story, the upside-down Chan master is Deng Yinfeng.

Yuanwu Keqin (Chinese, 1063–1135) was the Chan master from the Linji school who took Xuedou's book of one hundred Chan stories and verses and added his own commentaries, creating the *Blue Cliff Record*, one of the most well-known and extensive koan collections in the vast Zen literature.

Zazen is the Japanese Zen term for sitting meditation.

Zhaozhou Congshen (Chinese, 778–887) was one of the greatest Tang dynasty Chan masters. He received Dharma transmission from Nanquan. Many koans in both the *Blue Cliff Record* and *The Gateless Gate* are from the records of his teaching. He seemed to have a particularly strong affinity with women. Also known as Chao-chou and Joshu (in Japanese).

Ziyong Chengru (Chinese, 1645–?) was a nun, abbess, and lineage holder in the Linji lineage. She trained on Mount Wutai and was Gulu Fan's Dharma successor. She spent much of her life on pilgrimage and was given an honorary title by the emperor. She was abbess of convents in Beijing, Zhuozhuo, and the Wu Mountains.

Zongchi (Chinese, fifth–sixth centuries) was the daughter of an emperor of the Liang dynasty of sixth-century China. She became a nun and disciple of Chan founder Bodhidharma and is sometimes considered one of his four Dharma heirs. She is sometimes known as Tsung-ch'ih, Soji, or Myoren.

Sources and Translations of Koans

For more complete bibliographic information on translations, see the bibliography.

Anne Aitken's "Get On and Go." From a commentary by Aitken in *The Gateless Barrier*, 219.

Anoja Seeks the Self. From the *Visuddhimagga* and *The Pali Dictionary of Proper Names*. Translated by Murcott in *The First Buddhist Women*, 68; and online at http://www.rinpoche.com/stories/kapilani.htm.

Asan Claps Both Hands. Original source unknown. Translated by Thomas Cleary in the *Kahawai Journal*, 1984; and John Stevens in *Three Zen Masters*, 83.

Asan's Dewdrop. Original source unknown. Translated by Thomas Cleary in the *Kahawai Journal*, 1984.

Asan's Rooster. Original source unknown. Translated by Thomas Cleary in the *Kahawai Journal*, 1984.

Awakening While Cooking. From the *Therigatha Commentary*. Translated by Murcott in *The First Buddhist Women*, 104–5; Gunaratna in *Message of the Saints*, 14; and Boucher in *Opening the Lotus*, 78.

Bhadda Kapilani and Mahakassapa. From the *Therigatha (Songs of the Elder Nuns)*. Translated by Murcott in *The First Buddhist Women*, 101–4; Rhys Davids in *Psalms of the Sisters*; and online by Hecker and Khema, http://www.accesstoinsight.org/lib/authors/hecker/.

Bhadda-Kundalakesa Cannot Answer. From the *Therigatha (Songs of the Elder Nuns)* and the *Dhammapada Commentary*. Translated by Murcott in *The First Buddhist Women*, 44–47; Rhys Davids in *Psalms of the Sisters*;

Tisdale in *Women of the Way*, 80–83; and online by Hecker and Khema, http://www. accesstoinsight.org/lib/authors/hecker/.

Bhikkhuni Kabilsingh Keeps the Precepts. Original story shared by Dhammananda (Chatsumarn Kabilsingh), unpublished, and used with her permission.

Changjingjin's No Obstructions. From the *Lidai fabao ji* (*The Record of the Dharma-Jewel Through the Generations*). Translated by Wendy Adamek in *The Mystique of Transmission*, 131–32; and online by Shih, "Women in Zen Buddhism," http://www. purifymind.com/WomenChan.htm.

Chen's Mountain Flowers. Original source unknown. Translated by Cleary in the *Kahawai Journal*, 1984; and Wu in *The Golden Age of Zen*, 242.

Chiyono's No Water, No Moon. From the *Shonan-katto-roku* (*The Shonan Koan Record*), the *Zenmonkaikiden*, and many biographies. Translated by Dutton in Addiss's *Zen Sourcebook*, 173–79; Kubose in *Zen Koans*, 120; Reps and Senzaki in *Zen Flesh, Zen Bones*, 48–49; Leggett in *Zen and the Ways*, 81–82; and others.

Darlene Cohen's Skillful Means. Original story shared by Beata Chapman, unpublished, and used with her permission.

Dieu Nhan's Without Words. From the *Thien Uyen Teap Anh (Outstanding Figures in the Vietnamese Zen Community)*. Translated by Nguyen in *Zen in Medieval Vietnam*, 97.

Dipa Ma and the Thief. Original story shared by Amita Schmidt, used with her permission.

Dipa Ma's Fearless Daughters. Original story shared by Amita Schmidt and used with her permission.

Dogen Sets the Record Straight. From Dogen's "Raihai Tokuzui" in *Shobogenzo*. Translated by Tanahashi in *Treasury of the True Dharma Eye*, 80; and online by Weinstein, "Raihai tokuzui," at http://scbs.stanford.edu/sztp3/translations/shobogenzo/translations/raihai_tokuzui/rhtz.html.

Dongshan and the Old Woman's Water Buckets. From the *Wujia yulu* (*The Records of the Five Houses*). Translated by Powell in *The Record of Tung-shan*, 33.

Eshun's Deep Thing. From the *Rentoroku*. Translated by Bodiford in *Soto Zen in Medieval Japan*, 44; Tisdale in *Women of the Way*, 242; and online at http://www.asahi-net.or.jp/~qm9t-kndu/saijoji.htm.

Faxiang's Recognition. From the *Biqiuni zhuan (Complete Biographies of Bhiksunis)*. Translated by Tsai in *Lives of the Nuns*, 56–57.

Fish-Basket Kuan Yin. From Chinese folklore. Translated by Yu in *Kuan-yin*, 419–20; Waddell in *Hakuin's Precious Mirror Cave*, 274–75; and online at http://buddhasutra.com/stories/origin_fish_basket_holding_guanyin. htm.

The Flower Hall on Buddha's Birthday. From the *Shonan-katto-roku (The Shonan Koan Record)*. Translated by Leggett in *Samurai Zen*, 116–17; and Morrell in *Zen Sanctuary of the Purple Robes*, 55.

The Goddess and the Flowers. From the Vimalakirti Sutra. Translated by Paul in *Women in Buddhism*, 226–27; Watson in *The Vimalakirti Sutra*, 87; and Thurman in *The Holy Teaching of Vimalakirti*, 58–59.

The Goddess's Transformations. From the Vimalakirti Sutra. Translated by Paul in *Women in Buddhism*, 230–32; Watson in *The Vimalakirti Sutra*, 90–91; Thurman in *The Holy Teaching of Vimalakirti*, 61–62; and Shih online at http://www.purifymind.com/WomenChan.htm.

Ganji's Family. Original source unknown. Translated by Thomas Cleary in the *Kahawai Journal*, 1984.

Ikkyu and Kannon's Messenger. Original source unknown. Translated by Sanford in *Zen-Man Ikkyu*, 79–80; and Stevens in *Three Zen Masters*, 283–84.

Iron Grindstone Liu's Feast. From the *Biyan lu (Blue Cliff Record)*, Case 24; the *Congrong lu (The Book of Equanimity)*, Case 60; and the *Jingde chuandeng lu (Jingde Records of the Transmission of the Lamp)*. Translated by Cleary in the *Blue Cliff Record*, 159; Wick in *The Book of Equanimity*, 187; Kubose in *Zen Koans*, 194; Heine in *Opening a Mountain*, 64; Hoffman in *Every End Exposed*, 89; and others.

Jiaoan's Sand in the Eye. Original source unknown. Translated by Thomas Cleary in the *Kahawai Journal*, 1981.

Jiyu-Kennett's Not Bigger, Not Smaller. From *Roar of the Tigress*, by Kennett and MacPhillamy, 50–51.

Joko Beck and the Thought of Enlightenment. Original story shared by Peg Syverson, unpublished, and used with her permission.

Kakuzan Shido's Dagger. From the *Shonan-katto-roku* (*The Shonan Koan Record*). Translated by Leggett in *Samurai Zen*, 158–59; Morrell in *Zen Sanctuary of the Purple Robes*, 56; and Tisdale in *Women of the Way*, 222–25.

Khujjuttara Teaches the Dharma. From the *Dhammapada Commentary* and elsewhere. Translated by Murcott in *The First Buddhist Women*, 142; and online at http://www.tipitaka.net/tipitaka/dhp /verseload.php?verse=021 and http://www.dhammawiki.com/index .php?title=Khujjuttara.

Kisagotami's Mustard Seed. From the *Therigatha (Songs of the Elder Nuns)*. Many translators, including Rhys Davids in *Psalms of the Sisters*, 106–10; Murcott in *The First Buddhist Women*, 84–86; and Tisdale in *Women of the Way*, 91–92.

Kongshi's Bathhouse. From the *Wudeng huiyuan (Collated Essentials of the Five Flame Records)*. Translated by Hsieh in *Buddhism in the Sung*, 163; Tisdale in *Women of the Way*, 155–56; Cleary in the *Kahawai Journal*, 1985; and Levering in "Dogen's Raihaitokuzui and Women Teaching in Sung Ch'an."

Laywoman Pang's Merit. From the *Pang jushi yulu (The Recorded Sayings of Layman Pang)*. Translated by Sasaki et al. in *The Recorded Sayings of Layman Pang*, 73; and Tisdale, *Women of the Way*, 130.

Let's Become Enlightened Together. Original story from Chi Kwang Sunim, unpublished, and used with her permission.

Ling's Question. From the *Jingde chuandeng lu (Record of the Transmission of the Lamp)*. Translated by Kirchner in *Entangling Vines*, 120, Tisdale in *Women of the Way*, 125–26, and Cleary in the *Kahawai Journal*, 1984.

Lingzhao Goes First. From the *Pang jushi yulu (The Recorded Sayings of Layman Pang)*. Translated by Sasaki et al. in *The Recorded Sayings of Layman Pang*, 41; Chung-Yuan in *Original Teachings of Ch'an Buddhism*,

176–77; Ferguson in *Zen's Chinese Heritage*. 96; Tisdale in *Women of the Way*, 134–35; and other sources.

Lingzhao's Helping. From the *Pang jushi yulu (The Recorded Sayings of Layman Pang)*. Translated by Sasaki et al. in *The Recorded Sayings of Layman Pang*, 75; Tisdale in *Women of the Way*, 133; and other sources.

Lingzhao's Shining Grasses. From the *Pang jushi yulu (The Recorded Sayings of Layman Pang)*. Translated by Sasaki et al. in *The Recorded Sayings of Layman Pang*, 74; Tisdale in *Women of the Way*, 134; online at http://www.jcrows.com/xuyunteachings.html; and other sources.

Linji Meets the Old Woman Driving the Ox. Unknown source, probably from the *Linji-lu (Record of Linji)*. Translated by Cleary in the *Kahawai Journal*, 1984.

Mahapajapati Opens the Door. From *Buddhagosa's Commentary on the Dhammapada*, the *Therigatha (Songs of the Elder Nuns)*, and the *Cullavaga*. Translated by Murcott in *The First Buddhist Women*, 13–30; Tisdale in *Women of the Way*, 30–32; Dhammananda online at http://www.mahindarama.com/e-library/dhammapada26a.html; and many other sources.

Manseong's No Cultivation. Unknown source. Translated by Samu Sunim in "Manseong Sunim, A Woman Zen Master of Modern Korea," *Spring Wind: Buddhist Cultural Forum* 6 (1986), 192.

Maurine Stuart's Whack. Original story shared by Susan Jion Postal, unpublished, and used with her permission.

Maylie Scott Meets Loneliness. Original story shared by Andrea Thach, unpublished, and used with her permission.

Miaodao's Falling into the Hole. From the *Liandeng huiyao (Essential Items from Successive Lamps)*. Translated by Miriam Levering in *Buddhism in the Sung*, 207 (and in other books and journals); and Tisdale in *Women of the Way*, 173.

Miaoxin's Banner. From "Raihai Tokuzui" in Dogen's *Shobogenzo*. Translated by Stryk in *Zen Poems, Prayers, Anecdotes, Interviews*, 94–95; Tanahashi in *The Treasury of the True Dharma Eye*, 75–77; Levering in "Dogen's Raihaitokuzui and Women Teaching in Sung Ch'an"; Tisdale in *Women* of the Way, 147–48; and Weinstein online at http://scbs.stanford.edu /sztp3/translations/shobogenzo/translations/raihai_tokuzui/rhtz.html.

Miaozong's Dharma Interview. From *Wujia zhengzong can* (*Poems of Appraisal of the Correct Tradition of the Five Schools*), and the *Shonan-katto-roku* (*The Shonan Koan Record*). Translated by Levering in Addiss's *The Zen Sourcebook*, 130–31; Hsieh in *Buddhism in the Sung*, 164–65; Waddell in *The Essential Teachings of Zen Master Hakuin*; Leggett in *Samurai Zen*, 133; and others.

Miaozong's Disappointment. From the *Rentian baojian* (*Precious Mirror of Humans and Gods*). Translated by Levering in *Women Saints in World Religions*, 192.

Moshan's Mountain Summit. From the *Wudeng huiyuan* (*Compendium of Five Lamps*) and "Raihai Tokuzui" in Dogen's *Shobogenzo*. Translated by Heine in *Opening a Mountain*, 96; Tanahashi in *Treasury of the True Dharma Eye*, 75; Grant in *Eminent Nuns*, 15; Shih online at http://ccbs.ntu.edu.tw/FULLTEXT/JR-NX020/15_09.htm; and Weinstein at http://scbs.stanford.edu/sztp3/translations/shobogenzo/translations /raihai_tokuzui/rhtz.html. Also many other translations.

The Naga Princess's Enlightenment. From the *Miaofa lianhua jing* (*The Lotus Sutra*). Translated by Paul in *Women in Buddhism*, 188–90; Shih online at http://www.purifymind.com/WomenChan.htm; and other sources.

Nyozen's Pale Moon of Dawn. From the *Shonan-katto-roku* (*The Shonan Koan Record*). Translated by Leggett in *Zen and the Ways*, 82.

Ohashi Awakens in a Brothel. Original source unknown. Translated by Waddell in Hakuin's *Precious Mirror Cave*, 218–19; Stevens in *Three Zen Masters*, 82–83; Tisdale in *Women of the Way*, 264–67; and Cleary in the *Kahawai Journal*, 1984.

The Old Woman and the Pure Land. Original source unknown. Translated by Leggett in *Encounters in Yoga and Zen*.

The Old Woman and Naropa. Original source unknown. Translated by Khenpo Karthar Rinpoche online at http://www.kagyu.org/kagyulineage /lineage/kag03.php; and Osho online at http://www.messagefrommasters .com/Osho/oshomystics/Osho-on-Naropa-Tilopa.html.

The Old Woman and the Fire Poker. Original source unknown. Translated by Reps and Senzaki in *Zen Flesh, Zen Bones,* 100; and Cleary in the *Kahawai Journal,* 1984.

The Old Woman Burns Down the Hermitage. From the *Shaseki-shu (Collection of Stone and Sand),* the *Sumon Kattoshu (Entangling Vines),* and the *Wudeng huiyuan (Collated Essentials of the Five Flame Records).* Translated by Kirchner in *Entangling Vines;* Reps and Senzaki in *Zen Flesh, Zen Bones,* 24; Sanford in *Zen-Man Ikkyu,* 158; Hoffman in *The One Hand,* 193–94; and other sources.

The Old Woman of Mount Wutai. From the *Jingde chuandeng lu (Jingde Records of the Transmission of the Lamp),* *The True Dharma Eye* (Koans of Dogen), *Summon Kattoshu (Entangling Vines),* *Wumen guan (Mumonkan, Gateless Gate,* Case 32), and the *Congrong lu (Shoyoroku in Japanese, Book of Serenity,* Case 10). Translated by Loori and Tanahashi in *The True Dharma Eye,* 181–82; Ogata in *Transmission of the Lamp,* 351; Heine in *Opening a Mountain,* 91; Aitken in *The Gateless Barrier,* 195; Cleary in *The Book of Serenity,* 42; and many other sources.

The Old Woman Recognizes Mazu. Original source unknown. Translated by Wu in *The Golden Age of Zen,* 95.

The Old Woman Steals Zhaozhou's Bamboo Shoots. From the *Kosonshukugyo and the Zhaozhou lu (Joshuroku* in Japanese). Translated by Green in *The Recorded Sayings of Zen Master Joshu,* 166; Hoffman in *Radical Zen,* 156; and Cleary in the *Kahawai Journal,* 1981.

The Old Woman, Zhaozhou, and the Tiger. From the *Kosonshukugyo* and the *Zhaozhou lu (Joshuroku* in Japanese). Translated by Green in *The Recorded Sayings of Zen Master Joshu,* 206; Hoffman in *Radical Zen,* 76; and Cleary in the *Kahawai Journal,* 1981.

The Old Woman's Enlightenment. From the *Keikyoku Sodan (Thornbush Tales).* Translated by Stevens in *Three Zen Masters,* 84; Tanahashi in *Penetrating Laughter,* 15; and Cleary in the *Kahawai Journal,* 1984.

The Old Woman's Miraculous Powers. From the *Jingde chuandeng lu (Record of the Transmission of the Lamp).* Translated by Cleary in the *Kahawai Journal,* 1981; and Hsieh in *Buddhism in the Sung,* 169–70.

The Old Woman's Relatives. From the *Wu-deng-hui-yuan* (*Compendium of Five Lamps*). Translated by Cleary in the *Kahawai Journal*, 1981; and Hsieh in *Buddhism in the Sung*, 169.

The Old Woman's Rice Cakes. From the *Biyan lu* (*Blue Cliff Record*), commentary on Case 4. Many translators, including Heine in *Opening a Mountain*, 94; Hsieh in *Buddhism in the Sung*,172; Cleary in the *Blue Cliff Record*, 24; Kubose in *Zen Koans*, 92; and others.

Patacara's Presence of Mind. From the *Therigatha (Songs of the Elder Nuns)*. Translated by Murcott in *The First Buddhist Women*, 32–34; Rhys Davids in *Psalms of the Sisters*, 68–78; Tisdale in *Women of the Way*, 72–76; and many others.

Permanence and Impermanence. From the *New Chan Forum* vol. 42, 32, John Crook, ed.

Punna's Offering. From the *Saddharmaratnavaliya* (*Jewel Garland of the True Dharma*). Translated by Obeyesekere in *Portraits of Buddhist Women*, 199–201.

Punnika and the Brahman's Purification. From the *Therigatha (Songs of the Elder Nuns)*. Translated by Murcott in *The First Buddhist Women*, 190–93; Tisdale in *Women of the Way*, 69–70; and other sources.

Qiyuan and the Lotus Sutra. From *Fushi qiyuan chanshi yulu* (*Discourse Records of Chan Master Fushi Qiyuan*). Translated by Grant in *Eminent Nuns*, 66.

Qiyuan Gives Birth. From *Fushi qiyuan chanshi yulu* (*Discourse Records of Chan Master Fushi Qiyuan*). Translated by Grant in *Eminent Nuns*, 47.

Ryonen Scars Her Face. From *Shijitsu Ryonen-ni* (*A Factual Account of the Life of Ryonen*). Translated by Reps and Senzaki in *Zen Flesh, Zen Bones*, 65–66; Ruch in *Engendering Faith*, lxv-lxvix; and Addiss, "The Zen Nun Ryonen Genso," in *Spring Wind: Buddhist Cultural Forum* 6 (1986), 180–87.

Satsujo Overthrows Hakuin. From the *Keikyoku Sodan* (*Thornbush Tales*) and the *Chronological Biography of Zen Master Hakuin*. Translated by Tanahashi in *Penetrating Laughter*, 14; Cleary in the *Kahawai Journal*, 1984; Waddell in Hakuin's *Precious Mirror Cave*, 199–200; Stevens in *Three Zen Masters*, 80; and other sources.

Satsujo Sits on the Lotus Sutra. From the *Keikyoku Sodan (Thornbush Tales)* and the *Chronological Biography of Zen Master Hakuin*. Translated by Tanahashi in *Penetrating Laughter*, 14; Cleary in the *Kahawai Journal*, 1984; Waddell in Hakuin's *Precious Mirror Cave*, 199, 238; Stevens in *Three Zen Masters*, 80; and other sources.

Satsujo Weeps. From the *Keikyoku Sodan (Thornbush Tales)*. Translated by Cleary in the *Kahawai Journal*, 1984; Waddell in Hakuin's *Precious Mirror Cave*, 238; Seung Sahn in *Dropping Ashes on the Buddha*, 190; and other sources.

Senjo and Her Soul Are Separated. From the *Lui-shwo-li-hwan-ki* and the *Wumen guan (Mumonkan, Gateless Barrier)*. Translated by Kubose in *Zen Koans*, 8, Hearn in *Exotics and Retrospectives*, 84–89; Shibayama in *Zen Comments on the Mumonkan*, 252–53; and Heine in *Opening a Mountain*, 185–86.

Seven Wise Women in the Charnel Grounds. From the *Congrong lu (Shoyoroku, Book of Serenity)*, *Poisonous Leavings of Past Masters* (Hakuin), and *Dogen's Extensive Record*. Translated by Cleary in *The Book of Serenity*, 61; Waddell in *Essential Teachings of Zen Master Hakuin*, 31–32; Leighton and Okamura in *Dogen's Extensive Record*, 120; and other sources.

Shiji Doesn't Take Off Her Hat. From the *Chodang-chip (Patriarch's Hall Collection)* and the *Wumen guan (Mumonkan, Gateless Barrier)*. Translated by Heine in *Opening a Mountain*, 175; Senzaki in *Eloquent Silence*, 51–52; Ferguson in *Zen's Chinese Heritage*, 176; Aitken in *The Gateless Barrier*, 29; and other sources.

Shotaku's Paper Sword. From *Shonan-katto-roku (The Shonan Koan Record)*. Translated by Leggett in *Zen and the Ways*, 106; Morrell in *Zen Sanctuary of the Purple Robes*, 56; and Tisdale in *Women of the Way*, 234–36.

Soma Rebukes Mara. From the *Therigatha (Songs of the Elder Nuns)* and the *Bhikkhuni-samyutta (Discourses of the Ancient Nuns)* of the *Sagathavagga*. Translated by Rhys Davids in *Psalms of the Sisters*, 44–46; Murcott in *The First Buddhist Women*, 150–60; and Bhikkhu Bodhi online at http://www.accesstoinsight.org/lib/authors/bodhi/bl143.html.

Sona's Mother and the Thieves. From *Buddhagosa's Commentary on the Dhammapada*. Translated by Dhammananda in *The Dhammapada*;

and online by Daw Mya Tin, http://www.tipitaka.net/tipitaka/dhp /verseload.php?verse=368.

Songyong Doesn't Undress. From Martine Batchelor and Songyong Sunim, *Women in Korean Zen*, 100.

Sonin's Shadeless Tree. From the *Nihon tojo rentoroku*, Translated by Faure in *Visions of Power*, 42; and Tisdale in *Women of the Way*, 229.

Sujata's Offering. From the *Manorathapurani* (*The Wish Fulfiller*), the *Pathamasambodhi*, the *Jataka Tales*, and *Asvaghosa's Buddhacarita*. Translated by Herold in *The Life of the Buddha*, 83; Varma in *The Illustrated Jataka*, online at http://ignca.nic.in/jatak088.htm; Coomeraswami in *Buddha and the Gospel of Buddhism*, 31–31; Cowell in *The Buddha-carita of Asvaghosha*, Book XII, 135; and other sources.

Tara's Vow. From a text by Jo Nang Taranatha, translated by David Templeman, in *The Origin of the Tara Tantra*, 11. Also translated by Wilson in *In Praise of Tara*, 33 and Allione in "Tara, the First Feminist."

Uppalavana and the Precepts. From "Sutra on the Former Life of Nun Utpalavarna" in the *Jatakasutra* and "Kesa Kudoku" in Dogen's *Shobogenzo*. Translated by Tanahashi in *Treasury of the True Dharma Eye*, 124; Nearman in *The Shobogenzo*, 952–53; and Nishijima and Cross in *Master Dogen's Shobogenzo*, 170–71.

Vasumitra Teaches Freedom from Passion. From Cleary, *The Flower Ornament Sutra*, 1270–83.

The Woman in Samadhi. From the *Wumen guan* (*Mumonkan, The Gateless Gate*) and *Summon Kattoshu* (*Entangling Vines*). Many translators, incuding Heine in *Opening a Mountain*, 103; Hoffman in *The One Hand*, 207–8; Aitken in *The Gateless Barrier*, 256–57; and others.

The Woman Lets It Be. Original source unknown. Translated by Lu K'uan Yu in *Chan and Zen Teaching*, 95–100; and online by the Nan Hua Chan Buddhist Society, http://www.jcrows.com/xuyunteachings.html.

Yasodhara's Path. From the *Vinayapitaka of the Mulasarvastivada*. Translated by Bareau in *A Mysterious Being*, http://www. buddha-kyra.com /wife.htm; and retold by Fischer in "The Sacred and the Lost," http:// www.new-mag.com/1_2005/fischer_n_sacred_lost/detailpage.htm.

Yoshihime's "Look, Look!" From the *Shonan-katto-roku* (*The Shonan Koan Record*). Translated by Leggett in *Samurai Zen*, 76–79.

Yuanji Knocks the Body Down. From the *Jingde chuandeng lu* (*Jingde Records of the Transmission of the Lamp*) and the *Fozu guangmu*. Translated by Cheng Chien Bhikkshu in *Sun Face Buddha*, 135–36; Ogata in *The Transmission of the Lamp*; and Blyth in *Oriental Humor*, 93–94.

Yu Uses Her Full Strength. From the *Wanzi xuzangjing* (*Newly Compiled Continuation of the Buddhist Canon*). Translated by Hsieh in *Buddhism in the Sung*, 173–74; Cleary in the *Kahawai Journal*, 1984; and Tisdale in *Women of the Way*, 163.

The Zen Mirror of Tokeiji. From the *Shonan-katto-roku* (*The Shonan Koan Record*). Translated by Leggett in *Samurai Zen*, 95–100; and Morrell in *Zen Sanctuary of the Purple Robes*, 53.

Zhaozhou and the Old Woman's Obstacles. From the *Wudeng huiyuan* (*Collection of the Five Lamps*), the *Guzunsu yuyao* (*The Essential Teachings of the Ancient Masters*), and the *Zhaozhou lu* (*Joshuroku* in Japanese, *Record of Joshu*). Translated by Green in *The Recorded Sayings of Zen Master Joshu*, 436; and Hoffman in *Radical Zen*, 130.

Zhaozhou's Deeply Secret Mind. From the *Wudeng huiyuan* (*Collection of the Five Lamps*) and the *Kuzunsu yuyao* (*The Essential Teachings of the Ancient Masters*), and the *Zhaozhou lu* (*Joshuroku* in Japanese, *Record of Joshu*). Translated by Green in *The Recorded Sayings of Zen Master Joshu*, 319; Hoffman in *Radical Zen*, 103; and Wu in *The Golden Age of Zen*, 120.

Ziyong's Earth. From *Ziyong Ru Chanshi yulu* (*The Discourse Records of Chan Master Ziyong Ru*). Translated by Grant in *Eminent Nuns*, 179.

Ziyong's Last Teaching. From *Ziyong Ru Chanshi yulu* (*The Discourse Records of Chan Master Ziyong Ru*). Translated by Grant in *Eminent Nuns*, 181.

Ziyong's Ship of Compassion. From *Ziyong Ru Chanshi yulu* (*The Discourse Records of Chan Master Ziyong Ru*). Translated by Grant in *Eminent Nuns*, 173.

Zongchi and Bodhidharma's Flesh. From the *Jingde chuandeng lu* (*Jingde Records of the Transmission of the Lamp*), the *Lidai fabao ji* (*The Record* of the Dharma-Jewel Through the Generations) and "Katto" and "Raihai Tokuzui" in Dogen's Shobogenzo. Translated by Wu in The Golden Age of Zen, 47; Tanahashi in The Treasury of the True Dharma Eye, 479; Tisdale in Women of the Way, 117; and Adamek in The Mystique of Transmission, 154.

Permissions and Copyrights

Bibliography

Adamek, Wendi Leigh. *The Mystique of Transmission: On an Early Chan History and its Contexts.* New York: Columbia University Press, 2007.

Addiss, Stephen. "The Zen Nun Ryonen Genso (1646–1711)." In *Women in Buddhism, a Special Issue of the Spring Wind: Buddhist Cultural Forum* 6 (1986): 180–87.

Addiss, Stephen, with Stanley Lombardo and Judith Roitman. *Zen Sourcebook: Traditional Documents from China, Korea, and Japan.* Indianapolis, IN: Hackett Publishing Company, 2008.

Aitken, Robert. *The Gateless Barrier: The Wu-Men Kuan (Mumonkan).* Berkeley, CA: North Point Press, 1990.

Allione, Tsultrim. "Tara, the First Feminist." *Buddhadharma,* November 2010. Accessed July 31, 2012: http://bdtest1.squarespace.com/web-archive/2010/11/13/tara-the-first-feminist.html.

Arai, Paula. *Women Living Zen.* Oxford: Oxford University Press, 1999.

Bareau, Andre. *A Mysterious Being: The Wife of the Buddha.* Accessed August 12, 2012: http://www. buddha-kyra.com/wife.htm.

Batchelor, Martine, and Songyong Sunim. *Women in Korean Zen.* Syracuse: Syracuse University Press, 2006.

Bhikku Bodhi, trans. "Discourses of the Ancient Nuns (Bhikkhuni-samyutta)." *Access to Insight,* 2010. Accessed July 31, 2012: http://www.accessto insight.org/lib/authors/bodhi/bl143.html.

Blyth, R. H. *Games Zen Master Play.* New York: New American Library, 1976.

———. *Oriental Humor.* Tokyo: Hokuseido Press, 1959.

———. *Zen and Zen Classics, Volume Four: Mumonkan.* Japan: The Hokuseido Press, 1966.

Bodiford, William. *Soto Zen in Medieval Japan.* Honolulu: University of Hawai'i Press, 1993.

Boucher, Sandy. *Opening the Lotus: A Woman's Guide to Buddhism*. Boston: Beacon Press, 1997.

Cheng Chien Bhikshu (Mario Poceski). *Sun-Face Buddha: The Teachings of Ma-Tsu and the Hung-Chou School of Ch'an*. Fremont, CA: Asian Humanities Press, 1992.

Chung-Yuan, Chang, trans. *Original Teachings of Ch'an Buddhism: Selected from the Transmission of the Lamp*. New York: Pantheon Books, 1969.

Cleary, Thomas, trans. *Blue Cliff Record*. Boston: Shambhala, 1992.

———. *The Book of Serenity*. Hudson, New York: Lindisfarne Press, 1990.

———. "Kahawai Koans." Maui, Hawai'i: *Kahawai Journal of Women and Zen* (1981–85).

———. *The Flower Ornament Scripture: A Translation of the Avatamsaka Sutra*. Boston: Shambhala, 1993.

Coomaraswamy, Ananda Kentish. *Buddha and the Gospel of Buddhism*. New York: G. B. Putnam's Sons, 1916.

Cowell, E. B. *The Buddha-karita of Asvaghosha*. Oxford: Clarendon Press, 1893.

Crook, John. *New Chan Forum: Buddhist Journal of the Western Chan Fellowship* 42, 32 (Summer 2010). Bury, England.

Daw Mya Tin, trans. *The Dhammapada: Verses and Stories*. Rangoon, Myanmar: Myanmar Pitika Association, 1986. Accessed July 31, 2012: http://www.tipitaka.net/tipitaka/dhp/verseload.php?verse=368.

Dhammananda, K. Sri, trans. *The Dhammapada*. Kuala Lumpur: Sasana Abhiwurdi Wardhana Society, 1988.

Ewing, Jiden, and Taigen Leighton. "Zen Women Ancestors' Biographies." Accessed July 29, 2012: http://www.ancientdragon.org/Dharma/chants.

Faure, Bernard. *The Red Thread: Buddhist Approaches to Sexuality*. Princeton, NJ: Princeton University Press, 1998.

———. *Visions of Power: Imagining Medieval Japanese Buddhism*. Translated by Phyllis Brooks. Princeton, NJ: Princeton University Press, 1996.

Ferguson, Andy. *Zen's Chinese Heritage*. Boston: Wisdom, 2000.

Fischer, Norman. "The Sacred and the Lost." *New Magazine*, issue 1 (2005). Accessed July 17, 2012: http://www.new-mag.com/1_2005/fischer_n _sacred_lost/detailpage.htm.

Foster, Nelson, and Jack Shoemaker. *The Roaring Stream*. Hopewell, NJ: The Ecco Press, 1996.

Grant, Beata. *Eminent Nuns*. Honolulu: University of Hawai'i Press, 2008.

Green, James, trans. *The Recorded Sayings of Zen Master Joshu*. Boston: Shambhala, 1998.

Gunaratna, V. F. *The Message of the Saints: Thera-Theri-Gatha*. Kandy, Sri Lanka: Buddhist Publication Society, 1969. Online edition, 2008: www .bps.lk/olib/wh/wh135.pdf.

Haskel, Peter, trans. *Bankei Zen: Translations from the Record of Bankei*. Edited by Yoshito Hakeda. New York: Grove Press, 1984.

Hecker, Helmuth. *Buddhist Women at the Time of the Buddha*. Translated by Sister Khema. Kandy, Sri Lanka: Buddhist Publication Society, 1994. Online edition, 2012: http://www.accesstoinsight.org/lib/authors /hecker/wheel292.html.

Heine, Steven. *Opening a Mountain: Koans of the Zen Masters*. Oxford: Oxford University Press, 2001.

———. *Dogen and the Koan Tradition*. Albany, NY: State University of New York Press, 1994.

———. "Women in Zen Buddhism." Accessed July 17, 2012: http://www .purifymind.com/WomenChan.htm.

Hearn, Lafcadio. *Exotics and Retrospectives*. Boston: Little Brown & Co., 1898. Fully digitized at: http://archive.org/details/exoticsandretros 00heariala and forgottenbooks.org.

Herold, Andre Ferdinand. Translated by Paul C. Blum. *The Life of the Buddha*. New York: A & C Boni, 1927. Fully digitized at: sacredtexts.com and forgottenbooks.org.

Hoffman, Yoel. *Every End Exposed: The 100 Perfect Koans of Master Kido with the Answers of Hakuin-Zen*. Brookline, MA: Autumn Press, 1977.

———. *Radical Zen: The Sayings of Joshu*. Brookline, MA: Autumn Press, 1978.

———. *The One Hand: 281 Zen Koans with Answers*. New York: Basic Books, 1975.

Hopkinson, Deborah, Michele Hill, and Eileen Kiera, eds. *Not Mixing Up Buddhism: Essays on Women and Buddhist Practice*. Fredonia, NY: White Pine Press, 1986.

Hori, Victor Sogen. "Koan and Kensho in the Rinzai Zen Curriculum." In *The Koan: Texts and Contexts in Zen Buddhism*, edited by Steven Heine and Dale Wright, 280–309. Oxford: Oxford University Press, 2000.

Hsieh, Ding-wa. "Images of Women in Ch'an Buddhist Literature of the Sung." In *Buddhism in the Sung*, edited by Peter Gregory and Daniel Getz. Honolulu: Kuroda Institute, University of Hawai'i Press, 1999.

Kapleau, Philip. *Straight to the Heart of Zen*. Boston: Shambhala, 2001.

Kennett, Jiyu-, and Daizui MacPhillamy. *Roar of the Tigress*. Mount Shasta, CA: Shasta Abbey Press, 2000.

Khenpo Karthar Rinpoche. "Naropa." Accessed August 1, 2012: http://www.kagyu.org/kagyulineage/lineage/kag03.php.

Kirchner, Thomas Yuho. *Entangling Vines: Zen Koans of the Sumon Kattoshu*. Kyoto: Tenyryu-Ji Institute for Philosophy and Religion, 2004.

Kubose, Gyomay. *Zen Koans*. Chicago: Regnery, 1973.

Leggett, Trevor. *Encounters in Yoga and Zen*. Rutland, VT: Routledge and Kegan Paul, 1983.

———. *Samurai Zen*. London: Routledge Press, 2003.

———. *The Tiger's Cave*. Rutland, VT: Tuttle, 1995.

———. *Zen and the Ways*. Rutland, VT: Tuttle, 1978.

Leighton, Taigen Dan, and Shohaku Okamura, trans. *Dogen's Extensive Record*. Boston: Wisdom, 2004.

Levering, Miriam. "Dogen's Raihaitokuzui and Women Teaching in Sung Ch'an." *Journal of the International Association of Buddhist Studies* 21, issue 1 (1998).

———. "Miao-tao and her teacher Ta-hui." In *Buddhism in the Sung*, edited by Peter Gregory and Daniel Getz. Honolulu: Kuroda Institute, University of Hawai'i Press, 1999.

———. "Women Ch'an Masters: The Teacher Miao-tsung as Saint." In *Women Saints in World Religions*, edited by Arvid Sharma. Albany, NY: State University of New York Press, 2000.

Loori, John Daido, ed. *Sitting with Koans: Essential Writings on Zen Koan Introspection*. Boston: Wisdom, 2005.

Loori, John Daido, and Kazuaki Tanahashi, trans. *The True Dharma Eye: Zen Master Dogen's Three Hundred Koans*. Boston: Shambhala, 2009.

Lu K'uan Yu (Charles Luk). *Chan and Zen Teaching*. Berkeley, CA: Shambhala, 1970.

Maraldo, John C. "Liberating the Koan." In *The Journal of Chinese Religions* 31 (2003).

Miura, Isshu, and Ruth Fuller Sasaki. *The Zen Koan: Its History and Use in Rinzai Zen*. New York: Harcourt, Brace & World, 1965.

Morrell, Sachiko Kaneko, and Robert E. Morrell. *Zen Sanctuary of the Purple Robes: Japan's Tokeiji Convent Since 1285*. Albany, NY: State University of New York Press, 2006.

Mu Soeng Sunim. *Thousand Peaks: Korean Zen—Tradition and Teachers*. Berkeley, CA: Parallax Press, 1987.

Murcott, Susan. *The First Buddhist Women: Poems and Stories of Awakening*. Berkeley, CA: Parallax Press, 1991.

Nakagawa, Soen. "Passover Teisho." In *Sitting with Koans*, edited by John Daido Loori. Boston: Wisdom, 2005.

Nearman, Hubert, trans. *The Shobogenzo by Great Master Dogen*. Mount Shasta, CA: Shasta Abbey Press, 1996.

Nguyen, Cuong Tu. *Zen in Medieval Vietnam: A Study and Translation of the Thien Uyen Tap Anh*. Honolulu: University of Hawai'i Press, 1998.

Nishijima, Gudo, and Chodo Cross, trans. *Master Dogen's Shobogenzo*. Bristol, UK: Windbell Publications, 2007.

Obeyesekere, Ranjini. *Portraits of Buddhist Women: Stories from the Saddharmaratnāvaliya*. Albany, NY: State University of New York Press, 2001.

Ogata, Sohaku, trans. *The Transmission of the Lamp: Early Masters*, compiled by Tao Yuan. Wolfeboro, NH: Longwood Academic, 1989.

Osho. "Osho Story on Tantra Master Naropa and Tilopa." Accessed August 1, 2012: http://www.messagefrommasters.com/Osho/oshomystics /Osho-on-Naropa-Tilopa.html.

Paul, Diana. *Women in Buddhism*. Berkeley, CA: University of California Press, 1985.

Powell, William, trans. *The Record of Tung-shan*. Honolulu: Kuroda Institute, University of Hawai'i Press, 1986.

Rajneesh, Bhagwan Shree. *No Water, No Moon: Ten Discourses on Zen Stories*. Poona, India: Rajneesh Foundation, 1975.

Reps, Paul, and Nyogen Senzaki. *Zen Flesh, Zen Bones*. Rutland, VT: Tuttle, 1957.

Rhys Davids, Caroline. *Psalms of the Sisters: Psalms of the Early Buddhists* (Therigatha). London: Pali Text Society, Henry Frowde, 1909. Reissued as an Elibron Classics Reproduction in 2007. Fully digitized at: http:// www.forgottenbooks.org/info/Psalms_of_the_Sisters_1000914349 .php.

Ruch, Barbara, ed. *Engendering Faith: Women and Buddhism in Pre-modern Japan*. Ann Arbor, MI: Center for Japanese Studies, University of Michigan, 2002.

Samu Sunim. "Manseong Sunim, A Woman Zen Master of Modern Korea." In *Women in Buddhism, a Special Issue of the Spring Wind: Buddhist Cultural Forum* 6 (1986): 188–93.

Sanford, James H. *Zen-Man Ikkyu*. Harvard Studies in World Religions, no. 2. Chico, CA: Scholars Press, 1981.

Sasaki, Ruth Fuller, trans. *The Record of Linji*. Edited by Thomas Kirchner. Honolulu: University of Hawai'i Press, 2008.

Sasaki, Ruth Fuller, Yoshitaka Iriya, and Dana Fraser, translators. *A Man of Zen: The Recorded Sayings of Layman Pang*. New York: Weatherhill, 1971.

Schireson, Grace. *Zen Women: Beyond Tea Ladies, Iron Maidens, and Macho Masters*. Boston: Wisdom, 2009.

Schmidt, Amy. *Dipa Ma: The Life and Legacy of a Buddhist Master*. New York: BlueBridge, 2005.

Senzaki, Nyogen. *Eloquent Silence*, original commentary on the *Gateless Gate*, edited by Roko Sherry Chayat. Boston: Wisdom, 2008.

Seung Sahn. *Dropping Ashes on the Buddha*. New York: Grove Press, 1994.

———. *The Whole World Is a Single Flower: 365 Kong-ans for Everyday Life*. Rutland, VT: Tuttle, 1992.

Shakya, Ji Din. Compiled by Ming Zhen (Chuan Yuan) Shakya and Upasaka Richard Cheung. *Empty Cloud: The Teachings of Xu Yun—A Remembrance of the Great Chinese Master*. Nan Hua Chan Buddhist Society, 1996. Accessed July 29, 2012: http://zbohy.zatma.org/Dharma/zbohy/Literature/xybook/introp1.html.

Shibayama, Zenkei, translated by Sumiko Kudo. *Zen Comments on the Mumonkan*. New York: Harper and Row, 1974.

Shih, Heng-Ching. "Chinese Bhiksunis in the Ch'an Tradition." Accessed July 17, 2012: http://ccbs.ntu.edu.tw/FULLTEXT/JR-NX020/15_09.htm.

Stevens, John. *Lust for Enlightenment: Buddhism and Sex*. Boston: Shambhala, 1990.

———. *Three Zen Masters: Ikkyū, Hakuin, and Ryōkan*. Tokyo: Kodansha International, 1993.

Stryk, Lucien. *Zen Poems, Prayers, Sermons, Anecdotes, Interviews*. 2nd ed. Athens, OH: Swallow Press, 1982.

Tadahiro Kondo. "Saijoji (Doryo-son)." In *A Guide to Kamakura* (online), 2012. Accessed August 12, 2012: http://www.asahi-net.or.jp/~qm9t-kndu/saijoji.htm.

Tanahashi, Kazuaki. *Penetrating Laughter: Hakuin's Zen & Art*. Woodstock, NY: Overlook Press, 1984.

———, ed. *Treasury of the True Dharma Eye: Zen Master Dogen's Shobogenzo*. Boston: Shambhala, 2010.

Taranatha, Jo Nang. *The Origin of Tara Tantra*, translated by David Templeman. Dharamsala, India: Library of Tibetan Works and Archives, 1981. Accessed July 30. 2012: www.earlywomenmasters.net/masters/kuanyin/tara.html

Thurman, Robert. *The Holy Teaching of Vimalakirti*. University Park: Pennsylvania State University Press, 1976.

Tisdale, Sallie. *Women of the Way*. New York: HarperCollins, 2007.

Tsai, Kathryn Ann, trans. *Lives of the Nuns: Biographies of Chinese Buddhist Nuns from the Fourth to the Sixth Centuries*. Honolulu: University of Hawai'i Press, 1994.

Varma, C. B., *The Illustrated Jataka and Other Stories of the Buddha*. Fully digitized at: http://ignca.nic.in/jatak.htm. Indira Gandhi National Centre for the Arts.

Waddell, Norman, ed. *Hakuin's Precious Mirror Cave: A Zen Miscellany*. Berkeley, CA: Counterpoint, 2009.

————, trans. *The Essential Teachings of Zen Master Hakuin*. Boston: Shambhala, 1994.

Watson, Burton. *Zen Teachings of Master Lin-Chi*. New York: Columbia University Press, 1993.

————. *The Vimalakirti Sutra*. New York: Columbia University Press, 1997.

Weinstein, Stanley, trans. "Getting the Marrow by Doing Obeisance." Soto Zen Text Project. Accessed July 30, 2012: http://scbs.stanford.edu/sztp3/translations/shobogenzo/translations/raihai_tokuzui/rhtz.html.

Wick, Shishin. *The Book of Equanimity*. Boston: Wisdom, 2005.

Willson, Martin. *In Praise of Tara*. London: Wisdom, 1986.

Wu, John C. H. *The Golden Age of Zen: Zen Masters of the T'ang Dynasty*. Reprint, World Wisdom, 2003.

Yampolsky, Philip B. "Letter in Answer to an Old Nun of the Hoke Sect." In *The Zen Master Hakuin: Selected Writings*. New York: Columbia University Press, 1971.

Yu, Chun-Fang. *Kuan-yin: The Chinese Transformation of Avalokitsvara*. New York: Columbia University Press, 2003.

About the Contributors

Kokyo Meg Porter Alexander is a Soto Zen priest and teacher in the Everyday Zen community led by Zoketsu Norman Fischer, in the lineage of Suzuki Roshi. She leads a sitting group in Healdsburg, California. Her reflection can be found on page 72.

Shosan Victoria Austin is a certified Iyengar yoga instructor, a Soto Zen priest in Suzuki Roshi's lineage, and a Dharma teacher at San Francisco Zen Center. Her publications include "Zen or Yoga?" in *Freeing the Body, Freeing the Mind*. Her reflection can be found on page 125.

Nancy Mujo Baker is a Zen teacher who is a Dharma heir of Tetsugen Roshi, a member of the Zen Peacemaker Order, and a philosophy professor. She is the founder of No Traces Zendo and lives in New York. Her reflection can be found on page 138.

Martine Batchelor studied Zen under the guidance of the late Korean Zen Master Kusan at Songgwang Sa monastery in Korea. She leads meditation retreats worldwide. She's the author of *The Spirit of the Buddha*. She lives in France. Her reflection can be found on page 332.

Jan Chozen Bays is a Zen master in the Zen lineage of Maezumi Roshi and a pediatrician. She serves as priest and teacher at the Jizo Mountain-Great Vow Zen Monastery in Clatskanie, Oregon. Her reflection can be found on page 208.

Mitra Bishop, a Zen priest and Dharma heir of Kapleau Roshi, is the founder of Mountain Gate Temple in New Mexico and also teaches at Hidden Valley Zen Center in San Marco, California. She lives in Ojo Sarco, New Mexico. Her reflection can be found on page 250.

Melissa Myozen Blacker is a Zen priest and resident teacher at Boundless Way Temple in Worcester, Massachusetts, and abbot of Boundless Way Zen. She is the coeditor of *The Book of Mu* and does private spiritual direction and mindfulness consulting. Her reflection can be found on page 188.

Gyokujun Layla Smith Bockhorst is a Soto Zen priest with Dharma transmission in the lineage of Suzuki Roshi. She leads a sitting group in Larkspur, California, and travels regularly to Montana to teach. Her reflection can be found on page 283.

Angie Boissevain, a Soto Zen teacher in the lineage of Chino Roshi, is the guiding teacher of Floating Zendo in San Jose, California. Her reflection can be found on page 59.

Sylvia Boorstein is a cofounder of Spirit Rock Meditation Center and a senior teacher at the Insight Meditation Society. She is the author of several books on Buddhism in daily life. She lives in Sonoma County, California. Her reflection can be found on page 283.

Sandy Boucher, a Theravada practitioner, has been chronicling Western women's participation in Buddhism for twenty years. She has published five Dharma books, including *The Hidden Spring*, and leads retreats called "Dharma and Writing" and, with her partner Martha Boesing, "Joy in Mindfulness." Her reflection can be found on page 20.

Merle Kodo Boyd is a Zen priest and teacher in the Maezumi/Glassman lineage and a member of the Zen Peacemaker Community. She leads the Lincroft Zen Sangha in Monmouth County, New Jersey. Her reflection can be found on page 38.

Myokei Lynda Caine-Barrett, resident priest at Myoken-ji in Houston, Texas, is the first Western woman to be ordained as a Nichiren Shu priest. She is a Dharma teacher in the prison system and facilitates dialogues on diversity and conflict resolution. Her reflection can be found on page 228.

Gyokuko Carlson is a Soto Zen teacher and cofounder of the Dharma Rain Zen Center in Portland, Oregon, and was a student of Jiyu-Kennett Roshi at Shasta Abbey. Her reflection can be found on page 335.

Eido Frances Carney is a Soto Zen priest in the lineage of the poet Ryokan, founder of Olympia Zen Center, abbess of Fukujuji Temple in Japan, and editor of *Receiving the Marrow: Teachings on Dogen by Soto Zen Women Priests*. Her reflection can be found on page 164.

Shinge Roko Sherry Chayat, a Rinzai Zen teacher in the lineage of Soen Nakagawa Roshi, is abbot of the Zen Studies Society and the Zen Center of Syracuse, New York. Her books include *Subtle Sound: The Zen Teachings of Maurine Stuart*. Her reflection can be found on page 51.

Viveka Chen is ordained in the Triratna Buddhist Order and teaches and cocreates learning communities at the San Francisco Buddhist Center and internationally. She also loves working as a consultant, coach, facilitator, and trainer advancing social change and justice. Her reflection can be found on page 65.

Chi Kwang Sunim is a nun who trained in Korea under Masters Ku San and Myong Seong Sunim. She is the abbess of the Seon (Zen) Center, living in Victoria, Australia, and teaching throughout Australia and in Korea. Her reflection can be found on page 135.

Eijun Linda Ruth Cutts is a Soto Zen priest practicing in the lineage of Suzuki Roshi and an abbess of San Francisco Zen Center. She lives at Green Gulch Farm Zen Center in Marin County, California. Her reflection can be found on page 158.

Laura del Valle (Kyo Kai Dai) is a Mexican physician, a teacher with the Soto Zen Everyday Zen community under the direction of Zoketsu Norman Fischer, and the founder of Wellness Center Mar de Jade in Nayarit, Mexico, where she lives. Her reflection can be found on page 264.

Dhammananda (Chatsumarn Kabilsingh), a Thai Buddhist nun, received full bhikkhuni ordination in Sri Lanka, in the Theravada ordination lineage. She is abbess of Songdhammakalyani Monastery in Thailand. Her reflection can be found on page 315.

Anna Prajna Douglas is a cofounder of Spirit Rock Meditation Center. She teaches retreats and offers ongoing psycho-spiritual mentoring. Her teaching focus is on aging as spiritual opportunity. She is the guiding teacher of Insight Meditation Tucson. Her reflection can be found on page 198.

Heila Downey received teaching permission from Korean Zen Master Seung Sahn. She teaches in Europe, the United States, and South Africa, where she lives. Her reflection can be found on page 86.

Christina Feldman is a guiding teacher at the Insight Meditation Society in Barre, Massachusetts, and cofounder of Gaia House in England. Her reflection can be found on page 176.

Anita Feng teaches with the Blue Heron Zen Community, Seattle, in the Korean lineage of Zen Master Seung Sahn. She is a poet, the author of *Sid*, and ceramic artist making raku buddhas, and she lives in Issaquah, Washington. Her reflection can be found on page 80.

Hoka Chris Fortin is a Soto Zen priest in the lineage of Suzuki Roshi. She is a teacher in the Everyday Zen community and a spiritual counselor. She leads the Sebastopol women's Lotus Sangha and lives in Sebastopol, California. Her reflection can be found on page 108.

Nancy Genshin Gabrysch is a Zen teacher and member of the White Plum Asangha, which was established by Maezumi Roshi. She is the founder and resident teacher of Kannon-ji in Bilsborrow, Lancashire, England. Her reflection can be found on page 192.

Tamara Myoho Gabrysch is a Zen teacher and member of the White Plum Asangha, which was established by Maezumi Roshi. She is cofounder and a resident teacher of Zen River Temple, located on the northern coast of the Netherlands. Her reflection can be found on page 62.

Natalie Goldberg studied with Soto Zen teacher Katagiri Roshi and is ordained in the Order of Interbeing with Thich Nhat Hahn. She is the author of twelve books including *Writing Down the Bones*. She lives in New Mexico. Her reflection can be found on page 68.

Beth Kanji Goldring is a Zen priest and student of the late Maurine Stuart Roshi. A former humanities professor, she founded Brahmavihara Cambodia, a chaplaincy organization for destitute AIDS patients in Phnom Penh, where she lives and works. Her reflection can be found on page 34.

Jisan Tova Green is a Soto Zen priest ordained by Eijun Linda Cutts. She lives and teaches at San Francisco Zen Center's City Center, where she cofounded the Queer Dharma Group. She currently serves as vice-president of Zen Center. Her reflection can be found on page 338.

Rita M. Gross was a professor, theologian, author, and senior teacher in the Tibetan tradition of Jetsun Khandro Rinpoche. She authored several books, including the groundbreaking feminist critique of Buddhism *Buddhism After Patriarchy*. Her reflection can be found on page 216.

Joan Halifax is a Soto Zen priest, anthropologist, and author of *Being with Dying*. She is founder, abbot, and head teacher of Upaya Zen Center in Santa Fe, New Mexico. Her reflection can be found on page 256.

Diane Musho Hamilton is a Zen priest and teacher in the White Plum lineage of Maezumi Roshi. She is the cofounder of Earth and Sky Zen Group in Utah and Colorado. She works with Ken Wilber and the Integral Institute. Her reflection can be found on page 144.

Zenkei Blanche Hartman is a Soto Zen teacher in the lineage of Suzuki Roshi. She was the first woman abbot of San Francisco Zen Center, where she currently lives. Her reflection can be found on page 101.

Nancy Brown Hedgpeth is a teacher in the Kwan Um school of Zen founded by Korean Zen master Seung Sahn. She is co-guiding teacher at the Providence Zen Center and lives and farms in Rhode Island. Her reflection can be found on page 17.

Emila Heller has been a lay resident and leader within the Soto San Francisco Zen Center for several decades. She lives at Green Gulch Farm Zen Center, where she spends her days farming. Her reflection can be found on page 26.

Jane Hirshfield is a poet, essayist, and teacher, lay ordained in the Soto Zen lineage of Suzuki Roshi. Her most recent book is *Come, Thief*. A former resident of San Francisco Zen Center's three practice communities, she lives in northern California. Her reflection can be found on page 342.

Amy Hollowell is a poet, journalist, and teacher in the Zen lineage of Maezumi Roshi. Her latest book is *Giacomettrics*. She lives in France, where she is the founder of the Wild Flower Zen Sangha. Her reflection can be found on page 303.

Mushim Patricia Ikeda is a writer, peace activist, and core teacher at the East Bay Meditation Center in Oakland. She teaches retreats for people of color, women, and social justice activists nationally. She has practiced as a monastic and layperson. Her reflection can be found on page 154.

Leslie James is the abiding teacher at Tassajara Zen Mountain Center in the Soto Zen lineage of Suzuki Roshi. She lives in Jamesburg, California. Her reflection can be found on page 348.

Ursula Jarand is a Dharma heir of the Japanese Zen Master Morinaga Roshi. She is one of the founders of Daishu-in West, a temple in Garberville, California, where she leads daily practice. Her reflection can be found on page 234.

Karma Lekshe Tsomo is a professor of Buddhist studies at the University of California–San Diego and a fully ordained nun. She is active in Sakyadhita International Association of Buddhist Women and Jamyang Foundation, an educational initiative for women in developing countries. Her reflection can be found on page 268.

Stephanie Kaza is a professor of environmental studies at the University of Vermont, writer, and Soto Zen practitioner. Her most recent book is *Mindfully Green: A Personal and Spiritual Guide to Whole Earth Thinking*. She lives in Burlington, Vermont. Her reflection can be found on page 274.

Eileen Kiera was given Lamp transmission by Thich Nhat Hanh in 1990. She is the founding teacher of sanghas in Seattle and at Mountain Lamp

Community near Bellingham, Washington, and leads retreats in the United States, Canada, and Mexico. Her reflection can be found on page 277.

Daijaku Judith Kinst is a priest and teacher in the Soto Zen tradition of Suzuki Roshi and a faculty member at the Institute for Buddhist Studies in Berkeley, California. She co-leads the Ocean Gate Zendo in Santa Cruz, California. Her reflection can be found on page 213.

Sunya Kjolhede is a Zen priest and Dharma heir of Kapleau Roshi. She cofounded, teaches, and lives at Windhorse Zen Community, near Asheville, North Carolina. She is also the spiritual director of the Bodhidharma Zen Center in Warsaw, Poland. Her reflection can be found on page 54.

Anne Carolyn Klein Rigzin Drolma is a professor of religious studies at Rice University in Houston, Texas. Her seven books include *Meeting the Great Bliss Queen*. She founded Dawn Mountain Temple and Dawn Mountain Community Center & Research Institute. Her reflection can be found on page 237.

Jean La Valley is a community Dharma leader with the Bellingham Insight Meditation Society in Bellingham, Washington. Her reflection can be found on page 309.

Joanna Macy is a scholar of Buddhism and general systems theory and the root teacher of the Work That Reconnects. She's the author, along with Chris Johnstone, of *Active Hope: How to Face the Mess We're In without Going Crazy*. She lives in Berkeley, California. Her reflection can be found on page 57.

Jacqueline Mandell was one of the first Western Vipassana teachers and has also received teaching authorization from Adzom Rinpoche in the Tibetan tradition. She is the founding teacher of Samden Ling and lives in Portland, Oregon. Her reflection can be found on page 151.

Rachel Mansfield-Howlett is a Zen master in the Hakuin koan lineage; founder of CityZen, a koan school in Santa Rosa, California; contributor to *The Book of Mu: Essential Writings on Zen's Most Important Koan*; a passionate gardener; and an environmental attorney. Her reflection can be found on page 253.

Zenju Earthlyn Manuel is an author and Soto Zen priest in the lineage of Suzuki Roshi. She's the author of *Tell Me Something About Buddhism* and *The Way of Tenderness*. She lives in Albuquerque, New Mexico, and Oakland, California. Her reflection can be found on page 128.

Eve Myonen Marko is a founding teacher of the Zen Peacemaker Order; her focus has been spiritually-based social action. She is a writer and teacher at Green River Zen Center in Greenfield, Massachusetts. Her reflection can be found on page 241.

Heather Martin is a midwife and Vipassana teacher who guides the Salt Spring Island Vipassana Community and teaches internationally. She lives on Salt Spring Island, British Columbia, Canada. Her reflection can be found on page 322.

Myoshin Kate McCandless is a Soto Zen teacher in the lineage of Shunryu Suzuki Roshi. She is a resident priest of Mountain Rain Zen Community in Vancouver, British Columbia, Canada. Her reflection can be found on page 182.

Misha Shungen Merrill is a Soto Zen priest in the lineage of Suzuki Roshi. She is the teacher of Zen Heart Sangha in Menlo Park and Woodside, California, where she lives. She also teaches tea ceremony in the Mushanokoji style. Her reflection can be found on page 296.

Kuya Minogue trained in the Soto Zen lineage of Jiyu-Kennett Roshi and received lay ordination from Kyogen Carlson. She is the resident teacher at Creston Zendo in Creston, British Columbia. Her reflection can be found on page 96.

Zenki Mary Mocine is a Soto Zen priest in the lineage of Suzuki Roshi, the abbess of Clear Water Zendo, the founding teacher of the Contra Costa Zen Group, and a retired labor attorney living in Vallejo, California. Her reflection can be found on page 90.

Susan Murphy is a writer, filmmaker, Dharma heir to John Tarrant Roshi and Ross Bolleter Roshi, founding teacher of Zen Open Circle, Sydney, Australia, and teacher for the Melbourne Zen Group. She's the author of *Upside-Down Zen* and *Minding the Earth, Mending the World*. Her reflection can be found on page 48.

Wendy Egyoku Nakao is the abbot and head teacher of Zen Center Los Angeles. She is a member of the Maezumi/Glassman lineage and is a founding member of the Zen Peacemaker Community. Her reflection can be found on page 118.

Tonen Sara O'Connor trained at temples of the Soto school in Japan and received Dharma transmission from Tozen Akiyama Roshi. She is the resident priest at the Milwaukee Zen Center. Her reflection can be found on page 201.

Barbara Joshin O'Hara is a teacher in the Zen lineage of Maezumi Roshi, a psychotherapist, and cofounder of the Village Zendo. She grew up in Ireland and lives in New York. Her reflection can be found on page 210.

Pat Enkyo O'Hara is a Zen priest and teacher in the Maezumi-Glassman line. She is abbot of the Village Zendo in New York, a founding teacher in Zen Peacemakers, and formerly a professor of interactive media at New York University. Her reflection can be found on page 161.

Mary Grace Orr is a Vipassana teacher, member of the teachers council at Spirit Rock Meditation Center, and a retired therapist. She was the guiding teacher for Vipassana Santa Cruz from 1989 to 2011. She lives in Hawaii and California. Her reflection can be found on page 312.

Catherine Genno Pagès is a teacher in the Zen lineage of Maezumi Roshi and the founder of the Dana Zen Center. She lives in Paris, France. Her reflection can be found on page 185.

Alexandra Porter is a Zen master and vice head teacher in Europe in the Kwan Um school founded by Korean Zen master Seung Sahn. She lives in Warsaw, Poland. Her reflection can be found on page 345.

Jo Potter is a teacher in the Kwan Um school of Zen in the Korean Zen lineage of Zen master Seung Sahn. She teaches in Europe and North America and leads the Whole Heart Zen Center in Vienna, Austria. Her reflection can be found on page 260.

Byakuren Judith Ragir teaches in the Soto Zen tradition of Katagiri Roshi. She is the guiding teacher at Clouds in Water Zen Center in St. Paul, Minnesota. Her reflection can be found on page 147.

Judith Randall is a Soto Zen priest in the tradition of Shunyru Suzuki Roshi. She lives and practices at Tassajara Zen Mountain Center in the Los Padres Wilderness of California. Her reflection can be found on page 41.

Caitriona Reed was ordained as a Dharma teacher by Thich Nhat Hanh in 1992. She is cofounder of Ordinary Dharma in Los Angeles and Manzanita Village Retreat Center, near Warner Springs, California. Her reflection can be found on page 167.

Barbara Rhodes (Soeng Hyang) received Dharma transmission from Korean Zen master Seung Sahn and is the school Zen master and guiding teacher of the International Kwan Um school of Zen. She lives in Rhode Island. Her reflection can be found on page 30.

Hilary Richards is a retreat leader for the Western Chan Fellowship and a student of Chan Master Sheng Yen and Chan Master John Crook. She is a retired medical doctor and lives in Bristol, England. Her reflection can be found on page 194.

Diane Eshin Rizzetto received Dharma transmission from Charlotte Joko Beck. She is a founder of the Ordinary Mind Zen school and abbess of Bay Zen Center in Oakland, California. Her most recent book is *Waking Up to What You Do*. Her reflection can be found on page 111.

Shinshu Roberts ordained in the Soto Zen lineage of Suzuki Roshi and received Dharma transmission from Sojun Weitsman. She holds *kokusaifukyoshi* (teacher qualification) from the Sotoshu in Japan. Shinshu is cofounder and teacher at Ocean Gate Zen Center in Capitola, California. Her reflection can be found on page 231.

Judith Roitman (Zen Master Bon Hae) has received Dharma transmission with the Kwan Um school in the Korean Zen lineage of Master Seung Sahn. She is the guiding teacher of the Kansas Zen Center, a mathematics professor, and a poet. She lives in Lawrence, Kansas. Her reflection can be found on page 280.

Adrianne Ross is guiding teacher for British Columbia Insight Meditation Society based in Vancouver. A retired physician, she leads retreats in Canada and the US and teaches Mindfulness-Based Stress Reduction to people with chronic pain and illness. Her reflection can be found on page 306.

Miriam Sagan is a poet, essayist, memoirist, and student of Zen. Her most recent book is *Map of the Lost*. She lives in Santa Fe, New Mexico. Her reflection can be found on page 68.

Anne Seisen Saunders is a Zen priest in the Maezumi Roshi lineage. She received Dharma transmission from Bernie Glassman in the Zen Peacemaker Order. She is the abbot of Sweetwater Zen Center in National City, California. Her reflection can be found on page 121.

Myoan Grace Schireson is a Soto Zen priest and teacher in the Suzuki Roshi lineage, abbess of Central Valley Zen, Empty Nest, Modesto Zen, and Fresno River Zen Groups. She is the author of *Zen Women* and lives in Central California. Her reflection can be found on page 286.

Amita Schmidt is the author of *Dipa Ma: The Life and Legacy of a Buddhist Master*. She is a psychotherapist in Hawaii, specializing in trauma and anxiety. She also leads retreats in the Vipassana and Advaita traditions. Her reflection can be found on page 141.

Myokaku Jane Schneider is a Soto Zen priest in the lineage of Suzuki Roshi. She is an artist and with her husband Peter founded the Beginner's Mind Zen Center in Northridge, California. They spent twenty-two years in Japan. Her reflection can be found on page 83.

Furyu Nancy Schroeder is a Soto Zen priest and teacher in the Suzuki Roshi lineage. She has lived at Green Gulch Farm Zen Center in Sausalito, California for more than thirty years. Her reflection can be found on page 170.

Laurie Schley Senauke received Soto Zen lay teacher recognition in the Suzuki Roshi lineage. She lives and practices at Berkeley Zen Center, in Berkeley, California. Her reflection can be found on page 247.

Judith Simmer-Brown (Könchok Namgyal) is a professor at Naropa University and an acharya in the Shambhala Buddhist lineage of Chogyam Trungpa Rinpoche. She is the author of *Dakini's Warm Breath*. She lives in Boulder, Colorado. Her reflection can be found on page 131.

Karen Sundheim practices and is a lay teacher at the Berkeley Zen Center, in the Soto Zen lineage of Suzuki Roshi. She is also a librarian and lives in Oakland, California. Her reflection can be found on page 114.

Joan Sutherland is a teacher in the Zen koan tradition and the founder of Awakened Life in Santa Fe, New Mexico. She is a widely published author and translator, currently working on a new translation of the *Blue Cliff Record*. Her reflection can be found on page 293.

Peg Syverson trained with Charlotte Joko Beck and is a Soto Zen priest in the lineage of Suzuki Roshi. She is the cofounder of Appamada, a center for contemporary Zen practice and inquiry in Austin, Texas. Her reflection can be found on page 23.

Sobun Katherine Thanas was a Soto Zen priest who practiced and trained at San Francisco Zen Center with Suzuki Roshi and was the former abbot of Santa Cruz Zen Center in Santa Cruz, California. She passed away in 2012. Her reflection can be found on page 220.

Thanissara, former Buddhist nun in the Theravada Forest school of Ajahn Chah, is also a practitioner of Chan and Pure Land. She teaches internationally and is cofounder of Dharmagiri Meditation Center in South Africa. She currently lives in the US. Her reflection can be found on page 225.

Thubten Chodron is an American Tibetan Buddhist nun, student of His Holiness the Dalai Lama, and founder and abbess of Sravasti Abbey, a monastic community for Westerners near Newport, Washington. She is the author of *Buddhism for Beginners* and other books. Her reflection can be found on page 319.

Sallie Jiko Tisdale is a writer and Zen teacher at Dharma Rain Zen Center, in the lineage of Jiyu-Kennett Roshi. Her book *Women of the Way* provides biographies of many ancient Buddhist women. She lives in Portland, Oregon. Her reflection can be found on page 244.

Bonnie Myotai Treace is a teacher in the Zen lineage of Maezumi Roshi. She is the founder of Hermitage Heart and Bodies of Water Zen for the protection of water. She teaches at Gristmill Hermitage in Garrison, New York. Her reflection can be found on page 45.

Ikushin Dana Velden is a Soto Zen priest, culinary writer, and teacher in the Suzuki Roshi lineage who trained at San Francisco Zen Center and lives in Oakland, California. Her reflection can be found on page 104.

Vimalasara, aka Valerie Mason-John, is the author of *Detox Your Heart*. She works as a life coach. Vimalasara is ordained into the Triratna Buddhist Order and currently teaches at the Vancouver Buddhist Center in British Columbia, Canada. Her reflection can be found on page 299.

Jisho Warner is a Soto Zen priest and teacher in the Tozen Akiyama lineage, trained in the US and Japan. She heads Stone Creek Zen Center in Sebastopol, California, which she founded in 1996, and is a writer and artist. Her reflection can be found on page 271.

Jan Willis is a writer and professor of religion at Wesleyan University. An African-American practitioner of Tibetan Buddhism, her latest book is *Dreaming Me: Black, Baptist, and Buddhist, One Woman's Spiritual Journey*. She lives in Connecticut. Her reflection can be found on page 326.

Diana Winston is a Vipassana teacher and the director of Mindfulness Education at UCLA's Mindful Awareness Research Center. She is the author of *Fully Present: The Science, Art, and Practice of Mindfulness*. She lives in Los Angeles. Her reflection can be found on page 93.

Amala Wrightson is a Zen priest and Dharma heir of Bodhin Kjolhede Roshi in the lineage of Philip Kapleau Roshi. She is cofounder and director of the Auckland Zen Centre in Auckland, New Zealand. Her reflection can be found on page 76.

Index

Note: Page numbers in bold type indicate story/koan text. Page numbers followed by "q" indicate quotations.

A

Abdi, Dr. Hawa, 138–39

absence:
vs. emptiness, 195
vs. presence, 194

acceptance: of Kisagotami, 177, 178

action (activity):
doing something one hundred percent, 139–40
fear and, 326
"merge subject and object into…,"
148
"nothing…to be done," 283, 285
responding to each moment/situation, 278, 304
"Then what do I do?," 284–85
See also everyday life; helping; work in the world

Adam (drug dealer), 265

Adzom Rinpoche: and Rigzin Drolma, 239

aging:
"Am I old? What is old?," 128–29
the remedy for, 82

aging father, 81, 82

AIDS patients: work and intimacy with, 35–36

airplane panic story, 141

Aitken, Anne, 355
her "Get On and Go" (#54), **192**–93

Akshobhya Buddha, 125, 355

Alexander, Kokyo Meg Porter, 73, 74,
397
on Yu Uses Her Full Strength (#18),
72–74

"Alive or dead?," 192

"All are blessed, all are blessed"
(Wumen), 158

"All things are…in…extinction," 230

aloneness, 174
See also loneliness

"Am I old? What is old?," 128–29

ambiguous genitalia, 208, 221

Amida Buddha (Amitabha), 355
the body as, 51, 52

An. *See* Bingdian An

Ananda: and the Buddha, 8, 224–25,
355

anger:
at the destruction of life on earth,
58
radio theft story, 322–23

angst of separation, 78, 157, 158, 159

Anne Aitken's "Get On and Go"
(#54), **192**–93

Anoja, 20, 355–56, 363

Anoja Seeks the Self (#2), **20**–22

appreciation of everything, 102, 103

approval, desire for, 274–76

arahants, 152, 355

butt/Satsujo's ass as the sutra, 253–55
Byron Katie, 199

C

Caine-Barrett, Myokei Lynda, 228–29,
  230, 398
  on Changjingjin's No Obstructions
    (#64), 228–30
the call of the crow, 49
"Can you sing like that?," 239
Caplow, Zenshin Florence, 174, 421
  on The Old Woman's Relatives
    (#48), 173–75
caregivers: Roxy, 192–93
caregiving, 310
caring: for ourselves, 76–79, 93–94
  See also compassion; helping; kind-
    ness; serving others
Carlson, Gyokuko, 398
  on Maurine Stuart's Whack (#96),
    335–37
Carney, Eido Frances, 399
  on The Old Woman Recognizes
    Mazu (#45), 164–66
cartoon by Hollander, 330
Cash, Johnny, 330
catalysts, spiritual, 269–70
celibacy, 102–3, 150, 319, 320
the cervix: symbolism, 133
the cessation of suffering, 151
chains of words, 284–85
challenge of taking the precepts, 242,
  319–21
change:
  "I must change my life," 282
  work for, 331
  See also impermanence
Changjingjin, 228, 229, 230, 356
Changjingjin's No Obstructions
  (#64), **228**–30
chanting:
  Dipa Ma chanting metta for the
    thief, 322–23
  the Heart Sutra, 242–43

the Metta Sutta, 103q, 300q
the names of women ancestors, 5,
  38, 118, 242
the three refuges, 116
charnel grounds: the seven sisters in,
  44, 45
Chayat, Shinge Roko Sherry, 399
  on The Old Woman's Enlighten-
    ment (#11), 51–53
checking/testing questions on koans,
  251
Chen, Laywoman, 57–58, 357
Chen, Viveka, 66, 399
  on Awakening While Cooking
    (#16), 65–67
Chen's Mountain Flowers (#13),
  57–58
Chi Kwang Sunim, 399
  and Kye Jeon Sunim, 345, 346, 347
  on The Old Woman, Zhaozhou, and
    the Tiger (#36), 135–37
Chiba-sensei, 84–85
Chicksaw understanding of buddha
  nature, 255
children:
  death of one's child, 176–78, 179–
    81; Layman Pang on Lingzhao's
    going first, 185, 186–87
  of Isabel, 265
  and practice, 303–4
China: women in, 173–74
Chiyono (Mugai Nyodai), 37, 38, 97,
  357, 361
  enlightenment poem, 37–38, 39,
    96–97
Chiyono's No Water, No Moon (#7),
  37–40
Chokan, 157, 357
choosing the time of death, 186, 187,
  188, 317
Christian teachings: the parable of the
  Good Samaritan, 326–27
A Christmas Carol (Dickens), 249

meeting a teacher, 31–32, 174–75;
getting an appointment with the
roshi, 251
meeting the Buddha, 54, 56
practice with, 14, 170–72
questioning, 32, 174–75
at San Francisco Zen Center, 222
students' ideas about, 232–33
women. *See* women teachers
women students match their male
teachers, 161–63, 167–69, 170–72
See also teaching; *and specific*
teachers
teaching:
the art of, 336
through everyday affairs, 83–85
gender imbalance in addressed, xii–
xiii, 5–6
"how will you teach?," 260, 261
as in relationships, 335–37
See also skillful means; teaching
styles; teachings
teaching styles:
open-handed spirit in *The Hidden*
Lamp, xii, xii–xiii
traditional complementary styles,
xi–xii
teachings:
Buddhist. *See* the teachings (of
Buddhism)
Christian: the parable of the Good
Samaritan, 326–27
lessons of the world, 232
Rachel Mansfield-Howlett's mother's teaching, 255
the teachings (of Buddhism), 271,
273
core teaching of Zen, 287–88
deathbed teachings, 184
engaging with as women, 108
heart-teachings vs. the rules, 326–27
on the nature of self, 159
no-self, 39, 81

shadow teachings re Khujjuttara,
309, 311
See also buddha nature; the Buddha's teachings; compassion; the
Dharma; emptiness; enlightenment; impermanence; intimacy;
nirvana; nonduality; reality;
suffering; truth; the Unborn; the
Way; wisdom; *and also* sutras
(suttas)
tears. *See* weeping
teller, rude: compassion for, 323
temples. *See* Zen temples
tenth-stage bodhisattva, 327
testing questions on koans, 251
Tetsumon, 48, 201, 370
Thailand: ordination of women in,
315
Thanas, Sobun Katherine, 408
on Dogen Sets the Record Straight
(#62), 220–22
Thanissara, 408
on Mahapajapati Opens the Door
(#63), 225–27
"Thank you for your trouble," 167
"Then what do I do?," 284–85
Theravada, 370
"...there is a remedy..." (Feng), 82
"There is a true person of no rank..."
(Yu), 72
"There's still this," 135, 137
"These many beautiful days..." (Berrigan), 74
the thief: metta for, 322–23
the Thieves, Sona's Mother and (#94),
329–31
things:
"All...are...in...extinction," 230
Eshun's deep thing vs. the monk's
long thing, 114–15, 116
keeping together, 38–39
letting be, 38–40, 62–64; pain and
fear, 78–79
letting come apart, 38–40

About the Editors

ZENSHIN FLORENCE CAPLOW is a Soto Zen priest in the Suzuki Roshi lineage. She has been practicing Vipassana and Zen for thirty years and is a Dharma teacher, Unitarian Universalist minister, field botanist, essayist, and editor. She recently coedited and contributed to an anthology of nature writing, *Wildbranch*, and her essays can be read in *Tricycle, Inquiring Mind*, and on her blog: *Slipping Glimpser, Zen Wanderings and Wonderings*. Her reflection can be found on page 173.

REIGETSU SUSAN MOON has been practicing in the Soto Zen tradition for forty years, at the Berkeley Zen Center, the San Francisco Zen Center, and now with the Everyday Zen Sangha, where she received entrustment as a lay teacher from Zoketsu Norman Fischer. Her previous books include *The Life and Letters of Tofu Roshi, This Is Getting Old: Zen Thoughts on Aging*, and most recently, with Zoketsu Norman Fischer, *What Is Zen? Plain Talk For a Beginner's Mind*. For many years she edited *Turning Wheel*, the journal of the Buddhist Peace Fellowship. She teaches writing workshops, is a serious student of photography, and an enthusiastic grandmother. She lives in Berkeley. Her reflection can be found on page 179.

Also Available from Wisdom Publications

ZEN WOMEN
Beyond Tea Ladies, Iron Maidens, and Macho Masters
Grace Schireson
Foreword by Miriam Levering

"Fascinating and delightful. This book will overturn many long-held stereotypes about Zen."
—Ruben L. F. Habito, author of *Living Zen, Loving God*

THE WAY OF TENDERNESS
Awakening through Race, Sexuality, and Gender
Zenju Earthlyn Manuel
Foreword by Dr. Charles Johnson

"Manuel's teaching is a thought-provoking, much-needed addition to contemporary Buddhist literature."
—*Publishers Weekly*

PURE HEART, ENLIGHTENED MIND
The Life and Letters of an Irish Zen Saint
Maura O'Halloran

"A grand adventure."—*New York Times Book Review*

Bow First, Ask Questions Later
Ordination, Love, and Monastic Zen in Japan
Gesshin Claire Greenwood

"Gesshin Greenwood is the real deal. That's what makes this book so valuable. It's rare that someone from the West does any of this stuff, rarer still when they write about it, and yet even more rare that their writing is as good as Gesshin's is. This is a truly unique document of a truly unique lived experience."
—Brad Warner, author of *Hardcore Zen and Don't Be A Jerk*

Zen Echoes
Classic Koans with Verse Commentaries by Three Female Zen Masters
Beata Grant
Foreword by Susan Moon

"Zen Echoes is an exquisite book reflecting the power of the female voice in Zen."
—Joan Jiko Halifax, abbot, Upaya Zen Center

Daughters of Emptiness
Poems of Chinese Buddhist Nuns
Beata Grant

"This beautiful book testifies to the power of Buddhist practice to nourish the human spirit even when war, physical hardship, class discrimination, and oppression seem insurmountable."
—*Turning Wheel*

About Wisdom Publications

Wisdom Publications is the leading publisher of classic and contemporary Buddhist books and practical works on mindfulness. To learn more about us or to explore our other books, please visit our website at wisdompubs.org or contact us at the address below.

Wisdom Publications
199 Elm Street
Somerville, MA 02144 USA

We are a 501(c)(3) organization, and donations in support of our mission are tax deductible.

Wisdom Publications is affiliated with the Foundation for the Preservation of the Mahayana Tradition (FPMT).